CU BY NUM

*A Complete Team History of the
Chicago Cubs by Uniform Number*

Al Yellon, Kasey Ignarski, and Matthew Silverman
Foreword by Pat Hughes

Skyhorse Publishing

Skyhorse Publishing books may be purchased in bulk at special discounts for
sales promotion, corporate gifts, fund-raising, or educational purposes. Special
editions can also be created to specifications. For details, contact the Special Sales
Department, Skyhorse Publishing, 555 Eighth Avenue, Suite 903, New York, NY 10018
or info@skyhorsepublishing.com.

www.skyhorsepublishing.com

10 9 8 7 6 5 4 3 2 1

Library of Congress Cataloging-in-Publication Data

Yellon, Al.
   Cubs by the numbers : a complete team history of the Chicago Cubs by
uniform number / Al Yellon, Kasey Ignarski & Matthew Silverman.
        p. cm.
   ISBN 978-1-60239-372-1
1.   Chicago Cubs (Baseball team)—History. 2. Baseball
uniforms—Numbers—Illinois—Chicago. I. Ignarski, Kasey. II. Silverman,
Matthew. III. Title. IV. Title: Complete team history of the Chicago Cubs
by uniform number.
   GV875.C6Y45 2009
   796.357'640977311—dc22

                                        2009000434

Printed in Canada

Al:

To my dad, who had no idea what he'd be starting, my lifelong love for the Cubs, when he took me to Wrigley Field for the first time on July 6, 1963, and to Bob Romain, friend and great Cubs fan, who passed away suddenly on October 3, 2008, and never had a chance to read this history of the team he loved.

Kasey:

To Wally, Shelby, Al, and John . . . my ballpark family.

Matt:

For the diehards.

CONTENTS

FOREWORD

Numbers are such an integral part of baseball and of Wrigley Field, it's hard to believe there was a time when the Cubs ran onto the field with blank shirts on their backs. Glad I wasn't announcing or trying to keep score back then. I can only imagine what spring training games must have been like with all those substitutions and no numbers.

The Cubs had been playing in the National League for more than fifty years—they helped start the league in 1876—before they finally sewed numbers on their uniforms in the middle of the 1932 season. This is the story of everyone that's hitched up the digits. The Stan Hacks, the Charlie Roots, the Phil Cavarrettas of the world, those you might have been able to tell without a number—Cubs fans have always been sharp—but the Dom Dallessandros and Harry Chitis of the world, they could now stand and be counted. And they've kept on counting; since then more than 1,300 Cubs have worn numbers. Only one player or manager or coach a number at a time can wear, though some have traded in numbers often enough you'd think they wanted to change that rule, too. Seems that as soon as one person gets traded or demoted or retires or just feels like a numeric change is needed, their number is right back in circulation waiting for the next in line. Unless, of course, you're talking about numbers 10, 14, 23, or 26, the only four numbers the Cubs have retired.

Can you imagine Ron Santo wearing a number other than 10? Or Billy Williams wearing a number besides 26? Well, they both did. Yes, my broadcast partner these last twelve years came into the world as a Cub wearing #15 in 1960. Billy also came along that year and wore #41. He'd worn #4 the previous season for his first sweet swings at Wrigley. It wasn't until 1961 that both Ronnie and Billy settled into the numbers that now fly on the flagpoles on each side of fair territory at Wrigley Field. You didn't know that? Well, there's a lot about the Cubs you'll learn from this fun book.

This isn't just some dry account of numbers worn through the years—though it's got everybody who's donned Cubs blue since '32—but there are fun to read stories and facts about both your favorites and guys you never heard of. Anyone who's worn a Cubs uniform even for one inning is included here, people whose names you should get to know if you call yourself a Cubs fan. And millions do. Those #16 jerseys that I see from Waveland Avenue to Petco Park are in tribute to slugging Cubs third baseman Aramis Ramirez, but that number has belonged to the great Jimmie Foxx, the late Kenny Hubbs, the last legal spitballer Burleigh Grimes, and even two-time World Series winning manager Terry Francona during a more humble assignment as a bench player for the '86 Cubs. And you know what? There've been more than thirty others who've worn that number, people with names like Wimpy, Tex, Howie, Whitey, Delino, and Sonny. Come to think of it, the name Aramis fits right in.

But the number that's fascinated me since I first learned to count by reading the backs of baseball cards as a kid—and it's great looking at all the Topps cards scattered throughout this book—is #3. Three seems to come up constantly in baseball. Three outs, three strikes, three-game series, .300 hitters, and three men on the bases, which always makes your heart beat a little faster whether it's your guy that put them there or your guy at the plate trying to bring them home. And how many Cubs have worn #3? Why, thirty-three, of course, from guys named Kiki (Cuyler) and Ripper (Collins) in the thirties to Chad (Hermansen) and Jeromy (Burnitz) in the twenty-first century. You can't make this stuff up.

Count yourself lucky that the Cubs now have a book that tells the history of this great franchise, one number at a time.

And away we go . . .

— **Pat Hughes**
September 2008

INTRODUCTION

Even before the Cubs wore numbers on their uniforms, they had made three numbers famous: 6-4-3. Tinker to Evers to Chance was one of the great infields of its day, but it was a short ditty penned by Franklin P. Adams, a transplanted Chicagoan living in New York, that provided meter and made their names eternal, transforming these ballplayers into a "trio of bear cubs, fleeter than birds." Oddly, in the nine seasons (1902–1910) that these three made up that famous DP combination, not once did the Cubs lead the National League in double plays. It just must have seemed so to Adams and the New York Giants, the team the Cubs so often kept from the World Series.

"Peerless Leader" Frank Chance led the Cubs to no fewer than ninety wins in each of his seven full years at the helm in Chicago—four times cracking 100, with four pennants and two world championships. Since then, the Cubs have had to earn everything they've gotten. They won two pennants between Chance's acrimonious exit in 1912 and the unpleasant removal of another future Hall of Famer, Rogers Hornsby, from the manager's chair during the 1932 season. Charlie Grimm took over on July 13. By then, the Cubs were wearing numbers on their backs. So was the whole National League. The Cubs dialed it up under "Jolly Cholly" and won the pennant.

Seventy-seven years later, these numbers are like an epic poem through four generations of Cubs, from the days when no team played night games, to the present day, now twenty-one years past when Wrigley Field finally switched the lights on. Each player, each number, is linked in a chain through the years. Through the 2008 season, 1,247 different players have buttoned up or pulled over a jersey with "Cubs" on the front and a number on the back. That number increases by eighty-nine when counting managers and coaches who never suited up as Cubs players, bringing the grand total to 1,336 numbered personnel in franchise history. Of course that's a temporary total if there ever was one, because the numbers just keep rolling on.

cubsbythenumbers.com/cubs-all-time.html) to see who's new in Cubs blue. The popular site bleedcubbieblue.com will also have updates, links, and book-related promotions on the site.

7. Each chapter comes with a sidebar or other bits of information about the Cubs that may not be generally known. A lot of chapters include lists of uniform numbers that have collected the highest amount in a given statistical category, such as home runs or wins. You won't find this information anywhere else. Though it might seem extraneous at first glance, you'll surely never look at a Cub wearing #7 the same way again.

8. An alphabetical roster is included at the end of the book for quick and easy reference.

9. This is the pitcher's spot—though not a pitcher's number. Start reading the book already.

#1: WHERE HAVE YOU GONE, JOSE CARDENAL?

When teams began to issue uniforms with numbers on the back, many of them did it in the simplest possible way—right down to the starting lineup, with the leadoff hitter getting #1, the second-place hitter #2, etc.

And that is why **Woody English** is the first player discussed in the first chapter of this book. He led off for the 1932 Cubs, and when the ballclub first appeared in numbered uniforms on June 30 of that year, Woody became #1. He had been the Cubs' regular shortstop since 1927, having his best year in the hitters' season of 1930 when he hit 14 homers, drew 100 walks, finished third in the NL with 152 runs scored, and hit .331. He finished fourth in the MVP voting that year.

A genial, likeable man, he even got along with the irascible Rogers Hornsby, rooming with him for a time. But it was also English, in his role as team captain, who called the famed 1932 clubhouse meeting in which the players voted not to give the unpopular Hornsby a World Series share.

After the 1932 season, English's performance began to decline due to various injuries. He was traded to the Dodgers following the 1936 campaign. After that, two managers (Charlie Grimm and Jimmie Wilson) wore the premier digit, and then it lay on the shelf until 1954. Unlike other teams, who often reserved #1 for their best players (the number is retired by seven teams: Pirates, Dodgers, Yankees, Reds, Red Sox, Cardinals, and Phillies), the Cubs at first issued #1 to players who had worn other numbers (**Bill Serena,** who wore #6 from 1949–53), weren't very good (**Jim Fanning,** who hit .170 over four seasons as a backup catcher

but who later had a long career as a major league manager and general manager), or who were good elsewhere (**Richie Ashburn,** who was long past his prime when he played his two Cub seasons, and whose #1 is retired by the Phillies).

So that leaves outfielder **Jose Cardenal** (1972–77) as perhaps the most popular and well-known of the Cubs who have worn #1. During his career he was also well-known for his many excuses as to why he couldn't play (including "I woke up and my eyes were swollen shut," and "Loud crickets kept me up all night").

Cardenal was acquired on December 3, 1971 from the Milwaukee Brewers in what was one of the Cubs' better trades of the seventies. In his first three seasons he hit .290 or better and along with his speed—25 steals in 1972 and 19 in 1973—that helped gain him one point in the MVP voting in '72 and six points in '73. His best year in the blue pinstripes was 1973, when he led the team in hitting (.303), doubles (33), and steals (19) and was named Chicago Player of the Year by the city's baseball writers. In 1975, Jose swiped 34 bases, and he also had his best overall season, hitting .317/.397/.423.

Jose also posted one of the best single-game lines in franchise history, going 6-for-7 with a double, home run and four RBI as the Cubs defeated the Giants, 6-5 in fourteen innings on May 2, 1976.

The number was also Lance'd (**Lance Johnson,** 1997–99) and became Strange (**Doug Strange,** 1991–92). **Kenny Lofton** wore it for a couple of games after his acquisition by trade from the Pirates in July 2003 before switching to his more familiar #7. **Dave Martinez** (1986–88) began wearing #1 as a speedy twenty-one-year-old outfielder and he reclaimed the number at Wrigley as a near-the-end-of-the-line bench player in 2000, a year when he played for four different teams.

Years from now, perhaps #1 will be best known for its current wearer, **Kosuke Fukudome** (2008), the Cubs' first Japanese-born player. Fukudome wore #1 for nine years as a Chunichi Dragon in Japan and decided to keep it in the major leagues. It is already among the best-selling replica jerseys at Wrigley Field. He was popular enough to be voted to the All-Star team as a "rookie," but he went hitless in both of his at bats in the game and slumped badly in the second half, eventually being benched.

Oddity: **Cookie Rojas** (1978–81) is listed as "player and coach" here, but you won't find his name in any of the encyclopedias as having played for the Cubs. At thirty-nine and in his first year on the coaching staff following a sixteen-year playing career, Rojas talked the brass into activating him as a player after rosters expanded on September 1. He is listed as "Coach-IF" on all the home scorecards dated September 4, 1978 to the end of the season. But he never got into a game, not even after the Cubs were mathematically eliminated from playoff contention, and he was reportedly miffed at GM Bob Kennedy for giving him the idea that he'd be able to play again, even in a token appearance, and then not having it happen.

MOST OBSCURE CUB TO WEAR #1: **Tommy Shields** (1993), who, despite having a fine name for an athlete, wasn't very good. He went 6-for-34 in twenty games, starting six of them.

GUY YOU NEVER THOUGHT OF AS A CUB WHO WORE #1: **Larry Bowa** (1982-85). Bowa, who was brought over along with many other Phillies by Dallas Green, never seemed quite comfortable or looked very good in Cubs pinstripes. He did right by Green, though, becoming part of the first Phillies world championship after ninety-seven years of Phutility and then being on the Cubs' first postseason team in thirty-nine years. He had worn #10 for the Phils, but he chose to wear #1 for the Cubs, probably just to be ornery (or maybe because he didn't feel like fighting incumbent Leon Durham for #10). Yet he just didn't fit right in Chicago. Oh, there was some other kid thrown into the Bowa-for-Ivan DeJesus deal. Kid named Sandberg. That one worked out OK.

First Things

June 30, 1932, a Thursday, was the first time the Cubs wore uniform numbers. American League teams had all gone with numbers the previous year (the Yankees had done so in '29 and the A's wore numbers only on the road until '37). The National League followed the trend, demanding all teams go to numbers at the league meeting on June 22, 1932. "The club owners felt that there was a general demand on the part of the public that the players be numbered," said NL president John Heydler. Though no National League team was regularly wearing numbers before the meeting, all eight clubs quickly stitched digits on their shirts within ten days of the edict. The Cubs waited until they returned to Wrigley to suit up in the numbers, making them among the last teams to comply.

Chicago went with a system that—like several teams before them—generally featured players wearing numbers that coincided with the spot in the order in which they batted, with some exceptions. This was the lineup on June 30,1932, the first with numbered Cubs:

1. Woody English, 3B
2. Billy Herman, 2B
3. Kiki Cuyler, CF
4. Riggs Stephenson, LF
49. Vince Barton, RF
6. Charlie Grimm, 1B
7. Gabby Hartnett, C
11. Billy Jurges, SS
12. Charlie Root, P

The regular right fielder, Johnny Moore, did get #5, but didn't play that day. Root blanked the Reds, 7-0, in the first of a three-game series. At the end of the day the Cubs trailed the first-place Pirates by half a game. They took over first place the next day and the two teams were in a nip-and-tuck fight for the flag throughout the season. The Cubs would get rid of the great yet grouchy Rogers Hornsby (#9) as manager on July 13 and replace him with first baseman Charlie Grimm (#6), aka "Jolly Cholly." Chicago went 55–34 with the numbers on their back en route to the '32 pennant.

#2: THE LIP AND THE RIOT

Isn't this the Cubs way? Three Hall of Famers (Billy Herman, Leo Durocher, and Gabby Hartnett) have all worn #2.

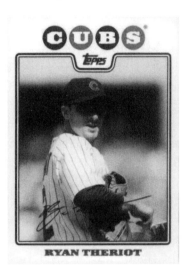

RYAN THERIOT

Yet, perhaps the most popular player ever to don this low digit is the current wearer, shortstop **Ryan Theriot.** There have been innumerable debates among fans about Theriot's perceived value to the ballclub, because he hits for virtually no power and doesn't really have the range or arm to be an everyday shortstop, but those who buy "The Riot" 's jersey, and who have made it among the biggest selling replica shirts seen at Wrigley Field, don't care about that. They admire what, for lack of a better term, is seen as his "scrappiness," his hustle, his willingness to get his uniform dirty. Popularity—and value to a team—can't always be measured on a stat sheet. And Theriot tried several other numbers out before settling on #2—wearing #55 when first called up at the end of the 2005 season, then switching to #3 in 2006, #7 when Cesar Izturis claimed #3 after arriving from the Dodgers, and #2 when Mark DeRosa joined the Cubs in 2007.

Gabby Hartnett is, without question, the greatest Cubs catcher of all time. In fact, when he retired in 1941, he was widely considered the best catcher in National League history, and he still ranks no worse than third (with Johnny Bench and Mike Piazza the only ones comparable). He was the first backstop to surpass 200 homers and 1,000 RBI, and his 163 double plays are still more than any other NL catcher. Hartnett played in four Cubs World Series (1929, 1932, 1935, and 1938), and managed the last of those teams. He was an All-Star six years running (1933–1938) and he was the one who told Carl Hubbell to throw nothing but screwballs when King Carl famously fanned Babe Ruth, Lou Gehrig, Jimmie Foxx, Al Simmons, and Joe Cronin in order in the 1934 All-Star Game. Hartnett was NL MVP in '35 when he batted .344 with 13 homers and 91 RBI. When he hit .339 and had career highs with 33 homers and 122 RBI in 1930, it was the only year between 1924 and present without a league MVP Award.

Fans could just barely make out the 2 on his back when he stepped up to the plate in the twilight of the afternoon of September 28, 1938. Hartnett had been named manager in July when the club was mired in third place. The Cubs, who'd rallied to sneak within a half-game of Pittsburgh, were tied 5-5 with the Pirates in the ninth. The umps were set to call the game because of darkness at the end of the inning when Hartnett ripped an 0-2 curve by Mace Brown over the not-quite-fully-covered-with-ivy walls (the ivy had been planted only a year before). The "Homer in the Gloamin'" put the Cubs in first place to stay.

Chicago followed with disappointing fourth and fifth-place finishes the next two years. Gabby, who'd gotten his name as a rookie because he wouldn't say a word to sportswriters, was let go and he finished his career as a player-coach for the Giants in 1941. He was elected to the Baseball Hall of Fame in 1955 and a decade later wore a uniform for the last time as a coach for the Kansas City A's.

In addition to #2, Hartnett was the first in club history to wear #7 (1932), and the following year started the rage of Cubs catchers

LEO DUROCHER

wearing #9 (1933–36), but #2 is his best-remembered number, a digit that perhaps ought to be retired someday.

After Hartnett, a series of forgettable players wore the "We Try Harder" number later popularized by Avis Rent-A-Car: **Marv Felderman** (1942), **Paul Gillespie** (1942), **Tony Jacobs** (1948), **Randy Jackson** (1950–55; Jackson's 21 HR, 70 RBI season got him on the All-Star team, and then, predictably, traded away), **Gale Wade** (1956), and **Lee Walls** (1957–59).

It was in 1966 that **Leo Durocher**, who had worn the number as Giants and Dodgers manager and for many years as a Brooklyn and Los Angeles coach, took the managerial reins on the North Side and donned #2. For several years prior to that, under the infamous "College of Coaches," coaches wore numbers in the 50s and 60s (and the club's win total was generally in that neighborhood as well). But no player wore #2 between 1959 and 1980, when **Mike "Not the Boxer" Tyson** joined the team. After serving as the regular second baseman in St. Louis for the better part of seven seasons, he was acquired in exchange for reliever Donnie Moore after the 1979 season. He spent a very forgettable year and a half as the second sacker for a sad sack Cubs team. Known as "Hitch" for constantly pulling up his pants, his biggest moment as a Cub came in '81, wearing #18, when he hit a three-run, pinch-hit homer off the Dodgers' Fernando Valenzuela at Wrigley Field on June 6, 1981, at the height of Fernandomania. That blast sent the Mexican-born pitcher, who'd been staked to a 4-0 lead against the 11–36 Cubs, to his shortest major league outing and worst loss to that date.

After that, players **Vance Law** (1988–89); **Rick Wilkins** (1991–95), who became only the second Cub catcher, after Hartnett, to have a 30-homer season (1993), perhaps one of the biggest fluke seasons in baseball history; and **Felix Fermin** (1996) wore #2 before it became a coach's number again from 1997–2006. And then "The Riot" started.

MOST OBSCURE CUB TO WEAR #2: Gale Wade, who bears the first name and surname of famous Chicago Bears but had the talent of neither, was #2 for 19 games in 1955 and 1956. He went 6-for-45 (.133) and vanished from the major league scene for good.

GUY YOU NEVER THOUGHT OF AS A CUB WHO WORE #2: Felix Fermin, who was once traded straight up for a young Omar Vizquel, was a Cub for the last stop of his career. A good glove man and career .259 hitter over ten seasons, in 1996 Fermin was released by the Mariners in April, the Yankees in May, and the Cubs in August. He hit .125 in eleven games as a Cub and called it quits.

Number 2 is Number 1

Charlie Grimm managed the Cubs wearing six different numbers (#1, #6, #7, #8, #40, #50), won pennants wearing two of them (1932, 1935, 1945), and had a record of 946–742 (second only in franchise wins to Cap Anson's 1,282, in the days before uni numbers). Yet it is #2—a number Grimm didn't wear—that reigns supreme as the winningest Cubs uni for managers. You can thank Gabby Hartnett, the man who replaced Grimm as manager in 1938 and went on to win the pennant, for getting #2 going. Leo Durocher later wore #2 for seven seasons. John Vukovich spent two days managing in #2. In fact, none of the three numbers (#4, #5, #25) worn for 500 managing wins belonged to Grimm. Sorry, Charlie.

Last Name	First Name	Uniform #	Years Managed	wins	losses	Total Wins	Total Losses
Grimm	Charlie	1	1937–38	138	97		
Wilson	Jimmy	1	1941–42	138	170		
						276	267
Hartnett	Gabby	2	1938–40	203	176		
Durocher	Leo	2	1966–72	535	526		
Vukovich+	John	2	1986	1	1		
						739	703
Frisch	Frankie	3	1949–51	141	196		
Franks	Herman	3	1977–79	238	241		
						379	437

Last Name	First Name	Uniform #	Years Managed	wins	losses	Total Wins	Total Losses
Elia	Lee	4	1982–83	127	158		
Fox+	Charlie	4	1983	17	22		
Michael	Gene	4	1986–87	114	124		
Zimmer	Don	4	1988–91	265	258		
						523	562
Boudreau	Lou	5	1960	50	78		
Amalfitano+	Joe	5	1979, 1980–81	66	116		
Lefebvre	Jim	5	1992–93	162	162		
Riggleman	Jim	5	1995–99	374	419		
Lachemann+	Rene	5	2002	0	1		
						652	776
Grimm	Charlie	6	1932	37	18		
Hack	Stan	6	1954–56	196	265		
Altobelli+	Joe	6	1991	0	1		
						233	284
Grimm	Charlie	7	1933–34, 1936	259	200		
						259	200
Grimm	Charlie	8	1935	100	54		
Frey	Jim	8	1984–86	196	182		
						296	236
Hornsby	Rogers	9	1932 (from 6–30 on)	18	16		
						18	16
Kimm+	Bruce	10	2002	33	45		
						33	45
Baker	Dusty	12	2003–06	322	326		
						322	326
Lockman	Whitey	16	1972–74	157	162		
						157	162
Gomez	Preston	18	1980	38	52		
						38	52

Last Name	First Name	Uniform #	Years Managed	wins	losses	Total Wins	Total Losses
Scheffing	Bob	25	1957–59	208	254		
Marshall	Jim	25	1974–76	175	218		
Baylor	Don	25	2000–02	187	220		
						570	692
Wilson	Jimmy	40	1943–44	75	88		
Grimm	Charlie	40	1944–49	406	402		
						481	490
Essian	Jim	41	1991	59	63		
Trebelhorn	Tom	41	1994	49	64		
Piniella	Lou	41	2007–08	182	141		
						290	268
Johnson+	Roy	42	1944	0	1		
Boudreau	Lou	42	1960	4	5		
						4	6
Cavarretta	Phil	44	1951–53	169	213		
						169	213
Grimm	Charlie	50	1960	6	11		
						6	11
Tappe*	El	52	1961–62	46	70		
						46	70
Craft*	Harry	53	1961	7	9		
Lucchesi+	Frank	53	1987	8	17		
						15	26
Himsl*	Vedie	54	1961	10	21		
						10	21
Klein*	Lou	60	1961–62, 1965	65	82		
						65	82
Kennedy*	Bob	61	1963–65	182	198		
						182	198
Metro*	Charlie	63	1962	43	69		
						43	69

- +designates interim manager
- *designates Head Coach during the College of Coaches Era

#3: KIKI

Hazen Shirley Cuyler was nicknamed "Kiki"—and if your name was "Hazen Shirley," wouldn't you want a nickname, too? The name is pronounced "Cuy-Cuy," as in the first part of his last name, not "Kee-Kee" as in Vandeweghe. Cuyler started his career with the Pirates, but he got into a dispute with Pirates manager Donie Bush and so the Cubs got him on November 28, 1927 for virtually nothing—just a couple of journeymen named Sparky Adams and Pete Scott.

Cuyler took off in 1929, hitting .360/.438/.532 and leading the National League with 43 stolen bases (one of four times he led the NL in steals), and the Cubs won the pennant. That stolen base number is even more impressive when you consider that steals were becoming less important in an era given over to power hitters. The next NL player to steal more than Cuyler's 43 in 1929 was Maury Wills, with 50 in 1960. No Cub would swipe as many as Cuyler until Bob Dernier stole 45 in 1984.

Cuyler suffered a broken foot in 1932, causing him to miss a third of the season, but he almost singlehandedly carried the Cubs to the pennant when he returned, hitting .365 from August 27 to the end of the season. He hit a walkoff homer on August 31 in one of the most dramatic games in Cubs history. For a time that homer held the reputation of being perhaps the greatest single Cubs moment, then Gabby Hartnett's "Homer in the Gloamin'" came along six years later, and the "Cuyler Game" is now forgotten except by history buffs.

Check out what Cuyler did in *one week* in late August and early September 1932 after returning from his injury:

8/27, a doubleheader vs. Giants. First game: three-run homer, Cubs win, 6-1, their eighth win in a row. Second game: single and run, the Cubs win their ninth in a row, 5-0.

8/28, vs. Giants. Three hits including an eighth-inning homer and game-winning sacrifice fly as the Cubs win their tenth straight, 5-4.

8/30, vs. Giants. Two hits, two RBI, eighth inning homer, another 5-4 win, the eleventh in a row.

8/31, vs. Giants. Four hits. Singles in a four-run ninth to tie the game at 5-5. The Giants score four in the top of the tenth, taking a 9-5 lead. In the last of the tenth, after the first two men are out, the Cubs score two to cut the lead to 9-7 and have two on for Cuyler, who hits a walkoff home run for a 10-9 win, their twelfth straight.

9/2, vs. Cardinals. Cuyler homers, his fifth in six games, leading the Cubs to their thirteenth straight win, 8-5. The Cubs' winning streak reaches fourteenth, then stopped, perhaps not coincidentally, on a day Cuyler was hitless.

And finally, as a fitting climax to this run, five years after they had unceremoniously dumped him, Cuyler got his revenge on Pittsburgh. On September 20, 1932, in the first game of a doubleheader, he stepped to the plate in the seventh inning against the Pirates with the game tied 2-2. He smacked a bases-clearing triple to break the game open and clinch the pennant for the Cubs, their second pennant in four seasons.

Injuries and age made for a rapid decline in Cuyler's abilities: after 1934, his playing time was reduced, and in 1935 he was released, signing with the Reds, for whom he put up one final salvo in 1936, hitting .326. He's in the Hall of Fame, but Cuyler is still nearly forgotten today. Had it not been for the injuries, he could have reached 3,000 hits (he finished with 2,299). He was one of the greatest hitters of his day.

And since Cuyler's day, #3 has become primarily a coach's and manager's number for the Cubs, although it bounced around to a few players in the 1930s and 1940s. **Ripper Collins,** better known as a Cardinal, was acquired by the Cubs after the 1936 season and was the starting first baseman for the 1938 NL champions, and **Walt Lanfranconi** pitched two games wearing #3 in September 1941. In all, only thirteen players besides Cuyler have worn this single digit, and between the end of the 1958 season, when utilityman **Jim Bolger** (.244 in 260 games as a backup infielder and outfielder from 1956–58) was traded to Cleveland, and 2002, when the Cubs acquired **Chad Hermansen,** a former number one draft pick of the Pirates, no player donned #3. Hermansen's greatest contribution to the Cubs (for whom he hit .209 in 43 at bats) was being part of the deal that sent Todd Hundley to the Dodgers on December 4, 2002, for infielders Mark Grudzielanek and Eric Karros.

There is one technical exception to the "no players wearing #3 between 1958 and 2002" rule: coach **Al Spangler,** who had played from 1967–70 for the Cubs as a backup outfielder wearing #20 and #21, wore #3 as a coach in 1971. The team activated him as a player on August 30. The Cubs, seven games out of first place and on the fringes of contention, perhaps thought that Spangler, a fine pinch hitter, could help them if they made the postseason. Spangler pinch-hit five times in 1971, had two hits, and the Cubs finished fourteen games out of first place.

In that forty-four-year interregnum, fourteen coaches and one manager (**Herman Franks,** 1977–79) sported the number. A great many of them were buddies with the manager they served under (1966 pitching coach **Freddie Fitzsimmons,** aka "Fat Freddie," had been a teammate of Leo Durocher's and coached under him in the 1950s with the Giants; **Joe Becker** had coached with Durocher in the Dodgers organization; **Larry Jansen** pitched for Durocher's Giants; **Herm Starrette** had been a pitching coach for the Phillies while Dallas Green was farm director there; **Dan Radison** was a minor league teammate of Jim Riggleman's; and **Gene Glynn** had been brought over with Don Baylor from Colorado, where he had been on Baylor's staff). And no mention of coaches wearing #3 would be complete without a nod to "Wavin'" **Wendell Kim** (another crony; he had coached under Dusty Baker in his Giants days), who got his nickname from all the runners he sent around third base into certain out-tagging at home plate.

When Hermansen departed the scene, #3 was returned to general circulation for players. It was briefly worn by **Ryan Theriot,** who also donned #55 and #7 before settling on his now-familiar #2; Theriot gave it up when veteran shortstop **Cesar Izturis,** who had worn #3 as a Dodger, was acquired on July 31, 2006. Izturis lasted less than a year in a Cubs uniform; when he was shipped to the Pirates on July 19, 2007, #3 again became available. It was taken two and a half weeks later by **Eric Patterson** when he made his major league debut on August 6. When the 2008 season began, coach **Alan Trammell**, outranking rookie Patterson, reclaimed #3, which he had worn throughout his great playing career with the Detroit Tigers.

MOST OBSCURE CUB TO WEAR #3: **Owen Friend** (1955-56). Friend, a middle infielder for four AL teams in the late 1940s and early 1950s, was rather pointlessly acquired by the Cubs via a waiver transaction on June 12, 1955. He played in eight Cubs games over parts of two seasons and had one hit in twelve at bats. After retiring as a player, he became a longtime minor league manager and was on the coaching staff of the 1969 expansion Kansas City Royals, where he became the first Royal to wear #5, later retired in honor of George Brett.

GUY YOU NEVER THOUGHT OF AS A CUB WHO WORE #3: **Jeromy Burnitz** (2005), the guy with the odd-spelled first name, played fourteen seasons in the majors, one of which was spent patrolling right field for the Cubs. He was signed as a free agent after posting a 37 HR, 110 RBI year for the Rockies. What Cubs management failed to recognize in making this signing was that: a) Burnitz was thirty-six years old, b) those numbers were compiled in the mile-high air of Denver, and c) Burnitz never spent a full season on a winning team during his long career; when 2005 was over, the Cubs fit right in with that group. Burnitz hit 24 homers and drove in 87 runs for the 79-83, fourth-place Cubs. He left via free agency after the season to finish his perfect record in Pittsburgh.

Pitching Low

What's the lowest uniform number worn by a pitcher in Cubs history? There are actually three different answers and they all occurred in the 1940s.

The lowest number to toe the rubber at Wrigley Field is #3. Walt Lanfranconi took the mound in relief in Chicago against the Phillies on September 12, 1941. He then got a start the last week of the season and lost at Crosley Field, 2-0. He reappeared six years later, following three-plus years in the military. He pitched his only other major league season in the more pitcher-friendly #34 as a member of the Boston Braves.

But he wasn't the lowest numbered Cub to ever pitch—that would be Tony Jacobs. Seven years after Lanfranconi pitched for the Cubs, Jacobs took the mound wearing #2. He threw two innings and allowed a run on three hits at Ebbets Field in an 8-1 loss. The Illinois native never pitched again for the Cubs, but he got two more innings seven years later as a Cardinal. Jacobs wore #1 for St. Louis, making his two career appearances the lowest number worn by a pitcher for two different clubs. Too bad his career ERA was above eleven.

Johnny "Bear Tracks" Schmitz holds the distinction of having the lowest number of any Cub to record a win. He debuted in #7 just six days before Lanfranconi, and won the first game of a doubleheader against the Dodgers on September 10, 1941. He won again four days later. The following year he moved up to #31 (which would later become the number of two famed Cubs pitchers, Ferguson Jenkins and Greg Maddux) and after missing three seasons in the military in World War II, Schmitz returned to Chicago to don #53. He wound up having a thirteen-year career wearing eleven different numbers for seven clubs, though he never again tarried in the single digits.

#4: THE HERMANS

Billy Herman was born in New Albany, Indiana, right across the Ohio River from Louisville, Kentucky, on July 7, 1909. As were many players (and just plain folks) born in that era, William Jennings Bryan "Billy" Herman was named after a popular politician of his day. During his playing career he was known for his stellar defense and consistent batting; in fact, he still holds many National League defensive records for second basemen, including the NL mark for most putouts in a single season (466 in 1933), and the most years leading his league in putouts (seven).

He broke into the major leagues in 1931 when the Cubs purchased his contract from AAA Louisville for $50,000. He asserted himself as a star the following season, starting all 154 games in 1932; he recorded 206 hits, scored 102 runs, and batted .314. A fixture in the Chicago lineup over the next decade, Herman was a consistent hitter and solid producer. He regularly hit .300 or higher, peaking at .341 in the pennant year of 1935, and the following year set a career high with 93 RBI.

After a sub-standard offensive year in 1940, Herman was traded to the Brooklyn Dodgers early in their pennant-winning 1941 season for Johnny Hudson, Charlie

Gilbert, and $65,000. Along with the earlier trade of Augie Galan, this was one of the deals that started the Cubs on their decline of the 1940s, stemmed only by the 1945 pennant.

Before Hall of Famer Billy Herman, another Herman, **Babe Herman,** wore #4 for two years, 1933 and 1934. Herman was best known for a baserunning gaffe he committed in 1926 while a member of the Brooklyn Dodgers. (He hit a double off the wall with two runners on base, but both of them stopped at third; when Herman tried to stretch the double into a triple, the Dodgers wound up with all three runners on third base, whereupon the third baseman tagged all three. Since only one runner was entitled to the base, Herman was said to have "doubled into a double play.")

While baserunning wasn't his forté, Babe could swing the bat. He had a .324 lifetime average and hit .296 with 30 homers and 177 RBI in 975 at bats as a Cub after being acquired from the Reds in 1932 for four players. Two years later, he was traded to the Pirates.

Ralph Kiner (1953–54) had two decent years in the Cubs outfield, hitting 50 homers in the blue pinstripes. Acquired on June 4, 1953 from the Pirates in a ten-player deal (massive trades were a popular device for teams in the 1950s, especially bad teams like the Cubs and Pirates, hoping major changes would improve their lot—it almost never worked), Kiner's better years were behind him. He was sent to Cleveland after the 1954 season. Had he not had serious back problems, he might have hit over 500 homers. As it was, his 369 homers in ten seasons—including an unmatched seven consecutive NL home run crowns (typical for those Cubs teams, the first year of his career without a home run title was as a Cub) got him elected to the Hall of Fame, and sent him to a long career as a broadcaster with the New York Mets.

Better remembered in Chicago is the first wearer of #4, **Riggs Stephenson,** who wore the number only in 1932, switching to #5 the following two seasons. Stephenson, a swift outfielder who spent his early years with Cleveland as an infielder, had suffered some shoulder injuries and was therefore made available to the Cubs in 1926. The next year he had a terrific season, hitting .344, and two years later his .362 average helped lead the Cubs to the pennant. In that 1929 season, each of the three Cubs starting outfielders (Stephenson, Kiki Cuyler, and Hack Wilson) had over 100 RBI.

At .336, Riggs Stephenson's lifetime batting average is the highest of anyone who is not in the Hall of Fame yet started his career in the twentieth century. That average still ranks twenty-second all-time in baseball history, and is the highest in the history of the Chicago National League ballclub (tied with Bill Madlock, though Stephenson batted almost 2,000 more times as a Cub). Had it not been for the shoulder injuries, which limited him to only four seasons of 136 or more games in his nine years with the Cubs, Stephenson might well be in the Hall of Fame today.

Ethan Allen—neither the early American patriot nor the furniture store—wore #4 in 1936, his only year as a Cub in a thirteen-year career. He had been acquired in the deal that sent Chuck Klein back to Philly, but he was sold to the Browns at season's end. **Wimpy Quinn** (1941) was a pitcher who pitched in three games—all with a different number: #4, #16, and #18. **Hal Jeffcoat** (1949–53) was a pitcher—wait, no he wasn't, no, wait, yes he was—well, let us explain. Jeffcoat was an outfielder from 1949–53 with little pop or sizzle, but, obviously, a strong arm. In 1954 he pulled what we might today call the "reverse Ankiel" and switched to pitching. He also switched numbers, from #4 to #19, and had some success as a reliever in 1955, at which time the Cubs traded him to the Reds. And **Billy Williams** spent his September call up in 1959 wearing #4 for the fifth-place Cubs: 18 games, 33 at bats, and a .152 average. You'd never have guessed that the skinny kid from Mobile, Alabama was on his way to the Hall of Fame.

And after that, much like #3, #4 became a coach's and manager's number starting with former great Cubs pitcher **Charlie Root** in 1960. With the sole exception of **Vic Harris**—who came over from the Rangers in 1974 and demanded to have his Texas number (and whose .191 average over two seasons made the Cubs think twice before listening to the likes of Vic Harris again)—no player wore #4 between Williams in '59 and **Glenallen Hill,** he of the rooftop bomb (hit while wearing #6 in 2000), in 1994. The best-known #4s were managers. **Lee Elia** started the trend with #4—the four-letter words in his fabled post-game tirade in 1983 were a different matter. Elia's interim replacement **Charlie Fox,** later followed by **Gene Michael** and **Don Zimmer,** kept #4 in the manager's office through most of the 1980s. Zimmer had worn #17 as a Cubs player in 1960 and 1961, but chose #4 when he returned as a coach in 1984 under manager Jim Frey. After Michael was fired, Zim reclaimed it when he came back to manage in 1988.

Since its return to player circulation, we cannot say that #4 has been worn with any distinction. **Jason Dubois** (2004–05), **Ben Grieve** (2005), **Freddie Bynum** (2006), **Rob Bowen** (2007), **Scott Moore** (2007), and **Eric Patterson** (2008) all wore the number briefly and with few accomplishments. On his second tour of duty as a Cub, **Doug Glanville,** who had worn #1 and #8 in his original Cubs incarnation, had one shining moment in uniform #4: a game-winning triple in the top of the eleventh inning in Game 3 of the 2003 NLCS.

MOST OBSCURE CUB TO WEAR #4: **Brian Dorsett** (1996). For some unexplainable reason, GM Ed Lynch decided that it was a good idea in the 1995–96 offseason to sign a thirty-five-year-old journeyman catcher who had failed for five different teams prior to 1996. Even worse, manager Jim Riggleman put him on the Opening Day roster. He started nine games behind the plate; somehow the Cubs managed to win six of them despite his .122 batting average. He was sent to the minors in June and released at the end of the season, never again reaching the majors.

GUY YOU NEVER THOUGHT OF AS A CUB WHO WORE #4: **Chuck Klein** (1935-36). He had put up big years for the Phillies from 1929-33, but immediately declined when he put on a Cubs uniform. Times were tight during the Depression, and he was traded to Chicago just months after capturing the 1933 Triple Crown (the Phillies were more intent on the $65,000 in the deal than the three live bodies sent back to the Baker Bowl). Wearing #6 in 1934, Klein switched to #4 for the following two seasons. When he got off to a bad start in '36, the Cubs sent him back to the City of Brotherly Love. Though some could quibble with his eventual selection to the Hall of Fame, there's no argument that his 25 home runs in 148 games as a Cub had little to do with the discussion either way.

Cubs Unis, Part I: Dressed for Success

One of the sidebars planned for this book was a brief history of the Cubs uniform. This is impossible. There are enough variations of the Cubs uniform to do a whole separate book (and for anyone planning on doing that, this book certainly proves that such an endeavor has an audience). This task was made easier by *Dressed to the Nines* by Marc Okkonen, at the Baseball Hall of Fame website, and by Paul Lukas of ESPN.com, the last word on all things uni related.

What follows are some of the most intriguing looks in Cubs fashion and the year they first appeared. The list is broken into three parts (1871–1932, 1933–81, 1982–2008). The other two parts are in the chapters immediately following this one.

1889: Hit Like an Egyptian—Starting in 1871, when the National Association forebears of the Cubs took to the diamond for pay, the team went through several styles. At various times in those early days, the club wore ties, pillbox caps, and high stockings, often white to go with the team's earliest name. For team president Albert Spalding's fabled round the world trip in 1889, Cap Anson's pre-Cubs posed on the Sphinx in their collared uniforms and you could read "Chicago" all the way from Cairo.

1900: Red Socks—Imagine the Cubs hosed in red? At the turn of the last century, they weren't really even known as the Cubs and the team we know as the Red Sox did not even exist. And Chicago's socks were probably closer to maroon, but the club was still getting it's feet wet. Frank Chance was a reserve catcher, Joe Tinker was still toiling in the minors, and Johnny Evers was just a teen growing up in Troy, New York.

Johnny Evers, pictured above, models the cadet uni in this 100-year-old baseball card originally distributed in a pack of cigarettes, though the cubs emblem is hidden by his bat.

1908: Cubby Bat—The team, now known as the Cubs, introduced the bear inside the "C" in silhouette and holding a bat. That emblem would be over every player's heart as the Cubs took the World Series that fall. The bear would return many times in many different forms through the years, but championships would be a different matter.

1909: Cadet Cubs—The two-time defending world champions were hard to miss, but the Cubs added a cool wrinkle to their pinstriped road uniforms. Called the "cadet collar," it spelled out "Chicago" vertically in white letters on a dark blue background. Next to it was "Cubs" spelled with the big "C," the first time that iconic logo appeared on the unis.

1932: Lots of Sewing—The year the Cubs added numbers to their uniforms in midseason they broke a few thimbles sewing on the new digits. The Cubs had four different uniforms: two each for home and the road. To be honest, the uniforms from this period—from 1931 up until the boys started leaving for the war in 1942—looked more like future White Sox garb than old-time Cubs togs.

#5: TAKE FIVE . . . PLEASE!

The Cubs' first #5, **Johnny Moore,** became a regular in 1932 after three years of playing sparingly. He hit .305 and knocked in 64 runs while patrolling the outfield that season, but he didn't get to be in the lineup the first day the Cubs wore uniform numbers. As the usual fifth-place hitter, he was assigned #5. But on June 30, Vince Barton, wearing #49, started in right field and hit fifth. It may have signaled the beginning of the end for Moore as a Cub, as after the season they shipped him to Cincinnati with three other players for Babe Herman. At the end of the 1945 season, the forty-three-year-old Moore made a brief seven-game reappearance with the Cubs wearing #5, after eight years out of the majors,

Billy Jurges (1937–38; he also wore #8 and #11 as a player) liked to be where the action was. The fiery shortstop was shot during the 1932 season by a distraught female fan (like in *The Natural*, only twenty years before Bernard Malamud's novel and more than fifty years before the film), yet Jurges came back in time to help the Cubs take the pennant and hit .364 in the World Series. On July 30, 1935, he picked a fight with rookie catcher Walter Stephenson of North Carolina about who won the Civil War, but that didn't stop him from helping the Cubs reel off winning streaks of eleven and twenty-one games in the second half as they grabbed the '35 flag. And in 1938... well, no bones were broken that year, but we're still talking three Cubs pennants with a shortstop not named Joe Tinker! So that winter the club traded the Bronx native to the New York Giants in a lousy six-player deal. Jurges returned to Chicago as a player-coach in 1946, wearing #45. He retired the following year and later went into managing. The most significant part of his two-year tenure as Boston's skipper was Pumpsie Green's debut in 1959, making the Red Sox the last team to integrate.

Many of the rest of the #5s were fringe players or those who had had better years with other teams. **Clyde McCullough** caught for the 1945 NL champion Cubs—becoming the first player to appear in a World Series without playing in that regular season (he had a good excuse: World War II service)—but in the Series McCullough wore #9, not the original #5 he'd worn in 1941 and 1942. A number of extraneous players—**Hank Schenz** (1947–49), **Bob Ramazzotti** (1949–53), **Bruce Edwards** (1954), **Vern Morgan** (1955), **Frank Kellert** (1956), **Bobby Del Greco** (1957), and **Frank Ernaga** (1957)—sported #5 without ever having much impact on even the bad Cubs teams of the 1950s. The best of the lot was Ramazzotti, and he wasn't very good; his best season was 1952, when he hit .284 and had three stolen bases in fifty games.

Tony Taylor (1958–60) could have reversed this trend, but he became another casualty of GM John Holland's failure to understand that young players, particularly those with a little bit of speed (Taylor stole 23 bases as Chicago's regular second baseman in 1959, ranking third in the NL), were becoming valuable in baseball at that time. Holland traded Taylor to the Phillies on May 13, 1960 for Ed Bouchee, a first baseman who couldn't run (zero steals in '59) but who had hit 15 home runs, and pitcher Don Cardwell. Though Cardwell made a splash by throwing a no-hitter in his first Cubs start (becoming the first player ever to do so in his debut with a team), he won only thirty games in three years in a Cubs uniform, while Taylor became a fine second baseman for over a decade, winding up with more than 2,000 career hits.

After **Jimmie Schaffer,** a backup catcher, wore #5 in 1963 and 1964, it became almost exclusively used by coaches and managers for the next four decades. Between 1964 and 2002, only **Adrian Garrett** (1974) and **Randy Hundley** (1976) wore it as players, and neither one of them had a particular affinity for #5. Garrett also wore #23, #25, and #28 in various Cub stints in the early seventies and Hundley had been much more famous as #9 in his first go-around as a Cub, taking #5 on his somewhat-less-than triumphant return in 1976 (3-for-18) because starting catcher Steve Swisher, an unlikely All-Star that year, already had #9.

Q. V. Lowe (1972) had been signed by the Cubs in 1964, and after never reaching the majors in eight years with the organization, the Cubs rewarded him with one year as a major league coach. Since leaving pro ball, Lowe has been a college baseball coach for more than thirty years. Less obscure was Hall of Famer **Lou Boudreau** (1960), a Chicago-area native who had played and managed the Cleveland Indians to a World Series title in 1948. Safely home and ensconced in the Cubs' radio booth, Boudreau was involved in one of the more unusual trades in baseball history when upper management decided to make a change in managers. They sent Charlie Grimm to do Boudreau's WGN radio job and moved the "Good Kid" to the dugout. Neither move was of any use—Grimm was horrid on the air and Boudreau, in his last managerial gig, went 54–83. The next season, Boudreau returned to the broadcast booth, where he would remain until 1987.

Three full-time managers (**Joey Amalfitano,** 1979–81; **Jim Lefebvre,** 1992–93, and **Jim Riggleman,** 1995–99) and one interim skipper—**Rene Lachemann,** who filled in for one game after Don Baylor was fired in 2002—wore #5; Amalfitano headed some of the worst Cubs teams in history, going 66–116. In 1992 Lefebvre became the first manager since Leo Durocher in 1971 to manage a Cubs team to a winning record in a non-playoff season, guiding the club to an 84–78 mark; he finished his Cubs managerial career exactly at .500 by reversing that record the following year. Riggleman had two winning seasons and a playoff berth in 1998 in his five seasons, but also had two 90-plus loss years and his Cubs managerial winning percentage was .472

(374–419). After Lachemann departed, #5, at last, returned to the player ranks. Two different speedsters, **Tom Goodwin** (who led the 2003 Cubs in steals with 19 despite playing in only 87 games) and **Tony Womack** (Goodwin switched to #24 when Womack was acquired) wore it for the 2003 NL Central champions.

The best player to wear #5 for the Cubs was likely **Nomar Garciaparra** (2004–05), but sadly, Nomar's All-Star days were behind him when GM Jim Hendry acquired him in a four-team deal at the trading deadline, July 31, 2004. Nomar appeared in his first game at Wrigley Field on August 1 to a standing ovation—wearing #8, since catcher **Michael Barrett** had been sporting #5 that year. Shortly afterward, Barrett offered #5—which Nomar had worn throughout his career in Boston—to the new Cubs shortstop, and he accepted. Shortly after the 2005 season began, Garciaparra suffered a serious groin injury and missed about half the year; when he departed, another shortstop, **Ronny Cedeno,** took over #5, after wearing #11 in a brief call up at the end of 2005 while Nomar was still on the team.

MOST OBSCURE CUB TO WEAR #5: **Vern Morgan** played in thirty-one games for two bad Cubs teams in 1954 (wearing #30) and 1955, playing seventeen of them at third base (and not very well, either, making six errors in those games for a brutal .864 fielding percentage). He hit .225 in 71 at bats with two doubles among his 16 hits. The Cubs might have figured this out three years earlier had they noticed that the woeful St. Louis Browns had selected him from the Cubs organization in the minor league draft—and then returned him before the next season even began.

GUY YOU NEVER THOUGHT OF AS A CUB WHO WORE #5: **Billy Rogell** (1940), who was the starting shortstop for two pennant-winning Detroit Tiger teams in 1934 and 1935 (and who hit .292 for Detroit in the '35 World Series against the Cubs), was acquired, as the Cubs sometimes did in those days, when he was thirty-five and long past being productive on the field. He hit .136 in thirty-three games in 1940 before his release. Meanwhile, the man the Cubs sent to Detroit for Rogell, **Dick "Rowdy Richard" Bartell,** another obscure #5 who played only one season for the Cubs (1939), finished twelfth in AL MVP voting in 1940 and was the starting shortstop for another Detroit World Series team.

Cubs Unis, Part II: Then Depression Set In

The Cubs enjoyed a prosperous period during the Great Depression. The Cubs won four pennants from 1929–38, taking the flag every three seasons like clockwork. Then the clock broke.

Here are the fashion highlights of a period that started out swell and eventually swelled shut.

1937: Zip Up—The Cubs were the first team to wear a zipper on a major league uniform, though they went back to buttons during World War II. The last team to go with zippers down the front was the Phillies in the 1980s.

1940: Three Stripes, You're Out—The Cubs brought the sleeveless vest look into the big leagues. It lasted a couple of years. The Cubs also went with three stripes on the socks and three on the sleeve of the sweatshirts on several varying home and road uniforms during the years World War II raged in Europe. The stripes remained on their pants and arms as the Cubs made it to the 1945 World Series. Then they disappeared.

jerry kindall

CHICAGO CUBS
INFIELD

1957: We Are the Cubs—The Cubs enjoyed little success in this decade and in '57, the club felt the need to explain exactly who they were. The '57 road uniform spelled out "Chicago Cubs," the last time the Cubs felt the need to specify on their uniform exactly which Chicago team they were (they'd also done so in 1917, the year the White Sox wound up winning the World Series), and the last time any team put both its city and nickname on a uni. The '57 Cubs drew heavily on lines: pinstripes on the home uniform, white lines on the hats, and blue and white stripes on their stirrups as opposed to blue and red (they dropped the striped stirrups and caps for good the next year).

1962: Face It—The '62 Cubs marked the first 100-loss team in franchise history and the nadir of the College of Coaches. It also introduced the "bear face" emblem that was, in various forms, on the home jersey every year through 1996 (with the exception of 1976, when it was trumped by the baseball centennial patch worn that year by every major league team).

1969: Count It—It was the best Cubs season since the war and the harshest finish yet. The Cubs tried something different with their numbers for the first time since 1932, placing them on the front of the road uniforms—something they have never done on the home duds. In 1972, after going to a pullover jersey, they would center the number below "Chicago" before switching the numbers back on the lower left front in '73.

1976: Baby Got Blue—The Cubs got funkadelic in 1976, breaking out powder blue road uniforms. Two years later, at the height of the disco rage, the Cubs kicked it up a notch with baby blue striped road threads, termed "pajamas" by some. The vertical stripes made even Herman Franks look thin and cool (well, almost).

#6: SMILIN' STAN

Before Ron Santo, **Stan Hack** was the best third baseman in Cubs history. Smiling Stan liked numbers—he wore seven different uniform numbers and was the first Cub to wear #31 and #39—but that made sense since he came to the Cubs from a bank. "Stanley got out of the banking business just as fast as he could and is now trying to forget the experience," *The Sporting News* said of the rookie in 1932. "Why can't the fans of Chicago forget he was an incipient banker and admire him for what he is today?" It gives you an idea where banks stood in the public's mind during the Depression. The Cubs were so impressed with Hack's Pacific Coast League pedigree they paid $40,000 to bring him to Chicago.

Hack was a lifetime .301 hitter, batting leadoff from the left side and rarely striking out. He led the team in runs eight times and batting four times while twice pacing the NL in hits and steals. With almost 2,200 career hits, scoring over 100 runs six straight times in a lower-offense era, and being an above-average third-sacker, he did get a handful of Hall of Fame votes in the 1940s and 1950s, peaking at 4.8 percent of the vote and eventually falling off the ballot. He retired following a disagreement with manager Jimmie Wilson in 1943, but after Wilson was fired midway through the next season **Charlie Grimm** (the original #6, now wearing #40 for his second tour of duty as manager) coaxed Hack out of retirement. It was a good thing, too. Hack hit .323 in 1945, finishing eleventh in MVP voting, and helped lead the Cubs to the pennant. He played in four World Series as a Cub—batting .348 in 18 Series games—and was a five-time All-Star. He tried to bring that talent to Cubs in the 1950s as manager, but in three years at the helm Hack never guided the team to higher than a sixth-place finish.

Truly, the Cubs should retire #6 in honor of Smilin' Stan, not just be-

JOHNNY CALLISON

cause he was one of the greatest players in Cubs history, but because the number hasn't been worn with much distinction since Stan's last year as manager in 1956. **Bill Serena** wore it from 1949–53, just before Hack's managerial stint, putting up mid-range power numbers (17 homers for a seventh-place Cub team in 1950, which earned him fifth place in the Rookie of the Year voting), but after that there were a number of players who either did little (**Fred Richards,** who went 8-for-27 in 1951, and then vanished from the baseball Earth),

poorly (**Jack Littrell,** .190 in 1957); went on to more success elsewhere (**Chuck Tanner** in 1958, a part-time outfielder who had a long career as a manager, including six seasons with the White Sox and later winning a World Series with the Pirates in 1979), or players like **Earl Averill** (1959–60), who hit 11 homers with the Cubs and 44 overall, 196 fewer than his Hall of Fame father whose name he bears, or **Jim McKnight** (1960), who played in three 1960 games before returning two years later wearing #15, perhaps giving a legacy to his yet-to-be-born son, Jeff (who didn't enter the world until 1963), who wore five different numbers for the New York Mets in the 1980s and 1990s.

In the 1960's, #6 was turned over exclusively to catchers. **Dick Bertell** had two tours of duty with the ball club and with the number (1960–65, 1967), hitting .252 as a Cub. He hit .302 in 1962 in about half a season's work (77 games, 215 AB), becoming the last .300-plus hitting Cubs catcher—in anything more than just a handful of at bats—until Michael

Barrett hit .307 in 2006. Catchers young—**Johnny Stephenson** (1967–68) and **Randy Bobb** (1968–69)—and old—**Ed Bailey** (1965)—wore #6 with little distinction. After outfielder **Johnny Callison** (1970–71) unsuccessfully tried to bring the achievements he'd had in Philadelphia wearing #6 to Chicago, the club turned the number over to coaches for several seasons. It wasn't until 1975 that another player, backup catcher **Tim Hosley,** put #6 on his back. In his single season in Chicago (and one at bat in 1976 before he was waived back to Oakland, whence he came), Hosley hit .255. He did manage one memorable moment in that Cub blue #6, though. On September 14, 1975, Hosley came to bat as a pinch hitter with the bases loaded and two out in the bottom of the ninth and hit a grand slam. The Cubs lost anyway, 13-7.

Ted Sizemore (1979) was yet another player who had tormented the Cubs as an opponent, mainly for the Cardinals and Phillies through the seventies. Acquired through the theory "If he's on our side, he can't beat us!" Sizemore tried his best to do that anyway, playing poor defense, hitting .248, and being seen as a malcontent. The Cubs dumped him to the Red Sox in August.

KEITH MORELAND

The player with the second-longest tenure in #6, six seasons, came to the Cubs from the Phillies as GM Dallas Green was seemingly intent on replicating his 1980 Phils World Series-winning team. (We'd have taken it.) **Bobby Keith Moreland** had played both baseball and football at the University of Texas and brought the gridiron mindset to the baseball diamond. Unfortunately, he didn't really have a position he could play well. The Cubs tried him behind the plate, but catching wasn't his thing. He played third base . . . like the proverbial statue. Without a DH in the National League, the Cubs had to find a position for his potent bat, and finally settled on right field once Bill Buckner was traded away and Leon Durham moved permanently to first base. Moreland was a bull in the outfield, but his bat made up for it (106 RBI in 1985 and 27 HR in 1987) and he loved getting and returning the "Hook 'em Horns" hand gesture with the bleacherites behind him.

In the second game of a doubleheader against the Mets at Wrigley Field on August 7, 1984, in the heat of a tight divisional race, Moreland embedded himself into Cubs lore forever. Mets pitcher Ed Lynch—later to become Cubs GM—hit Moreland with a pitch in the fourth inning. Moreland felt Lynch was throwing at him on purpose and charged the mound, tackling Lynch with one of his best linebacker moves. It triggered a bench-clearing brawl which some say helped galvanize the Cubs to the NL East title. Interestingly, neither player was ejected from that game, which the Cubs won, 8-4. Lynch was traded to the Cubs two years later and they became teammates.

After the 1987 season, the popular Moreland was traded to the Padres in a very unpopular deal that proved to be a bad one, too. It brought future Hall-of-Famer Rich Gossage to the Cubs, whose closing days were behind him by then, while Moreland stopped hitting in San Diego. Moreland finished his career with stints in Detroit and Baltimore, but he lives on in Cubs lore. Moreland and Ernie Banks are the only players actually mentioned in Steve Goodman's "A Dying Cub Fan's Last Request," the song that Dallas Green hated so much that WGN asked Goodman to write an upbeat Cubs song, which turned out to be "Go Cubs Go."

Since Moreland's departure, a number of coaches and backups have worn #6; coach **Joe Altobelli,** the manager of the 1983 world champion Orioles, also served one game as interim manager in 1991 between Don Zimmer's firing and Jim Essian's hiring. It also belonged to coach **Sonny Jackson** (2005–06), who was brought on board by his buddy Dusty Baker (the two had played together in Atlanta and Jackson had been on Baker's Giants coaching staff). No one seems to know exactly what Jackson did for the Cubs, except to wear uniform #6.

Journeymen make up the remainder of the #6 clan to the present day: **Glenallen Hill** (1998–2000), **Ross Gload** (2000), **Ron Coomer** (2001), **Darren Lewis** (2002), **Ramon Martinez** (2003–04), and **Micah Hoffpauir** (2008). Hill, who also wore #4 and #34 in two separate Cubs stints (the other from 1993–94), is the only one of this bunch rating more than a mere mention. On May 11, 2000, Hill hit a ball onto the roof of a building on Waveland Avenue, across the street from the left-field bleachers at Wrigley Field, a shot estimated at over 500 feet. The game itself became a note in baseball history: at the time, it was the longest nine-inning game by time in major league history, running four hours, twenty-two minutes (that record has since been surpassed). And naturally, that mammoth blast was hit in a Cubs loss, 14-8 to Milwaukee.

MOST OBSCURE CUB TO WEAR #6: **Mike O'Berry** (1980). Yet another in a very long line of pedestrian backup catchers acquired by the Cubs in the 1970s and early 1980s, O'Berry was the player to be named later in the trade that had sent Ted Sizemore to the Red Sox on August 17, 1979, a deal completed after the season was over. O'Berry caught ninteen games and hit .208 for the Cubs. His best contribution to the Cubs came after the 1980 season was over, when he was sent to Cincinnati for relief pitcher Jay Howell. In so doing, he began a trade chain that eventually helped win the Cubs the 1984 NL East title; Howell was sent to the Yankees for Pat Tabler, and Tabler eventually went to the White Sox in the deal that brought Steve Trout, a thirteen-game winner for the '84 Cubs, to the North Side. Thank you O'Berry much.

GUY YOU NEVER THOUGHT OF AS A CUB WHO WORE #6: **Willie Wilson** (1993-94). Long after he had back-to-back eighty-three- and seventy-nine-steal seasons for the Royals, led the AL in triples five times, helped lead Kansas City to five postseason appearances, the 1980 AL pennant, and the 1985 world championship, Wilson was signed as a free agent at age thirty-seven before the 1993 season. He couldn't hit triples any more (he had only one as a Cub), he couldn't really steal bases any more (he swiped only eight in 122 games), and frankly, he couldn't hit any more, either (batting .256 over a season-plus, more than thirty points below his lifetime average). Most of what Cubs fans remember about Wilson is his sulking on the bench when both Jim Lefebvre and Tom Trebelhorn wouldn't play him. His constant whining gained him his outright release on May 16, 1994, with many months left on his two-year, $1.4 million contract (and back then, that was a solid financial commitment to a ballplayer). His nineteen-year career was history.

Cubs Unis, Part III: Into the Now

Hand it to the Cubs to become more conservative with their uniforms as they marched deeper into modern times. The Cubs have gone with a pinstriped top as their de rigueur home uniform from 1957 straight through to the present. Still, they've tried a few things of note to stay styling as we get ready to click off the first decade of a new century.

1982: Goodbye Sister Disco—The Cubs shed baby blue on their road uniforms for a solid shade that more closely matched the stripes on the team's home uniform. They also added a red stripe on the sleeve and on the top of the pants, which were a solid white, the only team in that era to wear white road pants.

1990: Dress Gray—Coming off their second NL East title in five years, the Cubs switched road uniforms. They went from blue tops to gray with nondescript block lettering for "Chicago." The Cubs went from the best road record in the National League to limited success away from Wrigley and a fifth-place finish. New uniform, bad karma? Maybe the team ERA increasing by a full run had something to do with it, too.

1993: What's Your Name?—The Cubs put names on the back of the home uniforms (road unis had featured names since 1977). GM Larry Himes said it was partly because WGN was seen all around the country—apparently graphics and announcers prevented people watching at home from knowing who was batting. Once the names were on it was tough to go back. The Cubs did take them off in 2005–06 for tradition's sake, but marketing brought them back after replica jersey sales plummeted.

1994: Strike Three—The third road look in a dozen years didn't even make it through a full season as the Cubs—and everyone else—stopped playing in August. "Cubs" with a line under it wasn't overly inspired, and the script format made the wording resemble "Cuba". It was permanently embargoed three years later.

1997: New Bear in Town—The bear face sleeve emblem switched to the walking baby bear profile on the home and road uniforms. The Cubs also went back to block letters on the road unis. The result? They set a record for the most losses to start a season, but those basic road grays have become very popular with fans filling enemy venues from sea to shining sea to watch the Cubs come to town.

1997–2008: Alternate Ending—The Cubs first wore an alternate jersey on May 2, 1994; it wasn't an official shirt, but the batting practice jersey, done in an attempt to break a long home losing streak. It didn't work, as the Cubs lost to the Reds, 9–0. In 1997 they introduced an "official" blue alternate shirt, with the walking bear logo on the front and the forgotten National League insignia on the right sleeve harkening back to Chicago's role as founder of the NL. At first worn only for Sunday home games, in recent years the starting pitcher has had his choice of shirt on the day he starts. Carlos Zambrano remains a big fan of the little bear. It's hard to argue with Z.

#7: JO-DEE, JO-DEE DAVIS

Cubs fans of a certain age remember **Jody Davis** (1981–88) fondly. TV fans of a certain age remember a different Jody Davis, the little boy in the 1960s show *Family Affair* with Uncle Bill (cloyingly pronounced by child actor Johnny Whitaker as "Uncuw Biwl"); Mr. French; Cissy (it always seemed like a typo); Jody's twin, Buffy (not the vampire slayer, but the child actor who came to a tragic end); and a bespectacled doll called Mrs. Beasley. It was watchable for kids under ten, but that still didn't give the WB any earthly reason to re-make the show in 2002. First-hand reports claim the new show was harder to watch than the woeful, ninety-five loss, 2002 Cubs.

But Jody Davis the catcher was a productive Cub who called a good game and had some pop in his bat. Taken from the Cardinals in the 1980 Rule 5 draft, after a serious illness had nearly ended his career, he caught about half the games for the horrid 1981 Cubs (38–65 in the strike-shortened season). When Dallas Green and Lee Elia took over the following year, Davis was installed as the starting backstop. He produced immediately, hitting 12 home runs in 1982 and 24 the following year, becoming only the second Cubs catcher (after Gabby Hartnett) to hit 20 or more homers in a season. It was during that 1983 season that broadcaster Harry Caray helped Jody's popularity by singing (in his inimitable way) "Jo-dee, Jo-dee Davis, Catcher Without a Peer"— to the tune of "The Ballad of Davy Crockett." (It was better for everyone that he didn't try to hum the *Family Affair* theme.)

Caray's chorus led to chants of "Jo-DEE! Jo-DEE!" whenever he came up to bat. On September 14, 1984, with the Cubs still battling the Mets for first place in the NL East, Davis came to the plate with the bases loaded and the Cubs leading the Mets 2-0 in the sixth inning at Wrigley Field. He smacked a grand slam to seal the victory and put the Mets an insurmountable eight and a half games out of first place. That season Jody became the first Cubs catcher to play in an All-Star Game since 1969—when Randy Hundley struck out in his only at bat—and the first Cub to catch a postseason game since Mickey Livingston in 1945. One of his most heads-up plays occurred on June 8, 1987 when, in a tie game in the top of the ninth, he picked off Barry Lyons of the Mets at second while Mookie Wilson was being issued an intentional walk (the Cubs won the game in the last of the ninth on a Manny Trillo walkoff home run). Davis was traded to the Braves at the end of the 1988 season and struggled in Atlanta, managing just 20 RBI over 90 games.

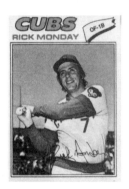

Apart from Davis, the best-known, and likely best, Cub to wear #7 was **Rick Monday** (1972–77). Monday played five seasons in Chicago as the regular center fielder, hitting 104 homers—peaking with 32 in 1976—and playing solid defense. He was the Cubs' best player in the first half of the lackluster 1976 season and had 15 homers at the All-Star break, but catcher Steve Swisher got the team's lone All-Star nod, primarily because the '76 NL All-Star squad already had too many outfielders and not enough catchers.

Monday's signature moment came on April 25, 1976 at Dodger Stadium, when, in the fourth inning, two protesters jumped on the field and tried to set an American flag on fire. Monday, playing center field for the Cubs that day, ran over, swooped up the flag and handed it to Dodgers pitcher Doug Rau. (The Cubs lost the game 5-4 in ten innings.) A month later when the Dodgers came to Wrigley Field, the flag was presented to Monday by Dodgers GM Al Campanis. Monday shrugged off the praise he received, saying, "It's the way I was brought up. You would have done the same thing." He has worked for many years as a Dodgers broadcaster since his retirement.

There haven't been many wearers of #7 who have made their marks as Cubs; players such as **Don Hoak** (1956), **Harvey Kuenn** (1965–66), **Eric Young** (2000–01), and **Kenny Lofton** (2003) all had their better years elsewhere. Hoak is part of Cubs lore in an odd way; between 1945 and 2001 only one team—the 1960 Pirates, where Hoak was the regular third baseman—won the World Series while having more than three ex-Cubs on the roster. Hoak apparently didn't like it in Chicago. He hit only .215 and asked to be traded after one last-place season; the Cubs obliged by sending him to Cincinnati. The "Ex-Cub Factor" as described above was finally broken in 2001, when the winning Diamondbacks had ex-Cubs Mark Grace, Luis Gonzalez, Miguel Batista, and Mike Morgan on their World Series roster.

Walt "Moose" Moryn was a popular Cubs outfielder of the 1950s acquired along with Hoak before the 1956 season; he took over Hoak's #7 in 1958 after sporting #43 his first two years on the North Side while a couple of nobodies, **Bobby Adams** (.251 in 60 games) and **Casey Wise** (.179 in 43 games), wore it in 1957. The left-hand-hitting left fielder hit 84 homers in a little over four seasons as a Cub and helped to provide a signature moment during the 1960 season, when he made a running, shoestring catch on Joe Cunningham's fly ball to preserve Don Cardwell's no-hitter on May 15. Jack Brickhouse's frenzied TV cry, "Come on, Moose!" is legendary in Chicago sports broadcasting annals.

Going back a little deeper in Cubs history, we find a #7 who became famous, but not for his play on the field. **Emil Verban** (1948–50) played in 199 games for three very bad Cubs teams, hitting only one career homer, a solo shot off Johnny "Double No-Hit" Vander Meer at Crosley Field in Cincinnati on September 6, 1948. After a decent 1949 season, he got off to a terrible start in 1950 and was waived. And that would likely be the end of any Cubs fan's remembrance, except that Verban had been a fan favorite for his hustle and positive attitude. In 1975, some expatriate Cubs fans living in Washington, D.C., decided they would honor the memory of this not-so-great ballplayer by creating the "Emil Verban Society," for far-flung Cubs fans everywhere. Popularized by the political columnist George Will, the Verban Society counts among its members Hillary Clinton, Barack Obama, Donald Rumsfeld, Dick Cheney, John Cusack, Pat Sajak, Jim Belushi, and until his death, Ronald Reagan.

The rest of the #7s are a motley lot ranging from mediocre catchers (**Sammy Taylor,** 1961–62; **Merritt Ranew,** 1963–64; **Bruce Kimm,** 1979; **Joe "Buy A Vowel" Kmak,** 1994; **and Tyler Houston,** 1996–99) to mediocre middle infielders (**Dick Culler,** 1948; **Ron Campbell,** 1964; **Roberto Pena,** 1965; **and Ramon Martinez,** 2003) to mediocre outfielders (**Dom Dallessandro,** 1942, and **John Herrnstein,** 1966, who was acquired in the Fergie Jenkins deal). And then there was **Cliff Johnson** (1980), yet another past-his-prime player acquired in an attempt to rev up a dormant Cubs offense. Although Johnson's primary position was catcher, he wasn't very good there, nor was he very good at first base. His best position was DH, but since the NL didn't and doesn't have one, and since the 1980 Cubs had both a regular catcher and a regular first baseman, manager Preston Gomez tried him for three games in left field. It was a disaster. Johnson made two putouts and committed one error for a laughable .667 fielding percentage. After the 1980 season Johnson was shipped to the A's for a minor leaguer, and he enjoyed several productive seasons as a DH in the American League.

Before we depart for #8, three other #7s deserve mention. **Augie Galan** (1937–41), who also wore #31 and #51, was a starting outfielder for two NL championship teams (1935 and 1938), primarily playing left field. He scored 133 runs in 1935, leading the National League in his first full season, and finished ninth in MVP voting. After five solid seasons, injuries curtailed his playing time, and the Cubs, thinking he was done, dealt him to the Dodgers on August 26, 1941, for Mace Brown (irony: Brown was the pitcher who, three years earlier, had given up the "Homer in the Gloamin'" to Gabby Hartnett). Galan revived his career and put up several more good years for the Dodgers and Reds.

Frankie Baumholtz (1951–55) was a speedy center fielder who was said to always be out of breath for having to cover both center *and* left field, where the immobile Hank Sauer played. In 1952 Baumholtz hit .325 and finished seventeenth in the MVP voting; he finished second in the batting race to Stan Musial, so on September 28, 1952, with the batting race well in hand, Musial stepped to the mound to pitch to Baumholtz, who batted right–handed for the only time in his career. Baumholtz hit a smash that Cards third baseman Solly Hemus couldn't handle; it was ruled an error, though Baumholtz maintained throughout his life that it should have been a hit. (Had it been so, his final average would have been .328.)

MOST OBSCURE CUB TO WEAR #7: **Mike Maksudian** (1994), who was rather pointlessly acquired after the 1993 season, spent much of 1994 at Triple-A Iowa, where he hit .318 in 58 games. Recalled to the horrid 1994 Cubs, he pinch-hit twenty-one times, going 4-for-14 with seven walks. For some reason, despite the fact that he was a catcher, his only starts as a Cub were two games at first base and one at third base. He was released at the end of the season and never played in the majors again.

GUY YOU NEVER THOUGHT OF AS A CUB WHO WORE #7: **Bobby Murcer** (1977-79) was acquired when Bill Madlock's contract demands angered owner P. K. Wrigley. Madlock and reserve infielder Rob Sperring were shipped to the Giants on February 11, 1977 for Murcer and Steve Ontiveros; the Wrigleys promptly signed Murcer to a more lucrative deal than the one Madlock had been asking for. And for a while, the five-time All-Star with the Yankees and Giants lived up to the contract. For the first three-quarters of the 1977 season, while the Cubs contended, Murcer produced. On August 22, with thirty-nine games remaining in the season, Murcer had 24 HR and 83 RBI, had scored 81 runs, and was seemingly on his way to his first 30/100 season. And then he almost literally stopped hitting. From August 23 to season's end he batted .216 with three home runs and six (yes, SIX) RBI in thirty-five games, and the Cubs stopped winning, going 11–28 the rest of the way. Murcer's power had gone—he hit only nine homers in 1978, and, off to a slow start in 1979, he was shipped back to the Yankees for a minor leaguer. Once ballyhooed as the "next Mickey Mantle"—he and the Mick were both from Oklahoma—Murcer took Mantle's number as a Cub. Murcer retired as a Yankee and spent two decades as a broadcaster for the team until his death from a brain tumor in 2008.

Bring 'em Home

While compiling the statistics for certain uniform numbers, sometimes the results make complete sense—such as #31 leading in most pitching categories. But then there are stat totals with no rhyme or reason, like #7 being the Cubs top RBI maker. Since the Cubs started wearing numbers in 1932, only one decade saw multiple RBI men wear #7 and wear out pitchers with runners on base. In the 1970s, the Cubs had Rick Monday, who knocked in a career high 77 runs in '76. He was promptly traded. The Cubs replaced him in the outfield with Bobby Murcer, who came from San Francisco in the Bill Madlock deal. Murcer uninspired play at Wrigley didn't make anyone in Chicago forget Madlock or Monday. The number returned to being a catcher's number—the great Gabby Hartnett had been the first to wear it in '32—and got a good one in Jody Davis, who racked up 467 RBI. It still doesn't explain how #7 knocked in more runs than any other number, but maybe it's better to just cross home plate and not worry so much who got credit.

Uni#	RBI	Uni#	RBI	Uni#	RBI	Uni#	RBI
7	2,622	6	2,080	12	1,599	25	1,254
9	2,576	11	2,057	26	1,569	24	1,229
10	2,484	17	2,027	23	1,419	22	1,134
21	2,431	14	1,708	2	1,364	43	1,088
8	2,137	18	1,674	16	1,357	4	1,067

#8: THE HAWK

Andre Dawson was born to play in an old-time grass field with reachable fences and adoring fans. Yet he played only a handful of home games on grass (as a twenty-two-year-old in the final days of Parc Jarry in Montreal) in his first decade in the major leagues. His knees paid the price. When Dawson finally became a free agent and wanted to play in a stadium where it didn't hurt him to run, major league owners were in their "collusion" phase, secretly and unethically agreeing not to sign each other's free agents. When Dawson showed up at spring training offering the Cubs his services, presenting GM Dallas Green with a contract with the dollar amount left blank, management relented. Green, after calling Dawson's arrival "a dog and pony show," filled in the blank with "$500,000," and for that sum the Cubs got their best outfielder since Billy Williams.

No one surpassed Dawson's 49 homers and 137 RBI in 1987, and he became the first league Most Valuable Player to play on a last-place team. One of the best moments for that substandard team occurred in the eighth inning on September 27, the final home game of the year against the Cardinals. It was a lovely fall afternoon and Dawson, in what all in attendance knew would be his final home at bat of the year, received a loud ovation. It got louder five pitches later, when Dawson sent a Bill Dawley offering onto Waveland for his forty-seventh homer of the year.

Dawson made five All-Star teams with the Cubs—he played in only three with the Expos—while surpassing twenty homers every year and driving in more runs than any Cub in five of his six seasons. Dawson remained one of the deadliest arms in right field and won two Gold Gloves as a Cub. The Hawk was beloved at Wrigley—right-field bleacher fans created "Andre's Army" T-shirts and would bow down to him when he would return to the outfield after one of his 174 Cubs home runs, which ranks tenth on the club all-time list despite the fact that he played only six seasons on the North Side. The only year he played fewer than 143 games was 1989, when Don Zimmer's army of super subs filled in amiably (Dawson still played 118 games and drove in 77). Dawson moved on to Fenway Park, a logical choice after Wrigley. He finished his career with the expansion Marlins—no classic park, mind you, but a grass field and in his hometown. No Cubs player has worn #8 longer than Andre, and he wore it every day with dignity and class. It's possible that if the Hawk is elected to the Hall of Fame, the Cubs might consider retiring it.

Of the thirty-seven other Cubs players to wear #8, there have been twenty-two catchers. And #8 became not only a catcher's number, but most of the backstops who wore it were fringe players or backups, from the 1960s until the 1990s. The roll call of mediocrity began with **Smoky Burgess** (1949), who was actually a good player . . . for other teams. He'd been originally signed by the Cubs in 1944, but as was the case with many talented players, the Cubs shipped him elsewhere to succeed, trading him to the Reds in 1951 for two players (Johnny Pramesa and Bob Usher) who had no impact with the Cubs. To be fair, several other teams also gave Burgess away before he became a premier pinch hitter in the 1960s.

Rube Walker (1948, 1949–51) actually wore #8 both before and after Burgess, but he went on to more success as a backup in Brooklyn and later helped introduce the concept of the five-man rotation as pitching coach under Gil Hodges for the Mets. Reserve backstops **Bruce Edwards** (1951–52), **Clyde McCullough** (1953–56), and **Charlie Silvera** (1957) filled out the number behind the plate, followed by a couple of years of the interesting career of first baseman **Dale Long** (1958–59). Long once homered in eight straight games (as a Pirate), still the NL record, and he remains the last Cub to catch left-handed (two games in 1958). Among the other catching #8s: **Moe Thacker** (1961–62; Thacker apparently couldn't make up his mind, as he also wore #19, #22, #23, and #25, five numbers all told in four Cub seasons); **Vic Roznovsky** (1964–65); **Bill Plummer** (1968), later a small cog in the Big Red Machine as Johnny Bench's backup and eventually a major league manager in Seattle; **Ken Rudolph** (1969–70); **Tom Lundstedt** (1973–74); **Ed Putman** (1976); **Dave Rader** (1978); **Barry Foote** (1979–81), who hit 16 homers behind the plate in his first year as a Cub; **Mark Parent** (1994–95); **Todd Pratt** (1995), who earned Cubs fans' ire when, on June 14, 1995, he reached third base in the bottom of the eleventh inning with one out, but failed to score the winning run on a wild pitch (the Cubs eventually lost the game in the 13th); and **Sandy Martinez** (1998). Martinez, who caught only thirty-three games for the 1998 NL wild card Cubs, had one that we'll all remember forever: he was behind the dish for Kerry Wood's twenty-strikeout game on May 6, 1998. The #8 catcher act even includes a non-Cubs catcher who later became a coach: **Duffy Dyer** (1983).

A couple of better backstops—**Joe Girardi** (2000), who also wore #7 and #27 in various Cubs stints, and **Michael Barrett** (2004–07), who took #8 after Nomar Garciaparra joined the team and took over the #5 Barrett had worn from the start of the 2004 season—brought the #8 catcher list into the millennium. There were even two pre–World War II catchers who donned #8—possibly because they hit eighth—

Rollie Hemsley (1932) and **Len Rice** (1945); Rice caught in thirty-two games for the '45 Cubs but didn't appear in the World Series.

One crazy 8 who didn't catch was first baseman **Joe Pepitone** (1970–73). Known for bringing the hair dryer into the major league clubhouse as a Yankee, Pepitone hit a career-best .307 in '71 as Ernie Banks spent most of his final season on the bench. Pepitone and **Lee Thomas** (1966–67, .229 in 340 Cub at bats) were the only non-catchers to wear #8 between 1961 and 1981, when the number was turned over to coaches as well as manager Jim Frey (1984–86), before the arrival of the Hawk.

MOST OBSCURE CUB TO WEAR #8: **Rick Stelmaszek** (1974), who through the 2008 season has spent twenty-eight consecutive seasons as a Minnesota Twins coach, the third-longest such tenure in major league history, lasted the final two months of the '74 season in a Cubs uniform after being acquired from the Angels in return for reliever Horacio Pina (that may be among the most obscure trades in Cubs history, too). Stelmaszek hit .227 in 44 Cubs at bats and was a career .170 hitter in 88 AB with four teams. On August 20, 1974, he hit his only major league homer, a high, arching blast onto Sheffield on a windy day against the Dodgers, off Hall of Famer Don Sutton. He drove in two runs, walked twice, and scored twice . . . in an 18-8 loss.

GUY YOU NEVER THOUGHT OF AS A CUB WHO WORE #8: **Gary Gaetti** (1998) spent most of his career in the American League with the Twins, Royals, and Angels. By 1998 he was with the Cardinals, and when the team he had grown up rooting for in Centralia, Illinois released him on August 14, 1998, Gaetti became a part of Cubs lore. Signing to play on the North Side five days later, Gaetti played just thirty-seven games with the Cubs, but he was a monster. He batted .320 with eight homers and 27 RBI and showed the form of a four-time Gold Glove third baseman. (He had established a big league first when he started two around-the-horn triple plays in the same game as a Twin in 1990.) Gaetti helped put the Cubs in the postseason by hitting a two-run homer in the wild-card tiebreaker game against the Giants on September 28, 1998, but like the rest of the Cubs, he stopped hitting in the Division Series against Atlanta (1-for-11). The next year Gaetti was the oldest player in the National League and he played like it (hitting .204 in 280 at bats), earning his release after the season.

Be Patient; Take a Number

The trite cry from Little League that a walk really is as good as a hit rings true at every level of the game. In some ways a walk is actually better, considering how a single can occur on one pitch, while a walk takes at least four. And with the importance of pitch counts in the modern game, every pitch you can get the other guy to throw—especially a starter—is to your advantage. So who are the all-time individual Cubs leaders in drawing bases on balls? Stan Hack (1,092) from the 1930s and Ron Santo (1,071) from the 1960s. There's proof that the greats play the game the right way regardless of the era. In the last few years, Hack's #6 has patiently worked its way into third place in this category, though Santo's #10 has the perpetual take sign since it was retired at the end of 2003.

Uni#	BB Drawn
7	2,317
11	1,945
6	1,915
10	1,908
9	1,755
21	1,740
17	1,610
8	1,300
18	1,204
12	1,149
1	1,134
23	1,116
2	1,108
25	1,096
26	1,027
20	1,011
16	1,005
24	926
4	913
28	880

#9: THE REBEL AND THE MAYOR

Randy Hundley was tough. He is the only player in major league history to catch 160 games in a season. That feat for the 1968 Cubs represented 98 percent of his team's games, and the 156 starts are 96 percent of the 163 available starts. Both of Hundley's numbers remain major league records, more than four decades later. The '68 Cubs had a tie game, and the other games were started by John Boccabella (four), Randy Bobb (two), and Gene Oliver (one). Four times that year Hundley came in to catch after beginning the game on the bench and fifteen times he caught both ends of a doubleheader, including consecutive twinbills at Wrigley on July 6 and 7.

Hundley, who came with Bill Hands in a 1965 heist from San Francisco, caught at least 140 games each year from 1966–69. He made just four errors in 1967 and earned a Gold Glove. A fair hitter, Hundley popularized the technique of catching one-handed and using a hinged mitt. While Johnny Bench is usually credited with that innovation, Bench actually followed Hundley

RANDY
HUNDLEY
CHICAGO CUBS   CATCHER

and didn't start catching one-handed until after he broke a finger in 1967. Hundley learned it from his father, Cecil, a hard-nosed, semi-pro catcher who didn't like busted up hands. Randy Hundley, who caught 1,026 career games, said he never missed a game because of a hand injury. His knees were another matter.

By the end of the 1969 season, the Cubs were exhausted and no one was more worn down than Hundley. His left knee went early in 1970 and his right knee failed the next year. He drifted to the Twins and Padres. He came back to the Cubs in 1976 (wearing #5) and served as a player-coach in '77 (wearing #4). Hundley became a minor league manager and later scouted and broadcast games for the Cubs. His nickname, "Rebel"? He was dubbed that for his birthplace, Martinsville, Virginia, a few miles from the site of a notorious prison for Union soldiers during the Civil War.

Both before and after Randy Hundley first donned %9 in 1966, the number has been a magnet for catchers. Backstops **Clyde McCullough** (1945–48), **Mickey Owen** (1949, long after his better days with the Dodgers), **Rube Novotney** (1949), **Gordon Massa** (1957), **Del Rice** (1960), **Jim Hegan** (1960), and **Cuno Barragan** (1961–63) wore #9 before Randy put it on and wore it for more seasons than anyone. Afterward, it belonged to **Steve Swisher** (1974–77), **Tim Blackwell** (1978–81), **Butch Benton** (1982), **Larry Cox** (1982), **Damon Berryhill** (1988–91), **Matt Walbeck** (1993), **Scott Servais** (1995–98)—who never did get to play on the same team with 1990s relief pitcher Scott Service, whose name was pronounced the same way—**Benito Santiago** (1999), **Paul Bako** (2003–04), and **Henry Blanco** (2005) have all worn the number since Hundley was traded to Minnesota after the 1973 season. Santiago deserves special mention here, because he didn't wear "9"—he wore "09". He claimed that having a single digit number felt "strange" with the catcher's equipment strapped to his back; wearing a two-digit number made the strap go down the middle, where it was unencumbered by twill. That he didn't just switch to another number (he wore six others during his long career), or deal with it like the other sixteen Cubs catchers named in this paragraph, places Benito in the Hall of High Maintenance.

The number was so popular Randy couldn't get it back when he returned in 1976 because it belonged to Swisher, the team's only All-Star that season. Randy's son, catcher **Todd Hundley,** was also out of luck when he became a Cub in 2001. Oddly, it was an outfielder and former Mets teammate, Damon Buford, who had the number. Todd took #99, a number Turk Wendell wouldn't even touch as a Cub (although Wendell wore #99 as Hundley's teammate with the Mets). The first issuance of #99 in Chicago lasted only three months. Todd grabbed #9 when Buford was cut. ("Sorry, buddy. Can I have that? Thanks.")

But while Randy Hundley once caught an unmatched 160 games in a season, Todd only caught 149 games in two years as a Cub. His tenure in Chicago began contentiously, after a widely-hailed four-year deal for $24 million signed prior to the 2001 season. Manager Don Baylor decided to start Joe Girardi on Opening Day, largely due to a favorable pitcher-batter matchup, and Todd, who had grown up in the Chicago suburbs, complained in the media. It went downhill from there, as Todd's bat (he had set a Mets team record, since tied by Carlos Beltran, with 41 homers in 1996) vanished; he hit .187 with 12 HR in 79 games and was routinely booed. In a dual salary dump that worked out great for the Cubs, Chicago sent Todd (and Chad Hermansen) to Los Angeles after the 2002 season for Eric Karros and Mark Grudzielanek.

In between all those catchers, #9 was the property of an outfielder: the popular **Hank Sauer** (1950–55; he also wore #43 in 1949). Sauer, whose 37 home runs in 1952 were second-most for a single season in club history at the time (tied with Gabby Hartnett), also drove in 121 runs that year and won the NL MVP award as the Cubs went 77–77. That may not sound like much of an achievement, but it is the only season between 1946 and 1963 that the Cubs did not have a *losing* record. Sauer, known as "The Mayor of Wrigley Field," used to have bleacher fans throw packets of tobacco at his feet after his homers. Yes, it was a different time. After five good years for the Cubs, Sauer was seen as washed-up and was sent to the Cardinals just before the 1956 season began. St. Louis released him and he was signed by the Giants, for whom he put up a 26 HR season at age forty in the franchise's last season at the Polo Grounds. He moved with them to San Francisco and played until he was forty-two.

In the pre-catcher, prewar days, #9's best occupant was **Frank Demaree** (1937–38; Demaree also wore #51 in his first year with the Cubs in 1932 and #5 in 1933 and in '35 and '36 after spending 1934 in the minors due to Kiki Cuyler's return from injury). Demaree was a solid part of three Wrigley pennant-winners (1932, 1935, 1938), but his best two years were put up in years the Cubs just missed winning the flag—in 1936 he hit .350 with 16 HR, and in 1937 batted .324 with 17 homers and 115 RBI, the latter total ranking second in the NL. The Cubs broke up the Thirties Gang after three World Series failures (they won a total of two games in the three Series losses) following the '38 season. Only three regulars returned in '39, with predictable results: they finished fourth. Demaree was sent to the Giants, where his career began to decline. **Hank Leiber,** for whom Demaree was dealt two months after the '38 Series, took over both the fielding position and number of Frank. Hank put up two decent years for middle-of-the-road Cubs teams in 1939 and 1940, declined in 1941, and was sent back to the Giants.

There is one further Cub who wore #9 who bears a footnote here, though he isn't "obscure" enough to rank as the *most* obscure Cub to wear the number. **Jody Gerut** (2005), a Chicago-area native who was Illinois High School Player of the Year in 1995, finished fourth in AL Rookie of the Year voting in 2003 when he hit 22 home runs for the Indians. He was acquired from the Tribe on July 18, 2005 in exchange for Jason Dubois. Before he could even get comfortable back in his hometown, he was shipped to the Pirates thirteen days later in an ill-advised deal for veteran Matt Lawton, who was dumped to the Yankees four weeks later. The 2005 Cubs were pretenders, not contenders, and this sequence summed up that year quite well.

MOST OBSCURE CUB TO WEAR #9: **Scott McClain** (2005). The thirty-six-year-old McClain played 17 pro seasons between the American minors and Japan, while recording more than 7,000 at bats and 358 home runs (287 in the minors and 71 in Japan). All he got out of the majors, though, were a few dozen at bats spread out over three seasons with three teams, one of which was the Cubs (he went 2-for-14 in September 2005). He lost a little of his obscurity tag on September 3, 2008, though, when he homered for the Giants at Coors Field, becoming the oldest player in history to hit his first major league home run. We should all have such perseverance.

GUY YOU NEVER THOUGHT OF AS A CUB WHO WORE #9: **Bobby Thomson** (1958-59). Thomson, famed for his "Shot Heard Round the World" that won the 1951 NL pennant for the New York Giants in a playoff over the Brooklyn Dodgers, appeared to be on his way to an excellent career, hitting 179 homers for New York by age twenty-nine. Traded to the Braves, he got hurt, and by the time the Cubs acquired him just before the 1958 season began, he was thirty-four years old and far past his prime (this is a recurring theme throughout this book, and Cubs history). He put up a decent season (.283, 21 HR, 83 RBI) in '58, declined in '59, and was subsequently traded to the Red Sox for right-handed reliever Al Schroll, who pitched in two games for the Cubs.

Scorecard Envy: Just What Are Those Scoreboard Numbers?

The old-fashioned manual scoreboard at Wrigley Field, which dates from the construction of the ivy-walled bleachers in 1937, puts the uniform number of the Cubs' pitchers and their opponents so that everyone can follow along. (In the early days of this board, catchers also had numbers posted on the board, but this practice ended after the 1952 season.)

But for the other eleven games being played on any particular day (quaintly, the board wasn't redone after the majors expanded past twenty-four teams, meaning that some games aren't shown), you might see that "#1" is pitching for, say, Detroit, against "#2" for, say, Minnesota. But wait, you're saying. Most pitchers don't wear single-digit numbers. So what does this mean?

The numbers correspond to lists that are published in the official Cubs scorecard, changed for every series. So, rather than have to have twenty-three copies of a panel reading "38," the scoreboard operators can get along, generally, with numbers 1–15, for most games. Since many Cubs games are still played in the afternoon, with the rest of the schedule at night (or N-I-T-E as it is abbreviated on the board), on those days the scoreboard folks don't need to make many pitcher switches at all.

So at Wrigley Field, for out-of-town-games, the old saying is true: you really *can't* tell the players without a scorecard.

#10: THE OL' THIRD BASEMAN

Ernie Banks may be "Mr. Cub," but perhaps no player in Cubs history is as big a Cubs fan, living and dying with all of us as a WGN radio broadcaster today, than **Ron Santo** (1960–73).

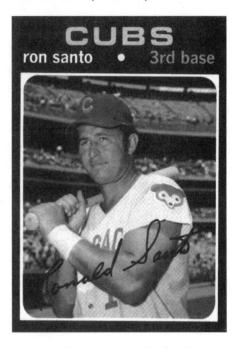

CUBS
ron santo • 3rd base

You can't get a real sense of his accomplishments and what he means to the Cubs franchise just by looking at his outstanding statistical line. That stat line, in fact, is even more remarkable when you consider the fact that he fought, and is still fighting, juvenile diabetes. Santo was the first high-profile professional athlete to reveal that he played sports at the major league level with this disease, which can debilitate and kill. In retrospect, knowing this makes his considerable accomplishments even more impressive. Even without that, his passion for playing the game could be seen every time he set foot on a baseball field.

Despite his diabetes—which he concealed even from his teammates for many years—Santo became one of the most durable players in baseball. He played in every game in 1961, 1962, 1963, 1965, and 1968. (Santo and Billy Williams played in a club-record 164 games in '65, including two tie games, which is the second-most games played in a season in major league history. Only Maury Wills, in the Dodgers' three-game playoff season of 1962, played in more.)

By 1964 Santo had established himself as the best third baseman in the National League, enjoyed the first of his six All-Star selections, and finished eighth in the MVP voting with a 30 HR, 114 RBI season in which he batted .312/.398/.564 with 86 walks. The patient Santo walked eighty-six or more times for seven consecutive seasons, from 1964 through 1970, leading the league four times in a period when walks were less frequent than they are today. For those of you who key on OPS as a Hall of Fame indicator, Santo was in the top six in NL OPS four consecutive seasons, from 1964 through 1967. And at a time when Brooks Robinson was synonymous with the Gold Glove Award at third base in the American League, Santo took the honor five straight times in the NL (1964–68).

The 1964 season was the first of four straight thirty-homer years for Santo, and though he had "only" four 100-RBI seasons, he came oh-so-close to having eight straight; from 1963 through 1970 his RBI totals were 99, 114, 101, 94, 98, 98, 123, and 114, averaging 105 RBI over the eight seasons.

His best overall season, and also his most eventful season, was likely 1966 (though some might choose 1964 or 1969). He had career highs in BA, OBP, and SLG (.312/.412/.538) that year, leading the league in on-base percentage. He also set a club record (since broken) by hitting safely in twenty-eight consecutive games.

At age thirty, and starting to feel the effects of a long career played with his disease, Santo's numbers began to decline in 1970. He had another 100-RBI season, but his average dropped to .267. The following year his power also began to decline as he drove in only 88 runs, the first time in nine years he drove in fewer than 94.

On August 28, 1971, the Cubs honored him with Ron Santo Day at Wrigley Field. That was the day that Santo at last revealed publicly his battle with juvenile diabetes, beginning a lifelong association with JD foundations, including the local Chicago-area JDRF chapter, which has hosted the Ron Santo Walk to Cure Diabetes every year since 1974.

At the end of the 1973 season, the team that shoulda, coulda won it all for all of us was broken up, and Santo was among those traded away.

Before leaving the Cubs, though, he became the first player to invoke the ten-and-five rule under the collective bargaining agreement signed after the 1972 strike (a player who had spent ten years in the major leagues, the last five with the same team, could veto any trade). The Cubs had agreed upon a deal to send Santo to the California Angels; the ballclub would have received in return two young lefties: Andy Hassler, who went on to have a middling career as a reliever/spot starter, and Bruce Heinbechner, a very highly-regarded prospect. Santo didn't want to play on the West Coast and vetoed the deal. Eerily and sadly, Heinbechner was killed in a car accident the following March, driving to Angels spring training in Palm Springs, California.

The Cubs still wanted to deal Santo, and since his preference was to stay in Chicago, they worked out a trade with the White Sox, acquiring catcher Steve Swisher and three young pitchers: Jim Kremmel, Ken Frailing, and one of Santo's future co-broadcasters, Steve Stone.

Santo's #10 was finally retired by the Cubs on September 28, 2003, the day after they clinched the NL Central title. It was a cloudy, cool afternoon, but the sun came out for about ten minutes, just when Santo was addressing the capacity crowd at Wrigley Field. He told the crowd, to a huge ovation, "*This* is my Hall of Fame."

On that date the Cubs *might* have retired #15. When Santo was first recalled on June 26, 1960, he replaced catcher Sammy Taylor on the roster while the Cubs were on the road. As was the practice in those days, if the shirt fit, the player wore it—thus Santo wore #15 until the Cubs came home, and clubhouse manager Yosh Kawano issued him the #10 that he would make so famous.

Twenty-one other players have worn #10 for the Cubs, but virtually none of them had any lasting impact. During the Wrigley ownership era, the Cubs refused to retire uniform numbers, so Santo's #10 was worn by nine subsequent players, starting with infielder **Billy Grabarkewitz** in 1974, and including one manager, **Bruce Kimm** in 2002. (Kimm actually asked Santo's permission before wearing it.) **Leon Durham** wore #10 longer than anyone not named Santo, logging eight seasons in the eighties. "Bull" Durham is famed most for a play he didn't make in the 1984 NLCS; nuff said about that, we suspect.

The best-known #10 besides Santo and Durham is probably **Dave Kingman** (1978–80), who hit homers of legendary length. Three of those home runs were hit in Dodger Stadium in a 10-7 Cubs win on May 14, 1978, leading Dodgers manager Tommy Lasorda to give a profanity-filled tirade when asked what he thought of Kingman's performance:

"What's my opinion of Kingman's performance!? What the BLEEP do you think is my opinion of it? I think it was BLEEPING BLEEP. Put that in, I don't give a BLEEP. Opinion of his performance!!? BLEEP, he beat us with three BLEEPING home runs! What the BLEEP do you mean, 'What is my opinion of his performance?' How could you ask me a question like that, 'What is my opinion of his performance?' BLEEP, he hit three home runs! BLEEP. I'm BLEEPING pissed off to lose that BLEEPING game. And you ask me my opinion of his performance! BLEEP. That's a tough question to ask me, isn't it? 'What is my opinion of his performance?'"

For those counting at home, that's twenty-seven fewer BLEEPs than Lee Elia would register in his fabled tirade three years later after a game at Wrigley against Lasorda's Dodgers.

Most of the other players who wore #10s prior to its retirement had little impact on the team; **Mike Sember** (1977) went 1-for-4 in a September call up and since Kingman had the number the following year, Sember was assigned #29 when called up in September '78. **Lloyd McClendon** (1989–90) caught and played a little outfield and first base, but his most memorable Cubs moment came in his very first Cubs at bat. On May 15, 1989, having been just recalled from Iowa and inserted in the starting lineup, McClendon hit a three-run homer off the Braves' Derek Lilliquist, snapping a five-game losing streak and helping the Cubs start a 14-5 run that would put them in first place. **Steve Lake** (1993), a backup catcher for the 1984 NL East champion Cubs wearing #16, returned for a curtain call in '93, donning #10 because all the other numbers in the teens were taken. So was his bat, apparently; he hit .225 in 44 games. For the rest of the 1990s #10 was given over to speedy outfielders: **Scott Bullett** (1995–96) hit seven triples in 1995 in only 150 at bats, finishing sixth in the NL, but hit only .212 the following year and left the majors and **Terrell Lowery** (1997–98) hit .241 in 29 at bats with the Cubs before leaving for baseball exile with the expansion Devil Rays.

MOST OBSCURE CUB TO WEAR #10: **Richie Myers** (1956), who pinch-ran in three games and pinch-hit in one for the Cubs. He scored one run and grounded out to shortstop in his only at bat, in a game the Cubs lost, 7-3. Well, we told you he was obscure!

GUY YOU NEVER THOUGHT OF AS A CUB WHO WORE #10: **Mickey Owen** (1949), who famously dropped a third strike as a Brooklyn Dodger in the 1941 World Series, allowing the Yankees a second chance, played three seasons as a Cubs backup, though only one wearing #10.

Running It Up the Flagpole

The Cubs have retired only four numbers in their history: #10 for Ron Santo, #14 for Ernie Banks, #23 for Ryne Sandberg, and #26 for Billy Williams. For decades, the Wrigley ownership refused to retire numbers even for greats like Gabby Hartnett, Stan Hack, and Phil Cavarretta, and, given that the Yankees have retired sixteen different numbers (including one for two different players), maybe it's better that the Cubs haven't run dozens of retired number flags up the flagpoles down the left- and right-field lines.

On the other hand, they've done pretty well in the four games played on number-retirement days, winning three, and there's an explanation for the one loss. Maybe they should save these ceremonies for critical pennant-race games!

August 22, 1982, #14 retired for Ernie Banks: The Cubs defeated the Padres, 8-7, in front of a modest crowd of 23,601. The Cubs rallied from 5-0 down and brought in closer Lee Smith in the ninth with the tying run on base to save it. Two players in the game—Cubs Larry Bowa and Bill Buckner—had played against Ernie in the early 1970s.

August 13, 1987, #26 retired for Billy Williams: Chicago defeated the Mets, 7-5, in front of a larger-than-usual weekday afternoon crowd of 35,033 (the reasons they chose a Thursday for this ceremony are lost to the mists of time). As in Ernie's ceremony game, the visitors blew a 5-0 lead, and once again, Smith was summoned with two out in the ninth—this time, he nearly blew the game, loading the bases on two singles and a walk before striking out Dave Magadan to end it. Irony: Billy was traded to the A's after the 1974 season for, among others, Manny Trillo; Manny pinch-hit for the Cubs in this game.

September 28, 2003, #10 retired for Ron Santo: Santo's emotional speech came prior to a meaningless game, the last of the 2003 regular season. The Cubs had clinched the NL Central the day before and though a handful of regulars started, they were all lifted by the middle innings. The sub Cubs blew a 2-0 lead and lost to the Pirates, 3-2, in front of 39,940.

August 28, 2005, #23 retired for Ryne Sandberg: Just a few weeks after his stirring Hall of Fame induction speech, Sandberg's number was run up the right-field flagpole before 38,763 on a gorgeous afternoon. The Cubs' play was beautiful, too—they demolished the Marlins, 14-3; the scoring barrage included two homers from Derrek Lee.

#11: KESS

More than three decades after he wore the uniform for the last time, **Don Kessinger** still stands as the best Cubs shortstop since Ernie Banks. And Kessinger played with Banks, slinging thousands of balls across the diamond to Mr. Cub at first base. Banks did not switch positions for Kessinger—Ernie's balky knees and diminished range had necessitated the move while Kessinger was still at the University of Mississippi—but they forged the premier NL infield of the late 1960s: Banks, Beckert, Kessinger, and Santo.

Kessinger was a six-time All-Star and rarely missed a game, playing in at least 145 games in ten of his eleven seasons as the Cubs' regular shortstop. He had little home run power, but he hit 254 doubles and 80 triples in his career. The ill-fated 1969 season was probably his best. He finished second in the NL with 38 doubles, scored 109 runs, and drove in 53, all career bests. To show how fielding expectations (or at least official scoring) has changed over the years, only once did Kessinger make fewer than 20 errors in a season as a Cub, yet he won two Gold Gloves. The shakier-fielding Nomar Garciaparra, by contrast, averaged about 15 miscues per year in the 2000s.

Kessinger, the last active member of that great Cubs infield, was traded to the Cardinals after the 1975 season for journeyman reliever Mike Garman and a minor leaguer. He'd complained that Leo Durocher never gave the Cubs regulars a day off in the heat of the 1969 season, and Kessinger got to show his stuff as player-manager for the 1979 White Sox, but the Pale Hose went 46–60 under Kessinger. He was replaced by Tony LaRussa, the fourth South Side manager in two years. LaRussa lasted a spell. Kessinger never again managed in the majors, though he served several years as the baseball coach at his alma mater, Ole Miss.

Kessinger spent more seasons—twelve in all, counting his brief September call up in 1964—than any other Cub wearing uniform #11. You'll note in the list above that **Paul Popovich** also wore #11 in 1964; Popo had made the Opening Day roster, but pinch-hit in only one game, singling, before being sent back to the minors, not to return until 1966 when Kessinger was already a regular. Popovich was then assigned #22.

For many years after Kessinger, #11 became known as "the shortstop's number." Next to wear it was **Ivan DeJesus** (1977–81), a solid Cubs shortstop for five years. DeJesus was a good leadoff hitter, got on base a lot, scored frequently—leading the league in runs with 103 in 1978—and rarely missed a game, playing in at least 155 games for his first four years with the Cubs and leading the team with 106 games played during strike-shortened 1981. Perhaps what's most memorable about his Cubs career, though, was how he arrived and how he left. He came to the Cubs as an unknown from the Dodgers in the Rick Monday–Bill Buckner trade. If there was any question as to who got the better of the deal, DeJesus emphatically gave Chicago the nod. He was traded to the Phillies for Larry Bowa in 1982, but Bowa was on the downward slope compared to the twenty-nine-year-old DeJesus, even though Ivan was coming off a poor 1981 in which he hit only .194 and drove in a meager 13 runs. Cubs GM Dallas Green insisted that to even things out, his old team had to throw in a minor league shortstop: Ryne Sandberg.

Other shortstops who wore #11 since Kessinger's departure were umpire's son **Jeff Kunkel** (1992), who played in only 20 games, hitting .138; **Rey Sanchez** (1993–97), of whom Harry Caray once said when watching him wait for an easy pop-up, "He's a fine fielder, he's never dropped one of those"—only to then watch him drop it; **Jose Nieves** (1998–00), and **Ronny Cedeno** (2005), who has sported #5 since Nomar Garciaparra departed after the 2005 season. **Alex Grammas,** better known as a Red and Cardinal, finished his career with 39 mediocre games for the 1962 and 1963 Cubs, hitting .218 in 87 at bats; Grammas was the Cub who wore #11 immediately before Kessinger (except for the brief one-game Popovich appearance). Another player better known for his days with other teams was not a shortstop, but third baseman **Luis Salazar** (1989–90), who started his Cubs career in #11 but switched to #10 when George Bell came to the Cubs in 1991. Salazar had his Cubs signature moment on September 9, 1989, when his double down the line in the tenth inning scored Andre Dawson, who had walked, with the winning run in a comeback 3–2 win over the Cardinals that cemented that division title-winning team's hold on first place.

In the pre-Kessinger days, the wearers of #11 were a mirror of the Cubs teams of the 1950s: nondescript backup catchers and outfielders, including **Bob Muncrief** (1949); **Carl Sawatski** (1950); **Smoky Burgess** (1951), who later became one of the American League's best pinch hitters with the White Sox in the 1960s; **Toby Atwell** (1952–53); **Joe Garagiola** (1953–54), who had a much more successful career with a mic than a mitt; **Bob Speake** (1955, 1957), of whose Cubs tenure we should not speak much; **Cal Neeman** (1958–1960), who until Geovany Soto did it in 2008 was the last Cubs catcher to hit an inside-the-park homer; and one first baseman, **Ed Bouchee** (1960–61). Bouchee was the first—and, to this point, the only—Cub ever born in Montana. Yet he actually came to Chicago via Philadelphia. The Cubs sent Tony Taylor and Neeman to the Phillies for Bouchee and Don Cardwell in May 1960. Although Bouchee was Chicago's regular first baseman for two seasons, he wasn't a huge threat with the stick. The Cubs weren't broken up when he was taken by the Mets in the '62 expansion draft. No surprise, as he couldn't even last more than fifty games with the 120-loss Mets in their inaugural season.

Perhaps the most famous player to don #11 post-Kessinger is **Ron Cey** (1983–86), much better known for his days manning third base at Dodger Stadium, where he played on four World Series teams. He was thirty-five when the Cubs acquired him for a couple of borderline pitching prospects just before spring training in 1983; the Dodgers thought Cey had nothing left. He was pretty immobile at third base, but "The Penguin" put up three 20-plus homer seasons in blue pinstripes, and his 97 RBI helped lead the Cubs to the NL East title in 1984. He wore #11 for the Cubs, instead of the #10 he had worn for more than a decade in Los Angeles, not because it was retired for Ron Santo (that wouldn't happen for twenty more years), but because an incumbent player, Leon Durham, had already claimed it. Ironically, Cey was only acquired because the Cubs failed to attract a free agent whom they wanted to take over at first base: Steve Garvey. We don't need to go over what Garvey means in Cubs history. And yes, Ron's wife's first name really is "Fran." (Say it out loud.)

A big-name player whose tenure in #11 was **George Bell** (1991). Signed with much ballyhoo from the Blue Jays as a free agent, he was just four years removed from a 47-homer MVP season in Toronto, and at age thirty-one it was hoped that Bell would solidify the Cubs outfield for several years. Instead, his lackadaisical play and attitude had fans turning on him and he wound up on the bench for the last ten games of the season. Bell's tenure as a Cub had a lasting legacy, though, when he was traded to the White Sox a few days before the 1992 season began for Sammy Sosa and Ken Patterson. In one of the last instances of a player being given the shirt off the previous wearer's back, Sosa wore #11 for the handful of games remaining in spring training, and also for an exhibition game played at Wrigley Field against the Brewers on April 4, 1992—which explains why some people have thought for years that Sosa briefly wore #11, as there are photos of him wearing that number taken at Wrigley Field. But two days later, when the 1992 regular season began, Sosa had taken his now-familiar #21, to honor the late Roberto Clemente. (He'd worn #25 for the White Sox.) Sosa never wore #11 in a regular-season game.

When uniform numbers first began, #11 was the property of **Billy Jurges,** who wore it from 1932–36, except for a brief switch to #8 in 1934. After Jurges gave up #11 following the '36 season and switched to #5, it was taken over by pitcher **Bill Lee** from 1937–42. Lee, who also wore #15, #19, #24, and #31 in his Cubs career, won 139 games in a Cubs uniform from 1934–43 (and a return in 1947 at age 37 when he went 0–2). He still ranks ninth on the all-time Cubs win list. Not to be confused with Bill "Spaceman" Lee, who wasn't even born when Big Bill was in his Cubs prime, the right-hander had his best year—22–9 with a 2.66 ERA—for the 1938 NL champions. He finished second in NL

MOST OBSCURE CUB TO WEAR #11: **Dan Briggs** (1982). Briggs was the very definition of a journeyman—prior to his acquisition during spring training in 1982, he had played for four teams in six years, and played well for none of them. He seemed a rather meaningless addition to the roster. He appeared in forty-eight games for the Cubs, starting only two of them, and pinch-hitting in 36. He hit .125 With no walks, extra-base hits, or RBI and on July 3 he was sent outright to Triple-A Iowa, never to return to the majors. The Cubs went 11–37 in games in which he appeared and 62–52 in all other 1982 games.

GUY YOU NEVER THOUGHT OF AS A CUB WHO WORE #11: **Jim Sundberg** (1987–88). Despite the fact that Cubs catcher Jody Davis had posted an All-Star, twenty-one-homer season in 1986, management felt they needed a better defensive catcher, so during spring training the following year, they traded Thad Bosley and Dave Gumpert to the Royals for the thirty-six-year-old Sundberg. He caught only 77 of his career 1,927 games in a Cubs uniform, hitting .212 in 85 games before being released on july 15, 1988. He did have two memorable moments in a Cubs uniform. On July 8, 1987, he was sent up to pinch-hit in the eighth inning of a game the Cubs were losing 8-4, and he hit a grand slam off San Diego's Lance McCullers, tying the game; the Cubs eventually won, 12-8. His other big moment came in a game that didn't count. In those years, the Cubs and White Sox played in-season charity exhibitions. And in the exhibition played on May 26, 1988, Sundberg pitched the 14th and 15th innings—allowing no runs and only one hit—because the teams had run out of pitchers (Steve Lyons did the same for the White Sox). Of his pitching appearance, Sundberg said: "This has got to be the greatest position on the field. I had more fun the last two innings pitching than I've had in a long time." The game ended in a 6-6 tie after the fifteenth inning.

MVP balloting that year to the Reds' Ernie Lombardi, but it was all for naught. Lee started and lost two games in the Yankees' sweep of the Cubs in the '38 World Series.

Active Wear

Some numbers are just more popular than others. While #11 has been issued every year the Cubs have worn numbers except for 1956 and 1976, all the numbers above #60 have only been used in thirty-three seasons all told by managers, coaches, and players alike. Not surprisingly, the least popular "low" number is #13. Is it a coincidence that only one wearer of that star-crossed number has played in the postseason for the Cubs? That would be also the first wearer of #13: Claude Passeau. His only World Series decision was a one-hit shutout of Detroit in the 1945 Series.

Below is a list of how many seasons each number issued by the Cubs has been used.

Uni Number	Total # of years used	Uni Number	Total # of years used	Uni Number	Total # of years used
11	75	39	60	14	32
6	73	15	59	50	32
7	73	31	59	52	31
12	71	33	59	53	30
22	71	25	58	13	22
5	70	37	58	55	19
9	70	23	56	56	19
18	69	28	56	57	14
20	69	43	56	59	14
8	68	27	55	58	13
17	67	10	54	54	12
21	67	42	54	61	8
2	65	46	53	62	6
24	65	48	53	63	6
19	63	38	52	60	5
34	63	26	51	64	2
36	63	45	51	72	2
41	63	1	50	76	1
4	62	29	48	81	1
40	62	47	48	94	1
3	61	49	47	96	1
30	61	35	44	99	1
32	61	44	44		
16	60	51	33		

#12: SHAWON

So who would you take? You're Cubs GM Dallas Green, it's June 1982, and you've got the first pick in the amateur draft. There are a lot of good players, a lot of future stars, but it comes down to Dwight Gooden or **Shawon Dunston**.

The Cubs chose Dunston, obviously, and received a dozen seasons of, shall we say, interesting baseball from him. He had speed but often ran himself out of plays with poor judgment. He had gap power but struck out more than one in every six at bats in his career, exactly 1,000 Ks in all. He had range and an amazing arm, but if it hadn't been for Mark Grace, many of his throws would have wound up heading in the general direction of Addison Street. He was one of the National League's best shortstops during his first seven seasons with the club, before a herniated disc in his lower back cost him the better part of three seasons. There wasn't a pitch he wouldn't swing at—in addition to the 1K of whiffs, he walked only 203 times in 1,814 games, giving him a .296 lifetime OBP, not very good for someone who often batted lead-off. His shortcomings notwithstanding, he was a popular player for the Cubs, frequently lauded by broadcaster Harry Caray for one of his acrobatic plays in the field.

As to whether Gooden, with his erratic and self-destructive behavior, would have had an even better career in Chicago, it's not ours to say. Dunston was, however, able to adapt. In 1997, during his second go-round with the Cubs, he played his first game as an outfielder after more than 1,200 games at shortstop. He added five years to his career as a spare flychaser, playing shortstop only eighteen times after '97, and making the postseason three times with three different teams (1999 Mets, 2000 Cardinals, 2002 Giants).

Apart from Dunston, no Cubs player has worn #12 for more than four seasons; it seems more a refuge for players in the early number days from another number. During the first two decades of Cubs uniform numbers, there was a large group of players who wore #12 and also had another number during their Wrigley tenure: **Charlie Root** (1932); **Mark Koenig** (1933); **Jim Weaver** (1934); **Lon Warneke** (1935–36), who had three 20-win seasons for the Cubs before he turned twenty-six in 1935, only to be dealt after 1936 to the Cardinals; **Ken O'Dea** (1937–38); **Rip Russell** (1940–42); **Billy Holm** (1943); **Chico Hernandez** (1943); **Roy Easterwood** (1944); **Dewey Williams** (1944–45), a backup catcher who squeezed in two at bats in the 1945 World Series; **Lou Stringer** (1946); **Cal McLish** (1949), another pitcher who showed great promise in his early years with the Cubs only to have his best success elsewhere; and **Mickey Owen** (1950–51), who also wore #9 and #12 as a Cub, perhaps trying to escape the memory of his momentary failure to catch a strike in Brooklyn.

The numbers seemed to be doled out to every **Tommy** (**Brown,** 1952–53), **Dick** (**Johnson**, 1958; **Gernert**, 1960) . . . and **Jerry** (**Tabb,** 1974). Sorry, no Harry ever wore #12 for the Cubs. It wasn't until 1968 that any Cub stayed in the number for more than two seasons. Back-up catcher **John Boccabella** (1966–68), who wasn't an original #12er (he wore #22 on his first call up in 1963), kept #12 while backing up Randy Hundley for most of three seasons; he was taken by the Montreal Expos in the 1968 expansion draft. He became far better known for the unique way the Jarry Park PA announcer would call out his name: "John Bocca-BEEEELLLLAAAAA!!!"

Andre Thornton first arrived in the major leagues with the Cubs in 1973, but he never really had a position. He played only part-time at first base while the Cubs were indulging the last good years of Billy Williams, and instead Andy became the poster child for the Lost Cubs of 1975. Thornton, the first Cub to wear #12 in more than three different seasons, who was sent to Montreal as a 1976 Olympic present for Larry Biittner and Steve Renko, never saw the postseason despite 253 homers and a .360 career on-base percentage. (He spent 1977–87 with Cleveland—nuff said.) Several other '75 Cubs won championships within a few years of being dealt: Manny Trillo (Phillies), Bill Madlock (Pirates), Milt Wilcox (Tigers), and Rick Monday and Burt Hooton (Dodgers). Trading future ace Larry Gura and longtime ace Ferguson Jenkins, who had a decade of good pitching left in him, marred the final years of John Holland's eighteen-year tenure as GM.

Pre-Dunston, #12 was inhabited by utilitymen, has-beens, and rookies who'd play their best baseball elsewhere. Of **Rudy Meoli** (1978), **Steve Macko** (1979–80), **Carmelo Martinez** (1983), and **Davey Lopes** (1984), the latter playing longer for the Cubs in the more familiar #15 that he had worn as a Dodger, the only player we will memorialize here is Macko. He was an infielder of some promise who was cut down far too young from testicular cancer at age twenty-seven in 1981. Steve's dad Joe Macko was a member of the College of Coaches (in 1964, wearing #64), and later, for many years the clubhouse manager for the Texas Rangers. Steve had served as a Rangers batboy as a teenager when the Senators first moved to Texas.

Mickey Morandini (1998–99) became popular for his slashing hitting and running style and solid defense at second base for the 1998 Wild Card Cubs, but his average declined fifty-five points from 1998 to 1999, the Cubs suffered a ninety-five-loss season, and Morandini departed as a free agent, almost as quickly as he was acquired for Doug Glanville after the 1997 season.

Perhaps the most controversial #12 was the only non-player to wear it, manager **Dusty Baker** (2003–06). Besides Thornton and Dunston, Baker is the only man, to date, to wear #12 in blue pinstripes for more than three seasons. Hailed as a potential franchise savior after leading the Cubs to within five outs of the World Series in 2003, Baker, noted as a player's manager, lost control of the clubhouse the following season, with players calling the press box to complain about calls; Baker got into a war of words with broadcaster Steve Stone, leading to Stone's leaving the club. By 2006, with Baker's managing philosophies leading the Cubs to hack away at pitches rather than "clog up the bases" with walks, the Cubs put together a ninety-six-loss season, one of the worst in club history, and Baker wasn't retained . . .

. . . which made #12 available for **Alfonso Soriano** (2007–08), signed by GM Jim Hendry to an eight-year, $136 million contract—the biggest free-agent signing in all of baseball that offseason—just weeks after Baker's departure and the hiring of new manager Lou Piniella, Soriano has prodigious power and baserunning speed, but he has been occasionally prone to injury, and possesses an annoying tendency toward making mental mistakes. Nevertheless, #12 Soriano jerseys are among the biggest sellers and there is no doubt that when he goes on a hot streak, he can carry a team for a month or more. Primary examples of this include Soriano's torrid September of 2007, which helped the Cubs win the NL Central, and his incredible July of 2008, when he returned from a stint on the disabled list to lead the Cubs to a 27–8 mark in their first thirty-five games after his reactivation.

MOST OBSCURE CUB TO WEAR #12: **Chris Kitsos** (1954). They don't come much more obscure than Kitsos, who, on April 21, 1954, came in to replace Ernie Banks (then in his rookie season) at shortstop in the bottom of the eighth in Milwaukee after Eddie Miksis had batted for Banks and grounded out with the Cubs trailing, 7-3. Kitsos had two assists and never played in the majors again. And that's all there is to know.

GUY YOU NEVER THOUGHT OF AS A CUB WHO WORE #12: **Bobby Darwin** (1977). Darwin, who had hit 64 homers from 1972–74 as a regular outfielder for the Twins, suffered a power outage in '75 and shuttled from the Twins to the Brewers to the Red Sox, from where the Cubs acquired him for Ramon Hernandez on May 28, 1977. It was a useless trade for both teams. Darwin played in just eleven games for the Cubs, going 2-for-12 before being released, and Hernandez pitched in twelve games for the Red Sox with a 5.68 ERA before being cut loose—the two releases coming within three days of each other, August 20 for Hernandez, August 23 for Darwin.

Helmet Head

By 1954, just about every Cub was wearing a batting helmet. Even after batting helmets became the official rule in 1971, you could still wear a protective liner in your hat—a practice used all the way until 1979, when lone holdout Bob Montgomery of the Red Sox retired.

Protecting batters' heads took long enough. A pitch had killed Cleveland's Ray Chapman in 1920 and beanballs had severely impacted the careers of many players before that, specifically one of the greatest Cubs: first baseman and manager Frank Chance. "The Peerless Leader" crowded the plate, barely flinched as the fastest pitch bore in on him, absorbed the impact, got up, and took his base. Chance was drilled 137 times in just 1,274 games as a Cub, including five times in a 1904 doubleheader in Cincinnati in which he was knocked unconscious in the opener, played the second game, and then was drilled twice more. Though Chance later took to wearing a crude cap liner, he suffered the effects of the beanings for the rest of his life, which ended at age forty-seven.

The adoption of the helmet helped cooler—and safer—heads prevail. The first helmets were made of fiberglass, but plastic became the material of choice. In 1983, it was mandated that players wear a helmet with a flap on the ear that faced the pitchers (switch hitters generally went with a double flap). Ron Santo had been one of the first to go to an ear flap, wearing one as protection after having his left cheekbone fractured in 1966. While it is not clear who the first Cub to wear a helmet during a game was—perhaps '54 leadoff man Bob Talbot?—the last to wear a helmet without an ear flap was Gary Gaetti. Grandfathered in from the old rule, Gaetti played his last game as a Cub on September 26, 1999. Although batboys and some catchers still used flapless helmets, these helmets reappeared in everyday use at Wrigley Field in 2008 when base coaches Matt Sinatro (first base) and Mike Quade (third base) were required to wear them following the death of minor league first base coach Mike Coolbaugh from a line drive the previous summer.

The Cubs were one of the first teams to wear the new Coolflo helmets, made by Rawlings, in 2006. The helmet is ugly enough, but a venting system keeps players' heads cooler than previous incarnations. And a head that's cool, comfortable, and safe can conceivably concentrate on the matter at hand: hitting a 95 MPH fastball on the inside corner.

#13: LUCKY CLAUDE

Thirteen isn't for everyone. It helps if you're not superstitious, and it helps even more if you're good. **Claude Passeau** was both. He was the first to wear #13 for both the Phillies and Cubs. Nearly seven decades later he is still the best Cub to wear the number.

Passeau arrived from Philadelphia in May 1939 in a trade for Kirby Higbe and two others having posted losing records in three years with the hapless Phils. In Chicago he reeled off eight consecutive winning seasons, leading the team in strikeouts seven times, complete games and ERA four times, and wins three times. Even today he still ranks fifteenth on the Cubs' all-time wins list, right behind Greg Maddux and Grover Cleveland Alexander. At age thirty-six he helped the Cubs claim the 1945 pennant, going 17–9 with a career-best 2.46 ERA. His first World Series appearance was magnificent: a one-hitter at Tiger Stadium in Game 3. The good-hitting Passeau, who had 15 career home runs, even drove in a run with a sacrifice fly. He was an All-Star five times—and still is the only Cubs pitcher to start an All-Star Game, doing so in 1946—but a lasting image is his serving up the game-ending homer to Ted Williams in the '41 Midsummer Classic in Detroit.

Only seven other players have taken the plunge and worn the number that so many avoid that there's a word—triskaidekaphobia—that specifically describes those who fear it. After the 1940s, no Cub dared wear #13 until **Bill Faul** (1965–66), a free-spirited right-hander who might have been a precursor to the more open days of the 1970s. Faul was purchased from the Tigers after the 1964 season, had limited success (6–6, 3.54 in 17 appearances, 16 starts) in 1965, and then was relegated mostly to the bullpen by Leo Durocher in 1966. Durocher, an old-school sort if ever there was one, probably was turned off by Faul's newfangled ideas, including self-hypnosis. Faul was sent to

the minors in mid-season 1966, later surfaced briefly with the 1970 Giants, and then found himself out of baseball.

After Faul, the #13 again sat hanging in a locker in the Cubs' clubhouse, waiting for another free spirit to claim it. No one did so for nearly three decades, until **Steven "Turk" Wendell** (1993–97) donned it upon making his inauspicious major league debut on June 17, 1993 as a starter against the Cardinals at Wrigley Field. He allowed eight hits, two walks, and five earned runs in a game the Cubs would eventually lose, 11-10. Wendell had been acquired in a trade made one week before the end of the regular season, on September 29, 1991, when the Cubs sent Damon Berryhill and Mike Bielecki to the Braves in exchange for Wendell and Yorkis Perez, both thought of at the time as good pitching prospects.

Wendell didn't do very well as a starter, but he improved when moved to the bullpen. Briefly made the Cubs closer in 1996, he led the team with 18 saves, which still stands as the lowest team-leading total since 1993. He might have done well had he continued in that role, but inexplicably, management signed Mel Rojas as a free agent to close in 1997. Rojas was so bad that he was dumped in a trade—along with Wendell and outfielder Brian McRae—to the Mets on August 8, 1997. Wendell turned in several decent years as a set-up man for the Mets, Phillies, and Rockies before retiring after the 2004 season.

Jeff Fassero (2001–02) was the next to try his luck with #13. After several years as a swingman—starter and reliever—mostly with the Expos, Mariners, and Red Sox, the thirty-eight-year-old Fassero was signed in December 2000 as a free agent with the intention that he'd compete for a spot in the Cubs rotation. But an injury to Tom Gordon forced the Cubs to try Fassero as a closer (prior to 2001, he'd had ten saves over his first three years as an Expo before converting to starting full-time). It worked, for a while. Fassero reeled off nine saves in April and when Gordon returned in May, Fassero became a top set-up man, recording twenty-five holds. But the next year, instead of putting out fires, he became a torch, lighting up NL bats to the tune of a 6.18 ERA before being traded to the Cardinals for a pair of minor leaguers.

Neifi Perez (2004–06) will always be fondly remembered by Cubs fans, but not for anything he did while a Cub. On September 27, 1998, literally thirty seconds after the Cubs lost their final regularly scheduled game to the Astros, Neifi, then playing for Colorado, hit a walkoff homer against San Francisco to beat the Giants, 9-8, forcing the September 28 winner-take-all tiebreaker in which the Cubs beat the Giants 5-3 to advance to the 1998 postseason. Little did we know that six years later, Neifi would join the Cubs in a desperation acquisition on August 19 after Nomar Garciaparra, who was supposed to help lead the Cubs to the postseason, got hurt. Neifi had the month of his life after the trade, going 23-for-62 with two homers, but the Cubs failed to qualify for the playoffs.

When Nomar went down again the following April, Neifi was pressed into service as the primary starting shortstop, a good six years after his best years had passed him by in Colorado. Manager Dusty Baker was quoted as saying, "Neifi saved us," leading Cubs fans to wonder, "From what?" since that club finished with a 79–83 record.

The following year, with the club in disarray, Neifi was dispatched to the Tigers for a minor league catcher on August 20. He should send Jim Hendry a Christmas gift every year for the rest of his life, because Hendry got him from a 96-loss last-place team into the World Series.

Right after Perez was sent to Detroit, **Will Ohman** (2006–07) claimed #13. Ohman was somewhat of a number vagabond—#13 was the fourth different number he had worn in several stints with the Cubs, beginning with #35 on his rookie call up in 2000. Arm surgery kept him from the majors for four years, from 2001 to 2005, and on his return he sported #45, then #50. Ohman had some success as a situational lefty, but he angered management and his teammates in 2007 when he, after being sent to the minors for poor performance, claimed he was injured and thus shouldn't have been optioned out. Upon his recall, he was assigned by the rest of the relievers to carry the pink backpack (filled with sunflower seeds and other paraphernalia relievers use in the bullpen), a task usually designated to the lowest-ranking rookie. Ohman was sent in a trade to Atlanta after the 2007 season . . . and for now, uniform #13 lays fallow at Wrigley Field.

MOST OBSCURE CUB TO WEAR #13: **Hal Manders** (1946). Manders, whose primary claim to fame is that Hall of Famer Bob Feller is his cousin, pitched in two games (one start) late in '46. Claude Passeau's season had ended due to a back injury and he had gone home in late August, presumably retired, so his #13 was available and, as was the custom in those days, if the club had an available shirt that fit and wasn't being used, it would be reassigned. Manders was not retained for 1947, and Passeau came back for a nineteen-appearance (six-start) encore, reclaiming his number in '47.

GUY YOU NEVER THOUGHT OF AS A CUB WHO WORE #13: **Rey Ordonez** (2004). Ordonez had been signed out of Cuba as a free agent by the Mets in 1993. They were dazzled by his glove, but quickly learned that he couldn't hit. His glovework was good enough to keep him a regular for seven seasons with the Mets, but they dealt him to Tampa Bay in 2003 for a couple of minor leaguers who never made it. He was signed by the Padres in 2004, but he never played in the majors for them and was released in May. Cubs manager Dusty Baker, liking supposedly scrappy middle infielders with good gloves, asked GM Jim Hendry to sign Ordonez. He hit .164 in twenty-three games (twenty-two starts) before being released; this eventually led Hendry to make the blockbuster Nomar Garcia-parra deal at the deadline that year.

Gassaway Got Away

Of the more than 1,200 men who have worn a Cubs uniform since 1932, we have a number to go with every name . . . except for one. Charlie Gassaway. And it's not for a lack of trying.

Gassaway was the starting pitcher in two games at the end of the 1944 season, both on the road, against teams long out of the pennant race. The fourth-place Cubs wound up thirty games behind the Cardinals, and they still had a double-digit lead on both opponents the final week of the season. The twenty-six-year-old southpaw from the eponymous locale of Gassaway, Tennessee, debuted on September 25, in the first game of a Monday doubleheader sweep of the Phillies at Shibe Park; he earned no decision in a 7-6 Cubs win. He started again four days later at Braves Field and lost, 5-1. The "crowd" for that Friday afternoon contest in Boston was 501.

Fifty years later, Kasey Ignarski was sifting through scorecards, media guides, and official documents in an attempt to verify every Cubs uniform number in history. But Gassaway's number was not in any source or on either of the lists Kasey got from the Cubs in 1995 and 1997. A few years later, when Jack Looney was working on his book, *Now Batting, Number . . .*, Looney contacted Kasey about Gassaway. Looney had found that Gassaway, though he never pitched again for the Cubs, had worn #3 in 1945 for the Philadelphia Athletics and #31 in Cleveland during his final season in 1946.

Kasey contacted the Boston Braves Historical Society to see if they had any source for scorecards from the game Gassaway pitched there in '44. Given that the team moved from Boston to Milwaukee in 1953, the paucity of that day's crowd, and the passage of time made it no surprise that this was a dead end. A search of Boston newspaper archives also proved unsuccessful. Attempts to find anyone in Philadelphia with information on the game he pitched there as a Cub also proved fruitless. Al Yellon contacted Gabriel Schechter, a researcher at the Hall of Fame, to see if the Hall had any information. But Schechter's research came up empty, too; there was nothing in his Cooperstown file mentioning a uniform number and no photos of Gassaway as a Cub.

Back in Chicago, Kasey searched the *Chicago Tribune* archives and found mentions of Gassaway in their game stories, but there was nothing on the number he wore. Kasey then went to his source for many past scorecard/program searches: AU Sports in Skokie. The 1944 programs they had did not list Gassaway on any roster—not exactly a surprise since he never pitched at home. There was no way on Earth to find out from the source, as Charlie Gassaway had already passed away by the time Kasey began his search in earnest,

So Gassaway's is the one number we never found. Given that during the last week of September 1944, Polish resistance in Warsaw was being crushed, repeated British attempts to take the Dutch bridge over the Rhine at Arnhem were failing, and American soldiers were pushing their way to the German border, people's minds were understandably focused on more than baseball.

#14: MR. CUB

Paul Schramka is the answer to one of the all-time Cubs trivia questions: Who was the last player to wear #14 before Ernie Banks? Originally signed by the Cubs in 1949 out of the University of San Francisco, Schramka, an outfielder, spent the next three-plus years playing in the Cubs' minor league system and in military service. But he impressed manager Phil Cavarretta enough during spring training in 1953 to make the Opening Day roster, and in fact, Cavarretta had told reporters that Schramka would be his Opening Day left fielder, becoming the first player to wear #14 in eleven years. When that day, April 14, came, Gene Hermanski was in left field and Schramka was on the bench. He did get into the game as a pinch runner, and two days later he replaced Hermanski in left field in the eighth inning. But that was the sum total of his major league career. He never again appeared in a game for the Cubs, and nine days after that, Schramka was sent to the Cubs' minor league affiliate in Springfield, Massachusetts, and #14 was put away in storage. Up to that time it had been worn by seven other players, some well-known (**Charlie Root**) and others not (**Zach Taylor**), some colorful (**Lou "The Mad Russian" Novikoff**), and some workmanlike (**Larry French**, winner of seventeen games with the '35 pennant winners and loser of nineteen when the Cubs won again in '38). Just short of five months after Schramka had his uniform taken back, a skinny shortstop was recalled by the Cubs and issued #14 on September 17, 1953.

Twenty-nine years later, Paul Schramka's uniform number was retired by the Cubs, having been worn with great distinction by **Ernie Banks** (1953–71, plus two more years as a coach). Schramka, who still lives in his hometown of Milwaukee, sent Banks a telegram after his number

Ernie Banks | 1ST BASE

was retired on August 22, 1982, reading: "I left all the base hits in the jersey for you."

Ernie Banks's standing as *the* greatest Cub has been apparent for so long, even evident during his days as an active player, that it has become a cliché, obscuring his true magnitude. He is not a first tier Hall of Famer (e.g. Henry Aaron, Willie Mays, Babe Ruth, Ty Cobb), but Banks is at the top of what may be called the "second class," and that's not intended as a slight. There is no question he was definitely headed for that first tier in the early years of his career, only to be derailed by serious injury. Indeed, a large part of Ernie's greatness is that he overcame that obstacle to achieve as much as he did.

It was in the years before those injuries that Ernie appeared to be heading for the top rank of the record books. From 1955 through 1960, he hit 40 or more home runs five times in six seasons. In the forty-eight seasons since then, only Sammy Sosa, Ken Griffey Jr., Harmon Killebrew, and Alex Rodriguez have accomplished that feat; Hall of Famers Mays and Aaron, Banks's contemporaries, never did. In 1955, he hit five grand slams, a record that stood for thirty-two years (and still stands as the NL record). The climax to all this production was the back-to-back MVP awards he won in 1958 and 1959, the first time a National Leaguer had won two in a row. Looking back on those awards from a 2009 perspective, they are even more impressive than they must have seemed at the time. The Cubs finished sixth in both those of seasons—losing eighty-two games and finishing twenty games out of first place in '58, losing eighty and winding up a closer, but still poor, thirteen games behind in '59. But Ernie dominated the league. In 1958, he led the National League in games, at bats, slugging, total bases, homers, RBI, and extra-base hits, finished second in OPS, and for good measure, second in triples with 11, though he was never much known for having much baserunning speed. He got sixteen of the possible twenty-four first-place MVP votes. He became only the third Cub to hit 40 homers in a season, after Hack Wilson and Hank Sauer, and it would take another dozen years (until Billy Williams hit 42 in 1970) for anyone else to join that exclusive club (since joined by Dave Kingman, Andre Dawson, Ryne Sandberg, Sosa, and Derrek Lee).

Injuries forced Banks to move from his original position, shortstop, where he played with grace and style and in many ways was the prototype for the power-hitting shortstops of today, to first base. As his knees got worse his mobility declined to the point where Leo Durocher openly campaigned to management to trade for a replacement. Perhaps as a reaction, Banks hit only 15 homers in 1966, the first year Durocher managed the club, but his power numbers came back in subsequent seasons. In 1969, Ernie drove in 106 runs at age thirty-eight. While that may not seem that "old" to us today, consider again the perspective of time—Ernie was the oldest position player in the major leagues that year.

As he approached retirement, Ernie became a player-coach. He continued those coaching duties for two years after his retirement as a player in 1971. Though his duties were somewhat undefined, he primarily coached first base—and Banks remained on the staff after Durocher was fired midway through '72. On May 8, 1973, manager Whitey Lockman was ejected in the third inning and Ernie took over for the rest of the game, technically becoming the first black manager in baseball history. In 1977, Ernie was elected to the Hall of Fame in his first year of eligibility, named on 83.8 percent of the ballots.

MOST OBSCURE CUB TO WEAR #14: **Vallie Eaves** (1941–42). One might call this "most obscure *name* to wear #14," or any other number, for that matter; Eaves is the only "Vallie" in major league history, and that is, in fact, his true given first name (Vallie Ennis Eaves is his full name). Eaves appeared in twelve games for the 1941 Cubs and two more in 1942.

GUY YOU NEVER THOUGHT OF AS A CUB WHO WORE #14: **Ken Raffensberger** (1940–41) won 119 games (and lost 154!) over a fifteen-year major league career, primarily with the Reds; he also played for the Cardinals and Phillies. Seven of those wins came in 1940 as a part-time starter for the 75–79, fifth-place Cubs; after ten uninspiring appearances in 1941, he was sent to the minors and eventually traded to the Phillies two years later.

The Number No One Knows About: Rose Breaks Record at Wrigley

Pete Rose, just as Ernie Banks did for the Cubs, set many records wearing #14 for the Cincinnati Reds. On September 11, 1985, Rose got his 4,192nd career hit against the San Diego Padres before a sellout crowd in Cincinnati and, in doing so, broke Ty Cobb's all-time career hits record.

Or did he? Later research corrected Cobb's hit total to be 4,189 instead of 4,191, the number it had been thought to be for decades. So to be historically correct, Rose's 4,190th hit should be the one denoted as the record-breaker.

Three days before the "official" record-breaking hit, Rose's Reds were in Chicago to play the Cubs. Rose, forty-four years old and a player-manager, no longer played against lefthanders, and was going to sit against the Cubs' scheduled starter, lefty Steve Trout. But it was reported that Trout "fell off a bicycle" that morning and right-hander Reggie Patterson replaced him. Rose put himself in the lineup and singled in the first inning, his 4,190th career hit. He singled again in the fifth for number 4,191.

So, the 28,269 on hand at Wrigley on Sunday, September 8, 1985 were the ones who really saw Pete Rose break Ty Cobb's record. Incidentally, that day started hot and humid and 88 degrees; midway through the game, a blinding thunderstorm blew through, delayed the game two hours, dropped the temperature to 58 and forced it to be called a tie when it got too dark to play. Perhaps forces other than Rose's bat were at work that afternoon.

#15: FAME ELUDED US

While #15 has been retired by the Yankees in honor of Thurman Munson, and by the Green Bay Packers in honor of Bart Starr, the lot of that number in Cubs lore is that it has been worn—very briefly, in many cases—by players who became better-known wearing other numbers, or for other teams.

Ron Santo, whose #10 is retired and flies proudly on a flag above the left-field foul pole at Wrigley Field, could have instead have sent #15 to its retirement. As we noted in chapter 10, Santo wore #15 for his first few games as a Cub, including a handful at Wrigley Field. As was the case for so many players of that era, Santo was simply handed the shirt off the back of the player he replaced on the roster, **Sammy Taylor.** At 6-foot-2, 185 pounds, Taylor wasn't that much different in size than the six-foot, 190-pound Santo. Taylor had been sent to the minors to make room for Santo in June 1960, and by the time he was recalled a month later, Santo had switched to his now-familiar #10, so Taylor took #15 back, wore it through the end of that season, then changed to #7 for 1961 and 1962.

It was ever thus with #15. **Pat Malone,** who went 15–17 for the NL champion Cubs in 1932, was the first player to wear #15, but changed to #19 in 1933 and 1934.

UNIFORM NUMBERS

1 Ashburn, OF	6 Averill, C	16 Kindall, IF	25 Thomas, OF	36 Elston, P	41 Hegan, C
2 Tappe, C	11 Bouchee, IF	17 Zimmer, IF	28 Will, OF	37 Ellsworth, P	43 Cardwell, P.
3 Craft, Coach	12 Gernert, IF	20 Murphy, OF	30 Drott, P	38 Morehead, P	46 Schaffernoth, P
4 Himsl, Coach	14 Banks, IF	21 Altman, IF	31 Freeman, P	39 Drabowsky, P	
5 Boudreau, Mgr.	15 Santo, IF	22 Thacker, C	32 Anderson, P	40 Hobbie, P	

The number then wended its way through reserves **Gilly Campbell** (1933), **Dick Ward** (1934), and **Jim Weaver** (1934) before pitcher **Bill Lee** sported it in 1935 and 1936—though Lee's best year came wearing #11, in 1938.

Lonny Frey (1937)? Better known as a Dodger and Red. **Tony Lazzeri** (1938)? A Yankee. **Bobby Mattick** (1939–40)? A Blue Jay (OK, much later, as their first manager). And the beat went on through the 1950s (after the number wasn't issued for ten seasons between 1943–52): **Carl Sawatski** (1953)? Cardinals and Braves. **John Briggs** (1956–57)? Wrong John Briggs; not the guy who was a solid outfielder for the Phillies and Brewers, this John Briggs was a run of the mill swingman (5–6, 4.70 in 26 Cubs games pitched).

KEN
RUDOLPH
CHICAGO CUBS   CATCHER

It wasn't until 1973 that anyone wore #15 for as many as four seasons; **Ken Rudolph,** a backup catcher, who had worn #8 in 1969, switched to #15 the following year, but he barely hit his weight in it (weight: 185, average wearing #15: .202). Another catcher, and the only other player to wear #15 for four years, **George Mitterwald,** traded to the Cubs before the 1974 season, hit three homers and drove in eight runs in an 18-9 win over the Pirates on April 17, just seven games into his Cubs career, but he hit only four other homers the rest of the '74 season. He wore #15 for more games than any other Cub (373).

Davey Lopes, stalwart of Dodgers World Series teams in the 1970s, had one last hurrah for the Cubs, stealing 47 bases at age forty in 1985—setting a record for the most steals for a player forty years old or over. **Gary Gaetti,** was picked up by the Cubs off the scrap heap on August 15, 1998, and would prove he still had a little something left. The third baseman wore #15 briefly until he reached an agreement to do a number swap for his familiar #8 with **Sandy Martinez**. In the eighties and nineties, #15 became the property of reserve infielders and catchers: **Steve Dillard** (1979–81), was an ordinary backup infielder except for one week in early August 1979, where he hit .600 (12-for-20) with three homers, nine runs, 10 RBI, and was named NL Player of the Week; **Junior Kennedy** (1982–83); **Mike Diaz** (1983); **Ron Hassey** (1984); **Domingo Ramos** (1989–90); **Rey Sanchez** (1991), who also wore #6 and #11, the well-known infielder numbers; and **Matt Franco** (1995), following the #15 trend set earlier, he's best remembered as a Met . . . and as actor Kurt Russell's nephew.

Julio Zuleta (2000–01) might have had a decent major league career if the NL had the DH rule; he wasn't about to displace Mark Grace at first base. His main claim to fame came in May 2001, when after a long Cubs losing streak, Zuleta decided to hold a ritual with his and his teammates' bats involving fruit, sunflower seeds, and liniment. The Cubs proceeded to win twelve games in a row. A .217 average, however, banished Zuleta and his voodoo to the minors by July, never to return.

Aramis Ramirez, far better known for wearing #16, gets a footnote in this chapter because when he was first acquired from the Pirates on July 22, 2003, coach **Sonny Jackson** was wearing the #16 that Ramirez had worn with the Pirates. It took a few games before Ramirez reclaimed the number he still wears today.

MOST OBSCURE CUB TO WEAR #15: **Norm Gigon** (1967). It's a mystery at times how certain players even get to wear a major league uniform. Gigon was signed out of high school by the Phillies in 1958. He spent eight years toiling in Philadelphia's farm system before being traded to the Cubs for Billy Cowan on June 22, 1966. It took nearly another year before he made his major league debut on April 12, 1967, walking as a pinch hitter. He played in thirty-three games, starting thirteen of them, some in the outfield, some at second base, and one at third base, and hit .171 with one home run, a three-run blast off Juan Pizarro in a 7-3 win over the Pirates. He was twenty-nine years old at the time of his major league service and one is made to wonder why the Cubs used a roster spot for him rather than a younger player.

GUY YOU NEVER THOUGHT OF AS A CUB WHO WORE #15: **Jim Edmonds** (2008). To say Cubs fans "never thought" of Edmonds as a Cub is an understatement. During his eight years as a Cardinal, he became one of Cubs fans' most hated opposing players; he hit .270/.394/.554 vs. the Cubs as a Cardinal, with 32 home runs in 126 career games. St. Louis sent him to San Diego before the 2008 season, but the Padres gave up on him after only a month; he was hitting .178 with one homer and many Cub fans thought Jim Hendry's signing of him was folly. But Edmonds surprised everyone by hitting for average and power, and showing flashes of that great center-field defense that had denied the Cubs so many times.

Popular

There have been a lot of Cubs and a lot of numbers. This list gets down to how many. The most popular numbers are generally the ones that have the fewest recognizable names, hence the quick turnover. Low numbers are also not as popular as one would think. No single-digit number made the top ten.

The one unknown number in Cubs history, Charlie Gassaway's, is listed as a question mark. Also note that this table includes the players in 2007 and 2008 who wore #42 for one day in honor of Jackie Robinson.

Uni #	Number of people who wore this #	Uni #	Number of people who wore this #
15	47	45	40
19	46	7	39
20	45	4	38
32	45	37	38
12	44	43	38
24	44	5	37
39	44	9	37
22	43	11	37
27	43	25	37
33	43	30	37
8	42	16	36
38	42	17	34
41	42	28	34
29	41	3	33
6	40	18	33

Uni #	Number of people who wore this #	Uni #	Number of people who wore this #
31	33	26	14
40	33	56	12
42	33	14	9
34	32	57	9
21	31	13	8
23	30	54	8
47	29	59	7
35	28	58	6
36	27	61	4
2	26	63	4
48	26	62	3
49	26	64	2
46	24	?	1
10	23	60	1
50	22	72	1
1	21	76	1
51	18	81	1
44	16	94	1
53	16	96	1
52	15	99	1
55	15		

#16 BITTERSWEET SIXTEEN

ALL-TIME #16 ROSTER:

Player	Year
Burleigh Grimes	1932
Ed Baecht	1932
Lon Warneke	1933–34
Tex Carleton	1935–38
Ray Harrell	1939
Ken Raffensberger	1940–41
Wimpy Quinn	1941
Babe Dahlgren	1941–42
Jimmie Foxx	1942
Don Carlsen	1948
Hank Edwards	1949–50
Harry Chiti	1950
Bob Addis	1952–53
Howie Pollet	1953–55
Bob Will	1957
Bobby Adams	1958–59
Randy Jackson	1959
Jerry Kindall	1960–61
Ken Hubbs	1962–63
Roger Metzger	1970
Garry Jestadt	1971
Gene Hiser	1971–72
Whitey Lockman (manager)	1972–74
Rob Sperring	1974–76
Steve Ontiveros	1977–80
Bill Hayes	1980–81
Steve Lake	1983–86
Terry Francona	1986
Paul Noce	1987
Greg Smith	1989–90
Jose Vizcaino	1991–93
Anthony Young	1994–95
Dave Magadan	1996
Jeff Reed	1999–2000
Delino DeShields	2001–02
Sonny Jackson (coach)	2003
Aramis Ramirez	2003–08

Number 16 is a number of great triumph and great sadness for Cubs fans. It currently belongs to **Aramis Ramirez** (2003–08), who was acquired in a salary-dump deal from the Pirates during the 2003 pennant race and who is already among the top five third basemen in club history (only Ron Santo, Stan Hack, and Harry Steinfeldt likely outrank him). Ramirez has solved the longtime third-base problem that was created when Santo was traded away after the 1973 season—more than 100 different players were tried there in the ensuing thirty years—and after only five and a half seasons in the blue pinstripes, Ramirez's total of 173 homers is one behind Andre Dawson for tenth in franchise history. If only his postseason hitting would measure up to his regular season prowess: Aramis has hit only .194 in sixty-seven October at bats, though he hit a grand slam in the '03 NLCS.

The sadness comes from wondering what might have become of **Ken Hubbs** (1961–63), one of the tragic figures in Cubs history. At age twenty he handled 418 consecutive chances without an error covering 78 games, both of which remained major league records for many years; the consecutive-chance

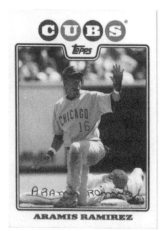

ARAMIS RAMIREZ

record stood until 1982, when it was broken by ex-Cub Manny Trillo, then playing for the Phillies. Hubbs was a free swinger, but his .260 average and 49 RBI garnered him nineteen of the twenty votes cast for the 1962 NL Rookie of the Year award. (Pirate Donn Clendenon kept it from being unanimous.) Although Hubbs slumped the next year, he was a key part of a club with improving pitching and a lineup of future Hall of Famers Ernie Banks, Billy Williams, and Lou Brock, not to mention Ron Santo.

Hubbs hated to fly and because of that, he decided to take flying lessons to conquer that fear. He earned his pilot's license at age twenty-two, in the 1963–64 offseason. On February 15, 1964, just a week before spring training, he was killed after taking off in a snowstorm in Utah. Though the Cubs didn't retire numbers in those years, it was announced that Hubbs's #16 would not be reissued for the 1964 season. Hubbs also wore #33 during his September call up in 1961.

Though the Cubs only promised to keep #16 out of circulation for one year out of respect to Hubbs, they let it lay vacant for six full seasons, when rookie hotshot **Roger Metzger** (1970) was called up and given the number. Metzger was a pretty good prospect, but he was blocked behind Don Kessinger and Glenn Beckert at both the middle infield positions and was traded to Houston in the 1970–71 offseason for the forgettable Hector Torres. Metzger became the Astros' regular shortstop for several seasons.

After Metzger left, the number was issued to a number of mediocre individuals, including the mediocre manager **Whitey Lockman** (1972–74), and after he was fired, to the non-prospect infielder **Rob Sperring** (1974–76). A future manager, **Terry Francona**, wore it in his brief Cubs career in 1986. The same was the case prior to Hubbs being issued the number at the end of the 1961 season: it was either worn by well-known players after they were famous (Hall of Famers **Burleigh Grimes,** (1932); **Jimmie Foxx,** (1942); and **Howie Pollet,** (1953–55), who had been a key part of the Cardinals pennant winners in 1942 and 1946, but as a Cub posted a 4.19 ERA in two-plus seasons) or by players who became famous for not-so-wonderful reasons (**Harry Chiti,** 1950, remembered as the player to be named later in a trade for himself as an original Met, and **Anthony Young**, 1994, who set the major league record for consecutive

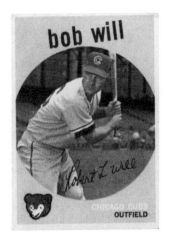

pitching losses, twenty-seven, the season before the Cubs traded for him—and the Cubs still gave the Mets everyday shortstop **Jose Vizcaino**, who preceded Young in #16).

Then there were the guys who wore #16 who weren't remembered by anyone, except in this book: **Bill Hayes** (1980–81), a catcher who played in five games for two of the worst Cubs teams ever; **Paul Noce** (1987), another middle infielder who couldn't hit (.228 in 180 at bats); **Greg Smith** (1989–90), ditto Noce; and **Jeff Reed** (1999–2000), who had a long career as a backup catcher with other teams, but his major distinction as a Cub was drawing the first pinch-walk by a major leaguer in Japan (in the Cubs/Mets game on March 30, 2000). Still others had more notoriety or recognition or just simple indecisiveness in other numbers: **Wimpy Quinn** was the first Cub to wear three numbers in one season, #4, #16, and #18 in 1941; **Bob Will,** best known as #28 from 1960–63, and **Dave Magadan,** best known as a Met, Marlin, or Padre. His one year as a Cub produced the second-worst season average of his career, .254.

A final perfect example of how the #16s had to get their fame off the baseball field is **Steve Ontiveros** (1977–80). He had slight power (10 homers, 32 doubles) and hit .299 for 1977's half-season overachievers. But the balding "Onty" became best known in Chicago for his TV commercials for "Hairline Creations."

MOST OBSCURE CUB TO WEAR #16: **Garry Jestadt,** who was acquired in an April 1970 trade from the Montreal Expos, spent the rest of that season in the minors, and somehow wound up on the Opening Day 1971 roster. He pinch-hit three times, all late in blowout losses, not getting a single hit, and then was traded to San Diego on May 19, 1971 for backup catcher Chris Cannizzaro.

GUY YOU NEVER THOUGHT OF AS A CUB WHO WORE #16: Hall of Famer **Jimmie Foxx,** who hit 534 career home runs and was second to Babe Ruth on the all-time list from his retirement in 1945 until Mickey Mantle passed him late in 1968, hit exactly ten of those homers as a Cub, long after the prime of his career, in 1942 and 1944. Double-X did wind up with a long association with the Wrigleys, as he managed in the All-American Girls Professional Baseball League, started by P. K. Wrigley in the 1940s. Tom Hanks's character in the film *A League of Their Own*, manager Jimmie Dugan, is said to be based loosely on Foxx.

Maybe They Shoulda Kept 'Em Blank

The Cubs and Braves are the only major league franchises in continuous operation since 1876, and the Cubs the only one that has stayed in the same city for those 133 seasons. The histories of the two ballclubs actually date back to their charter membership in the first professional baseball league: the National Association. Though it has never been classified a "major" league, the NA provided Chicago with its pro baseball debut in 1871 before the Great Chicago Fire that October idled the team for two years. Chicago had a thoroughly average record of 77–77 in the NA when they weren't being burned out or maneuvering to form the National League. Chicago won the inaugural National League pennant in 1876, the first of sixteen league titles they have won.

From 1876 through June 27, 1932—fifty-six and a half seasons—the Cubs wore number-less shirts. And from June 30, 1932 through the end of the 2008 season—seventy-six and a half seasons—the club has worn numbers on their backs.

So how did the team do, with blank shirts and with digits?

Without numbers: 4,276–3,143; .577

With numbers: 5,806–6,133; .486

We leave it to the reader to draw his or her own conclusions.

#17: GRACIE

Just hearing someone say the name **Mark Grace** is enough to make some Cubs fans stand and cheer. Not only was he the most smooth-fielding first baseman the Cubs have had—he fielded more balls cleanly than anyone in team history—but Gracie was an outstanding hitter. Only Cap Anson had more doubles in franchise

1B · MARK GRACE

history, and Grace's 51 two-baggers in strike-shortened 1995 were the most by any NL player since Pete Rose in 1978. He owned the 1990s, leading all Cubs in runs, triples, and batting. No player in either league had more hits or doubles during the decade.

The Cubs were lucky to get him. The Twins drafted Grace earlier and higher than the Cubs, but he stayed around San Diego State an extra year and Chicago took him in the twenty-fourth round of the 1985 draft. He rocketed through the minors and finished second to Chris Sabo in the 1988 Rookie of the Year balloting. The only problem was that the Cubs had another slick first baseman on their roster: Rafael Palmeiro. The Cubs were comfortable enough with Grace to trade Palmeiro, who had been a first-round pick the same years Grace was drafted. The multi-player deal with Texas brought back Mitch Williams, without whom the Cubs probably wouldn't have won the NL East in 1989. If lefties could play third base, the Cubs might have moved Grace there and found a way to keep both him and Palmeiro. But then he wouldn't have had so many people to talk to in the field. And he may not have won four Gold Gloves.

Grace was not a typical slugger-type first baseman, which may explain why he made only three All-Star teams. He didn't play in many postseason games, but his astounding .647 batting average in Chicago's 1989 NLCS loss to the Giants is the highest postseason average in franchise history. He left Chicago after the 2000 season (not of his own choice), went to Arizona as a free agent, and (sigh!) got a World Series ring in his first year as a Diamondback. He's still in Arizona, broadcasting D'backs games and Fox Saturday coverage.

Besides Grace, the best-known Cub to wear #17 is pitcher **Charlie Root.** He won 201 games, which, nearly seventy years after his retirement, remains the club record. He also served as a Cubs coach from 1951–53, wearing #49. Root pitched for the Cubs for sixteen years and also wore #12, which he was sporting when he gave up the alleged "called shot" to Babe Ruth in Game 3 of the 1932 World Series. He switched to #19 in 1933 and #14 the year after before finally settling on #17.

That World Series incident makes Root a central figure in one of the most debated moments in baseball history. Root, who never won a World Series game in six appearances over four different Series, had already allowed a homer to Ruth in the first inning on October 1, 1932, plus a drive that was caught at the wall in the second. The Cubs trailed by a run when Ruth stepped up in the fifth. Ruth stuck out his right hand after each of Root's first two pitches, both strikes. Ruth waved a single finger before the third pitch. The Bambino then, of course, clubbed that pitch for a home run to center field. Some swear the ball went to the exact spot he pointed to; some say he never even lifted his hand; still others were on line for the men's room and missed the whole incident. Root's feelings on Ruth? "He didn't point," Root said a few years before his death in 1970. "If he had, I'd have knocked him on his fanny." Root allowed a home run to the next batter, Lou Gehrig, and then manager Charlie Grimm pointed Root to the showers.

Some claim that Ruth's pointing at Wrigley Field in Game 3 was aimed at **Guy Bush,** who was a Cub for a decade before they ever wore uniform numbers, and who wore #17 immediately before Root (Bush was wearing #14 in 1932 when he drew the Bambino's attention). No one really knows whether Ruth called his shot, but it is true that Bush drilled Ruth with a pitch the next day. Ruth got him back, though.

Ruth was a washed-up Boston Brave, and Bush was a passable Pirate when they met on May 25, 1935. Bush came on in relief of Red Lucas, who had already given up a homer to the Babe. The Bambino crushed two homers off Bush, the last one—number 714 of his career—was called by eyewitnesses the longest ever hit at Forbes Field.

There's room for one last story about the Mississippi Mudcat, who also wore #14 as a Cub. Bush once complained to Cubs trainer Andy Lotshaw about an ache in his arm before a start, so he rubbed Bush with a dark "secret liniment." Bush pitched well and insisted that he receive a treatment of Lotshaw's miracle moisture before every start. When Bush went to the Pirates, Lotshaw gave away the secret: He'd been out of liniment that first day and he'd been rubbing Bush's arm with Coca-Cola ever since. Well, 176 major league wins makes a sweet pitcher.

Besides Grace, only one other Cub wore #17 for more than three seasons: pitcher **Bob Rush,** who was a mainstay of Cubs rotations for most of the 1950s, peaking at 17 wins in the .500 season of 1952, when he made one of his two All-Star appearances. He also hit well that year, batting .292 with 15 RBI. Rush won 110 games in all over ten seasons

(1948–57) as a Cub, wearing #30, switching to #17 in 1949, and after management felt he had outlived his usefulness, he was shipped to the Milwaukee Braves for some Taylors (Taylor Phillips and Sammy Taylor). Rush started and lost Game 3 of the 1958 World Series for Milwaukee.

Hi Bithorn wore #17 in his first major league season in 1942 and then, the following year, changed his number to #25 and had a great year with eighteen wins for a sixty-eight-win Cubs team, including seven shutouts and nine relief appearances. The next year Bithorn, the first Puerto Rican born major leaguer, went into the U.S. military. He returned to the Cubs in poor shape in 1946, and pitched twice on the South Side the following year, his last in the big leagues. He was shot to death on New Year's Day, 1952, attempting a comeback in the Mexican League. The stadium in San Juan is named after the former Cub. In this era of corporate stadium names, Bithorn is the first former player since Connie Mack to have his name on a "major league" ballpark. The Montreal Expos played official games at Bithorn's ballpark in 2003 (including a series against the Cubs in September) and 2004, before giving up the Canadian ghost and moving to Washington.

Four future major league managers wore #17 as Cubs infielders within a ten-season span: **Al Dark** (1958–59), **Don Zimmer** (1960–61), **Steve Boros** (1963), and **Joey Amalfitano** (1964–66). Lefty reliever **Dave LaRoche,** better known as the dad of Adam and Andy, wore #17 for ninety-four mediocre (5.17 ERA) appearances in 1973–74. He was a superstar compared to the players for whom the proverbial phrase "cup o'coffee" is too kind: **Jess Dobernic** (1948–49), **Frank Ernaga** (1958), **Jose Arcia** (1968), **Terry Hughes** (1970), **Frank Coggins** (1972), **Kurt Seibert** (1979), **Jesus Figueroa** (1980), **Joe Strain** (1981), **Jay Loviglio** (1983), **Dan "Not The WGN-TV Sports Guy, That's Spelled ROAN" Rohn** (1983–84), and **Mike Brumley** (1987). Another backup infielder, **Davey Rosello,** wore #17 off and on from 1972 to 1977, and while his .232 average as a Cub wasn't anything special, he did have one shining Cubs moment. Sporting a .170 batting average (8-for-47) on July 28, 1977, Rosello stepped to the plate in the bottom of the thirteenth inning and singled sharply up the middle, scoring pinch runner Rick Reuschel with the winning run in a 16–15 victory over the Reds, a game the Cubs had trailed 6–0, 10–7, and 14–10.

Lon Warneke was the Cubs' first #17 and he went 22–6 in 1932 as the runner-up for NL MVP, but he switched numbers the next year and wore five others as a Cub (#16, #12, #19, #32, #36) and did a stint in St. Louis without ever reaching the level of success he did the first year he wore a number. The current wearer of #17, **Mike Fontenot,** at first appeared to be nothing more than the answer to a trivia question: "Who did the Cubs acquire when they traded Sammy Sosa?" Fontenot, a former first-round pick of the Orioles, worked hard in the minors and impressed manager Lou Piniella enough that he made the 2007 roster as a backup infielder. Generously listed as 5-foot-8, 160 pounds, Fontenot has shown enough "sneaky power" to be nicknamed "Little Babe Ruth" by broadcaster Ron Santo.

MOST OBSCURE CUB TO WEAR #17: **Adam Greenberg** (2005). Perhaps "obscure" isn't the right word for Greenberg, since his only game in a Cubs uniform got considerable media attention. But he may have claim to the *shortest* Cubs career—one pitch, thrown by the Marlins' Valerio de los Santos, on July 9, 2005. The pitch hit Greenberg in the head, giving him a concussion. He left the game and has not made it back to the major leagues. Interesting bit of trivia: Carlos Zambrano served as the pinch runner for Greenberg and scored when Todd Walker doubled him in.

GUY YOU NEVER THOUGHT OF AS A CUB WHO WORE #17: **Bump Wills** (1982). Maury Wills's son, Elliott Taylor Wills, nicknamed "Bump" for unfathomable reasons, was acquired in an offseason trade with the Rangers, for whom he had had five average seasons as their second baseman, averaging over thirty steals a year. He started his Cubs career with a bang, connecting for a leadoff home run off Mario Soto in Cincinnati in the first game by any team in 1982, but Wills had another league-average season (102 OPS+) for the Cubs, stealing 35 bases and hitting .272 with a .347 OBP. Cubs management, however, had a kid third baseman they wanted to move across the diamond—someone named Sandberg—and when they acquired Ron Cey to play third base, Wills saw the handwriting on the wall. At age twenty-nine, he signed to play in Japan and never returned to the majors.

Double Your Pleasure

From Cap Anson to Mark Grace, the Cubs have had plenty of hitters able to pile up doubles. Anson (528) and Grace (456) had more doubles than any Cubs in history, with the pair ending their careers in Chicago about a century apart. Judging by this list below, though, you'd hardly know about their prolific two-base power. Anson never wore a number and Grace could barely pull #17 into the top ten in doubles as counted by uniform numbers in Cubs history. Grace had two-thirds of the doubles amassed by #17. That's nothing compared to the 93 percent (407 of 436) accounted for at #14 by Ernie Banks, and it still missed the top twenty. Just like one double doesn't do much to score runs, it takes people doubling before and after to really make the scoreboard jump. And #7 and #11 just seem lucky that way.

Uni #	Doubles
7	1,069
11	893
9	853
6	833
10	726
8	719
21	717
18	703
17	680
12	645
2	579
16	555
23	532
25	531
20	525
26	494
24	479
22	471
4	447
1	441

#18: BRUNO, MO, AND GEO

Glenn Beckert (1965–74) had a tough act to follow; he was the designated replacement for a deceased Rookie of the Year. When Ken Hubbs was killed in a plane crash before the 1964 season, the Cubs muddled through that year with four second basemen (Joe Amalfitano, Jimmy Stewart, Ron Campbell, and Leo Burke), but in '65 they decided to try the twenty-four-year-old Beckert, who had been acquired from the Red Sox in the first-year player draft in November 1962. A four-time All-Star, he was a future commodities trader nicknamed after a pro wrestler, and he broke Pirates second baseman Bill Mazeroski's stranglehold on the Gold Glove. Beckert and slick-fielding shortstop Don Kessinger made up a dependable double-play combination for nine straight years; Beckert, a solid if unspectacular hitter, hit .280 or better for six consecutive seasons, including a .342 mark in 1971 that was runner-up in the National League to MVP Joe Torre's .363.

Amid the Gold Gloves piled up by Kessinger and Santo, Beckert won the award in 1968, ending a string of seven Gold Gloves in eight years by Mazeroski (Hubbs was the only other winner in that time). Beckert's minor league teammate and friend Paul Popovich nicknamed him "Bruno" after wrestler Bruno Sammartino because of his aggressive nature chasing pop-ups. When the great team that never made the postseason was broken up

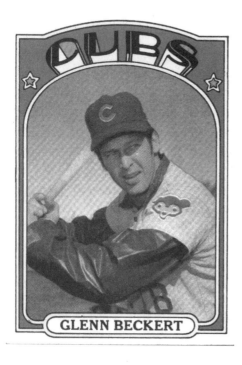

GLENN BECKERT

after the 1973 season, Beckert was sent to San Diego with a minor leaguer for outfielder Jerry Morales.

In future years, #18 may be remembered as the number of **Geovany Soto,** who began wearing it in 2008 after three September call ups wearing #58 (another catcher, **Jason Kendall,** who wore #18 for both the Pirates and A's, had worn it during his mostly forgettable two months as a Cub in 2007). Soto, who had not been considered a catching prospect in his first six professional seasons, had a breakout year in the minors in 2007, hitting .353 with 26 homers and 109 RBI and winning the Pacific Coast League MVP award. Called up and given the starting catcher nod in Game 2 of the Division Series, Soto homered in an 8-4 loss, the Cubs' only homer off Arizona pitching in that series. As the starting catcher beginning in 2008, Soto has received praise for his handling of the pitching staff and was appreciated enough in Chicago and elsewhere to become the first rookie catcher ever voted to start an All-Star Game.

Perhaps the best two players to wear #18 for the Cubs were a pair who each played three seasons in Chicago, enjoyed success on the North Side, but had many other good years elsewhere. **Bill Madlock** (1974–76) was another acquisition in the "Back Up the Truck" purge after '73, coming from the Rangers in the Fergie Jenkins deal. He started hitting immediately, posting a .313 batting average in his first season and finishing third in the Rookie of the Year voting. By hitting .354 in 1975 (a year in which he was All-Star Game co-MVP with similarly-named Met Jon Matlack), and .339 in 1976, Madlock became the first Cub since Cap Anson (1887–88) to win successive NL batting titles. When Madlock asked for a three-year contract, management's response was to trade him to the Giants for Bobby Murcer; they then proceeded to give Murcer a three-year deal for more money than Madlock had asked for. There were justifiable accusations of racism involved in this deal, and there is no doubt that Madlock could have helped the Cubs more than Murcer; "Mad Dog" won two more batting titles (both with Pittsburgh), wound up with over 2,000 hits, and was a key part of the 1979 Pirates World Series-winning team.

Moises Alou (2002–04), signed as a free agent after hitting .331 with 27 homers and 108 RBI for the Astros in 2001, disappointed in '02 by missing thirty games due to injury and hitting only 15 homers. In '03, though, he came back to form with a 22-homer, 91-RBI campaign, and he was even better in '04, smacking 39 dingers (leading a team with four 30-homer men) and both scoring and driving in 106 runs. But the most enduring memory, unfortunately, that most Cubs fans will have about this itinerant outfielder (he wore seven different major league uniforms in his career) is watching him slam down his glove in the eighth inning of Game 6 of the 2003 NLCS when a ball headed to the seats was interfered with by a fan. And of that incident, we shall say no more in this book.

An earlier long-time denizen of #18 was pitcher **Warren Hacker,** who wore it from 1949–56 (after beginning his Cubs career in #17 in 1948). Hacker was a mainstay in the Cubs starting rotation for nine years, but as was common for those poor Cubs teams, his record wasn't very good: 52–79 from 1948–56. The native of downstate Marissa, Illinois, had his best season in 1952, his first year as a regular starter, when he went 15–9 with a 2.58 ERA, finishing second in the National League in ERA to Hoyt Wilhelm. After that, hitters went up there hacking. In '53 he led the league in hits, earned runs, and home runs allowed, not to mention losses. His ERA stayed above 4.25 and he lost thirteen or more each season until he was dealt to Cincinnati in 1957.

Before the last pennant in 1945, #18 was mainly the property of pitchers. Two good ones, **Pat Malone** and **Clay Bryant,** were the primary wearers, Malone in 1933 and 1934, after his best years for the Cubs had ended, and then Bryant following for six seasons from 1935–40. Bryant had only one full season pitching for the Cubs, 1938 (though he had some appearances in each of the six seasons), and it was one that helped the Cubs to the NL pennant, He finished the season 19–11 in 44 appearances (30 starts, with 17 complete games). After Bryant's retirement he spent more than twenty years managing in the minor leagues and was briefly a major league coach with the Dodgers, in 1961.

Others who wore #18 in the early days are mostly forgotten today, like **Bob Smith** (1932) and **Johnnie Gill** (1935). **Zeke Bonura** (1940) hit 79 homers in four years for the White Sox but managed to club only four for the Cubs before leaving the majors, but later became known as the "czar of North African baseball" for organizing leagues and games in the Army during World War II; **Wimpy Quinn** (1941), one of only three Cubs (Ryan Theriot and Roberto Pena the others) to wear three different numbers in a single season—he also wore #4 and #16); **Red Adams** (1946); **Russ Bauers** (1946); **Carl Sawatski** (1948); **Jeff Cross** (1948); and **Bob Kelly** (1951).

One who might be remembered better today if not for injuries is **Dick Drott** (1957–58). Drott was a Kerry Wood prototype. As a twenty-year-old in '57 he went 15–11 with a 2.70 ERA, throwing three shutouts and striking out 170 in 229 innings. That K total may not seem high by today's standards, but in 1957 it was good enough to tie for second in the National League. On May 26, 1957, in Drott's ninth major league start, he struck out fifteen Braves, setting a team record that stood until it was broken by Wood forty-one years later. But in '58 Drott got hurt, and unfortunately for him, modern arm surgeries had not yet been invented. He drifted through three more poor Cubs seasons and eventually departed to Houston in the '62 expansion draft.

Other notable #18s include regular 1961–64 shortstop **Andre Rodgers,** the first major leaguer born in the Bahamas; **Gene Clines** (1977–79), a fine pinch hitter who retired to the coaching lines in the middle of the 1979 season and stuck around as a coach through 1981 (switching to #3 as a coach in 1980, when manager **Preston Gomez** claimed #18); **Dwight Smith** (1989–93), who finished second in the Rookie of the Year voting in '89 (taking the only two first-place votes not snagged by teammate Jerome Walton), hit .324 that year and had a memorable game on August 29, 1989, when he replaced Andre Dawson with the Cubs trailing Houston 9–0, and drove in three runs including the game-winner in an amazing 10–9 comeback win; and **Jose Hernandez** (1994–99), who hit twenty-three homers for the 1998 Wild Card Cubs.

MOST OBSCURE CUB TO WEAR #18: **Don Eaddy** (1959). Although Eaddy was a college baseball star at the University of Michigan and considered a "sure major league prospect" by Freddie Lindstrom, then coach for Michigan's Big Ten rival Northwestern, he appeared only on the margins of the majors. Signed out of school by the Cubs in 1955, it took him four years to make the major league roster. And then he did nothing but pinch-run—fourteen times (scoring three runs)—and appearing in the second half of a 12–3 blowout by the Reds on August 1, 1959, striking out in his only turn at the plate.

GUY YOU NEVER THOUGHT OF AS A CUB WHO WORE #18: **Richie Hebner** (1984–85). "The Hacker"— not to be confused with fellow #18 Warren Hacker of the 1950s—wore out Cubs pitching for virtually the entire 1970s as a Pirate and Phillie, hitting .331/.391/.547 with 30 homers in 647 at bats, his best marks against any National League opponent. Cubs management, figuring, "if we can't beat him, let's have him join us," signed him as a free agent before the 1984 season. The gambit worked; Hebner had only 81 at bats as a bench player in '84, but he hit .333 and was a key part of the NL East division champions that year.

Numbers Not Off Their Backs: Pre-existing Cubs (1871–1932)

1 City. The franchise has never played a season outside the Chicago city limits. Even after the Great Chicago Fire of 1871, they chose not to play in the National Association for two years rather than set up shop in another city. The Braves, the only other team left that started in 1871 (and who joined the National League along with the Cubs in 1876) have called three different cities home.

2 World Series championships—both over Detroit—in 1907 and 1908.

4 The actual number of fingers on Three-Fingers Brown's right hand.

6 Pre–1932 National League batting champions (including the first NL leader, Ross Barnes at .429, in 1876). The Cubs have won six batting titles since '32.

9 League strikeout crowns before 1932, compared to six since.

12 Pennants won before 1932, compared to four since.

27 The obscene number of home runs hit by Ned Williamson over the 196-foot left field fence at Lake Front Park in 1884. The previous year's NL champion had hit ten.

34 Losses by the pennant-winning 1886 club (out of 124 decisions); the NL's first 90-win season and no major league team has had that few defeats since.

56 The longtime National League and Cubs record for home runs in a season, set by Hack Wilson in 1930. The mark stood until the summer of 1998.

116 Wins for the 1906 club, a record unsurpassed in the National League.

#19: MANNY AND THE MAD RUSSIAN

ALL-TIME #19 ROSTER:

Player	Year
Harry Taylor	1932
Jakie May	1932
Charlie Root	1933
Bill Lee	1934
Red Corriden (coach)	1937–40
Barney Olsen	1941
Lou Novikoff	1941–42
Lon Warneke	1942
Doyle Lade	1946
Emmett O'Neil	1946
Hal Jeffcoat	1948–49, 1954–55
Dick Manville	1952
Joe Hatten	1952
Pepper Martin (coach)	1956
Bill Henry	1958
Moe Thacker	1958
Paul Smith	1958
Sammy Drake	1960–61
Elder White	1962
Daryl Robertson	1962
Billy Ott	1962
Jimmy Stewart	1963–67
Lee Elia	1968
Bill Heath	1969
Charley Smith	1969
Phil Gagliano	1970
Danny Breeden	1971
Pat Bourque	1971–73
Gonzalo Marquez	1973–74
Manny Trillo	1975–78, 1986–88
Pat Tabler	1981–82
Dave Owen	1983–85
Curtis Wilkerson	1989–90
Hector Villanueva	1991–92
Kevin Roberson	1993–95
Brooks Kieschnick	1996–97
Jason Hardtke	1998
Curtis Goodwin	1999
Jose Molina	1999
Gary Matthews, Jr.	2001
Hee Seop Choi	2002–03
Damian Jackson	2004
Brendan Harris	2004
Mike DiFelice	2004
Enrique Wilson	2005
Matt Murton	2005–08

Lou Novikoff, "The Mad Russian," was actually born in Arizona. The nickname came both from his last name and in reference to a popular radio character of the time portrayed by actor Bert Gordon. After posting a .363 batting average with 41 home runs and 171 RBI for the Cubs' minor league Los Angeles Angels team in 1940, he was called up to the Cubs in 1941. He played only one of his four Cubs seasons as an outfield regular (1942), in part because of his eccentric personality. He was reputedly afraid of the ivy at Wrigley Field, thinking it was "poison ivy," and this made him shy away from the wall. And, he once tried to steal third base with the bases loaded. When asked why he did it, he reportedly replied: "I got such a good jump on the pitcher." In keeping with his oddball nature, he switched numbers frequently, also wearing #45 and two numbers that were eventually retired: #14 and #26. He switched to a military uniform in 1944 and wore a Phillies uniform upon his return stateside in 1946. After his retirement from the major leagues, he continued to play softball under the name "Lou Nova," which he had also used before his major league career; he was eventually inducted into the Softball Hall of Fame in Long Beach, California.

MANNY TRILLO

Manny Trillo's method of getting the ball to first base after fielding it at second —seemingly stopping and reading the NL president's signature on the ball before firing it sidearm—became his trademark during his four solid seasons in Chicago from 1975–78. Trillo was traded to the Phillies along with Greg Gross and Dave Rader in an eight-player deal that brought Barry Foote, Ted Sizemore, Jerry Martin, Derek Botelho, and minor leaguer Henry Mack in a deal that clearly was better for the Phils. Trillo played every inning—and hit .381 in the epic NLCS—of Philadelphia's October run to the world championship in 1980 and set a record for consecutive errorless games for a second baseman in 1982 (a record since broken by Ryne Sandberg).

A singles hitter with little power, Trillo's best year as a Cub was 1977, when he hit .280; his value to the club was primarily defense. After stops in Montreal, San Francisco, and Cleveland, the Cubs reacquired the popular second sacker (some bleacher fans used to chant when he came to bat: "One-O! Two-O! Trillo!") and he hit .296 and .294 as a solid backup in 1986 and 1987. By 1988 he had declined.

One of the funnier sights of the end of the 1988 season occurred on September 20 when Randy Johnson, a September call up for the Expos, faced the Cubs for the first time. In the top of the seventh, Johnson, who threw his first complete game that night, singled for his first major league hit. When the 6-foot–11 Johnson reached first base, TV cameras showed him standing next to first baseman Trillo, who's listed at 6-foot–1 but might be shorter than that. Trillo looked like a bat boy standing next to the Big Unit.

Then there's the curious case of **Hal Jeffcoat,** who had been a middling-hitting outfielder starting in 1948, when he hit .279 playing mostly full-time (473 AB). That got him shipped to the bench, where he played part-time for the next five seasons, wearing #19 in 1948 and 1949, switching to #4 from 1950–52, to #3 in 1953, and then back to #19 when, at age thirty, he converted to hurling after the '53 season. Jeffcoat was photographed wearing #3 for his pitching debut in an exhibition game against the Orioles in New Orleans on April 7, 1954, but the likelihood is that it was a leftover jersey from '53 worn in spring training. Though coach Bob Scheffing said after Jeffcoat's debut that "he has the equipment to win," Jeffcoat spent most of 1954 in the bullpen, going 5–6 with 5.19 ERA in forty-three games, starting only three of them. The next year he cut that figure down to 2.95 in forty-nine relief appearances and one start, and naturally, that got him immediately shipped out of town, dealt to Cincinnati

JIM STEWART   inf-of

Bill Heath | CATCHER

that offseason for catcher Hobie Landrith, a career .233 hitter with no pitching promise.

The rest of the #19s bear little more than brief mentions. The only other one to wear the number for more than three seasons was **Jimmy "Not The Actor" Stewart**, a reserve infielder from 1963–67. **Lee Elia** (1968), later to become famous for a tirade given to a radio reporter while Cubs manager in 1983, went 3-for-17 as a Cubs player; **Bill Heath** (1969) had his moment in the sun when he caught most of Kenny Holtzman's first no-hitter on August 19, 1969. It was only "most of" a no-hitter because in the top of the eighth, Tommie Aaron fouled a ball off Heath's finger, breaking it; Heath left the game and never played again. Others who sported #19 briefly—but in less pain—included **Charley Smith** (1969), **Phil Gagliano** (1970), **Danny Breeden** (1971), and **Pat Bourque** (1971–73), a hot hitting prospect with many home runs in the minors who never got a chance with the Cubs; he later played a couple of seasons in the AL.

The revolving door at #19 continued with the player acquired in trade for Bourque, **Gonzalo Marquez** (1973–74). After Manny Trillo departed, it continued with **Pat Tabler** (1981–82); **Dave Owen** (1983–85), who also had a signature career moment and became the answer to a trivia question when he singled in the winning run in the eleventh inning of the "Sandberg Game" on June 23, 1984, one of only 27 hits he had in his career; **Curtis Wilkerson** (1989–90); **Hector Villanueva** (1991–92), a big bull of a man who had tremendous power (25 HR in 473 career AB) but no position; they tried him at catcher but he should have been a DH; **Kevin Roberson** (1993–95); **Brooks Kieschnick** (1996–97), who later in his career pulled a Jeffcoat while with the Brewers and put up a couple of decent years as a middle reliever/pinch hitter; **Jason Hardtke** (1998); **Curtis Goodwin** (1999); **Jose Molina** (1999); **Gary Matthews, Jr.** (2001); and the Cubs' first Korean-born player, **Hee Seop Choi** (2002–03), whose ascent through the minor leagues prompted the Cubs to let Mark Grace walk via free agency. Management hoped Choi would be the club's first baseman for years to come, but after a frightening collision with Kerry Wood chasing a pop-up on June 7, 2003 (Choi was taken off the field in an ambulance, the only time an ambulance has ever been driven onto the field at Wrigley), he was never quite the same player. His biggest contribution to the Cubs was being shipped to Florida for Derrek Lee.

To date, the last player to wear #19 is **Matt Murton** (2005–08), a popular outfielder nicknamed "Orange Guy" because of the color of his hair; unfortunately, his performance never lived up to his popularity, and after two years of less than outstanding play he was sent to Oakland in the Rich Harden deal.

MOST OBSCURE CUB TO WEAR #19: **Elder White** (1962). White, whose name makes him sound like a deacon in the Mormon Church, was one of three Cubs to wear #19 in the 1962 season, when the Cubs used forty-three different players en route to a 103-loss year, the worst in team history. White was the Opening Day shortstop—with Ernie Banks having moved to first base, it was the first time since 1953 that anyone but Ernie had played shortstop on Opening Day—but White quickly played himself to the bench, starting only thirteen more games and batting .151 in 53 at bats before vanishing forever from the major league scene.

GUY YOU NEVER THOUGHT OF AS A CUB WHO WORE #19: **Bill Henry** (1958). Henry, who also wore #37 in 1959, had two solid seasons as a Cubs reliever and then, because management apparently thought the team needed more power (they didn't; they ranked third in the league in '59 with 163 homers), traded him to Cincinnati for Frank Thomas (the "other" Frank Thomas, not the White Sox/A's DH). Thomas hit 286 HR in a sixteen-year career, mostly with Pittsburgh, yet only 23 in a year and a fraction of another with the Cubs. Henry, meanwhile, made the All-Star team in his first year as a Red and helped lead them to the NL pennant in 1961.

Numbers Not Off Their Backs: Since 1932 Edition

1 Home games played on foreign soil. On March 30, 2000, the Cubs lost to the Mets, 5-1, in eleven innings at the Tokyo Dome; the Cubs had won the previous day in Tokyo with the Mets serving as home team, 5-3.

2 The number of times shortstop Billy Jurges was shot by spurned girlfriend Violet Popovich Valli in 1932; he returned to the Cubs two weeks later, while she received a nightclub contract as a singer.

3½ Innings the Cubs and Phillies played in the first night game at Wrigley Field before the game was rained out on August 8, 1988.

4 Major league starts it took Cubs rookie Burt Hooton to toss a no-hitter; the victim was Philadelphia, April 16, 1972.

7 Total wins as a Cub, against 19 defeats, by Ernie Broglio after coming from St. Louis in the deal for twenty-four-year-old future Hall of Famer Lou Brock.

20 Strikeouts by Kerry Wood in just his fifth major league start, tying the big league record for most Ks in a game.

22 Runs scored against the Phillies at Wrigley on May 17, 1979. And the Cubs still lost by one!

36 Years between no-hitters by the Cubs. After the near perfect game by Milt Pappas (he issued his only walk on a close 3-2 pitch with two outs in the ninth) against the Padres on September 2, 1972, Carlos Zambrano next threw one against Houston in Milwaukee (moved there because of a tropical storm in Texas) on September 14, 2008.

60.75 Sammy Sosa's average annual home run production between 1998–2001.

123 Consecutive errorless games by Ryne Sandberg at second base in 1990.

#20: NOW DISAPPOINTING IN CENTER FIELD . . .

Seemingly for decades, the Cubs have trotted out young, "toolsy" center fielders and assigned them #20, perhaps in the hope that one of them would make that number worthy of a flag atop the Wrigley Field foul poles, just as Lou Brock's #20 was retired in St. Louis after his Hall of Fame induction. It was as if management was attempting to recapture what they lost when Brock was traded. They never got it back.

The first of these speedsters was **Adolfo Phillips** (1966–69), who was the third player acquired in the Fergie Jenkins trade with the Phillies on April 21, 1966. Installed as the center fielder for the 103-loss '66 Cubs at age twenty-four, he hit a respectable .262/.348/.452 with 16 homers and 32 stolen bases, which was the most for a Cub since Kiki Cuyler stole 37 in 1930 (the Cubs were late arrivers to the 1960s' stolen-base party). The following year, Phillips broke out and had a stellar season, with 70 RBI, 24 steals, and 80 walks, which ranked third in the National League. On June 11, 1967, in a doubleheader sweep of the Mets, Phillips hit four homers and drove in eight runs, earning him instant popularity among Cubs fans, who would yell "Olé, Adolfo! Olé!" when he came out to center field.

But it started to sour for Phillips in 1968. He hit .241—an average that in the Year of The Pitcher was not terrible—but his RBI count dropped to 33 and he stole only nine bases. And when he got off to a slow start in 1969, Leo Durocher benched him. Durocher, an old-school guy, couldn't communicate with the young Panamanian and the Cubs shipped him off to the expansion Expos, where his career fizzled.

Before that year was over, they again put a speedy youngster in uniform #20. **Oscar Gamble** (1969) wore it as a teenage call up for the 1969 Cubs. As the team tried desperately to hold off the Mets, Gamble got into twenty-four games in the final month. He showed enough power potential and on-base skill for other teams to crave him. Before his twentieth birthday, the Cubs traded Gamble and Dick Selma to the Phillies for Johnny Callison. Gamble accrued teams almost as easily as he added inches to his Afro in the 1970s but still wound up with 200 career homers. Those would have looked pretty good at Wrigley Field, or at least better than the 27 homers and .243 average the Cubs got in 250 games from Callison.

For more than a decade after Gamble's departure there was a succession of so-so infielders and outfielders who were each issued #20: **Boots Day** (1970), **Jose Ortiz** (1971), **Chris Ward** (1972,1974), **Mick Kelleher** (1976–80), **Scott Fletcher** (1981–82), **Wayne Nordhagen** (1983), and **Thad Bosley** (1983); none of them had any impact except for Kelleher. You may wonder why we say that, given that Kelleher's lifetime batting average was .213 and he never hit higher than .254 in his five seasons at Wrigley. We say "impact" because on August 7, 1977, in the second game of a doubleheader against the Padres, Kelleher took exception to Dave Kingman (then in his brief San Diego sojourn), sliding hard into him to break up a double play. He came up fighting. This sort of thing does happen occasionally on a baseball field when passions flare, but keep in mind that the 5-foot–9, 176-pound Kelleher gave away seven inches and nearly 35 pounds to the 6-foot–6, 210-pound slugger known as Kong. Nevertheless, Little Mick held his own in the brawl, earning the eternal admiration of Cubs fans. Both players were ejected from the game, which the Cubs won, 9-4. Mick and Kong wound up being teammates a year later and somehow managed to coexist.

The Cubs tried #20 again, as they did in 1966, with a fast-running center fielder they acquired from Philadelphia just before the 1984 season began. **Bob Dernier** (1984–87) helped lead the Cubs to the 1984 NL East title with stellar defense, a .278 average, 94 runs scored, and 45 stolen bases, the most for a Cub since Johnny Evers swiped 46 in 1907. But he would never again come close to those numbers and was allowed to leave via free agency three years later. Two years after that, Cubs fans had hope for yet another #20 in center field, **Jerome Walton** (1989–92). Again, a speedy guy helped lead the Cubs to the playoffs; Walton won the NL Rookie of the Year award, batting .293, hitting safely in 30 straight games, and stealing 24 bases as the Cubs won the NL East. He declined even more swiftly than Dernier; by mid–1991 he was benched, and eventually let go after 1992.

More forgettable bodies inhabited #20 for the rest of the 1990s: **Eric Yelding** (1993), **Todd Haney** (1994), **Bret Barberie** (1996), **Miguel Cairo** (1997), **Matt Mieske** (1998), and **Chad Meyers** (1999–2000). The name "Barberie" may ring a bell; Bret's ex-wife Jillian Barberie (now known as Jillian Reynolds) is a television personality perhaps best known for her "weather" segments on Fox NFL Sunday. Bret Barberie's career with the Cubs was brief and unsuccessful; signed as a free agent before the 1996 season, he started the year in the minors before being recalled on May 19. In his first Cubs appearance, he was sent up to pinch-hit for Rey Sanchez with a runner on first and the Cubs trailing the Marlins, 7-5. Barberie hit a two-run homer, tying the game. The Cubs eventually lost that game in eleven innings . . . and Barberie never had another hit as a Cub (or in the majors, for that matter). He went 1-for-29 (.034) before they sent him back to Triple-A.

And then there's the #20 with perhaps the greatest promise of all: **Corey Patterson** (2001–05). Patterson, the third overall pick in the 1998 draft, was rushed through the system because, well, the Cubs had had

so many failed prospects just like him and, ballyhooed as a "five-tool" player, management felt they finally had "the guy." But like Lou Brock many years before, no one quite knew what to do with him. Was he a speedster? Was he a power hitter? Various managers tried to squeeze him into various roles. Finally, in 2003 he was installed as the regular center fielder and on Opening Day at Shea Stadium, Patterson hit two homers and drove in seven runs in a 15-2 rout of the Mets. At age twenty-three he seemed to have arrived. He had a solid first half, hitting .298/.329/.511 with 13 HR and 55 RBI in 83 games, but then on July 6, in a 4-1 loss to the Cardinals, Patterson suffered a torn ACL and torn meniscus in his left knee trying to beat out an infield grounder. He missed the rest of the season and the playoffs; GM Jim Hendry picked up veteran Kenny Lofton two weeks later to play center field the rest of the year. Many felt the Cubs should have kept Lofton, but he was allowed to leave via free agency and Patterson regained the job. He had a good year in 2004, hitting 24 homers, driving in 72 runs, scoring 91 times, and stealing 32 bases. Yet he also struck out an alarming 168 times, often flailing at pitches far over his head.

In 2005, Patterson regressed. He had the worst offensive season for anyone who had more than 400 at bats since the pitchers' year of 1968. (Remember Adolfo Phillips?) Patterson hit .215/.254/.348 with 118 strikeouts in 451 AB and was frequently booed for the Ks and for inattentive play in the field. After the season he was unceremoniously dumped to the Orioles for two minor leaguers.

The most recent player to wear #20 was **Felix Pie** (2007-08), the latest in that long line of "we hope" centerfielders. Pie put up good numbers at every minor league level and played excellent outfield defense, but management never warmed up to him as an everyday player. On January 18, 2009, he was shipped to the Orioles for two minor leaguers, and #20 awaits its next "can't miss" prospect.

Before the center fielders and before expansion and before World War II, #20 was also worn by players who are remembered today only by their families. Included in this roll call of mediocrity are **Emil Kush** (1941); **Hank Gornicki** (1941); **Dewey Williams** (1946); **Dummy Lynch** (1948); **Dwain Sloat** (1949); **Elmer Singleton** (1957), a right-handed pitcher who won over 140 games in the Pacific Coast League in the 1950s, but only three as a Cub; **Ed Mayer** (1958); **Marcelino Solis** (1958); **Charlie (Chick) King** (1958–59); **and Irv Noren** (1959–60). King was traded for Noren on May 19, 1959, and Noren took over King's jersey and number. He's the only one of the players in this group who played more than thirty games as a Cub, hitting a solid .321/.384/.462 in sixty-five games as a part-time outfielder. Naturally, when he got off to a slow start in 1960, he was released. Noren, a reserve outfielder for three pennant-winning Yankees teams in the 1950s, was picked up by Chicago far past his prime, at age thirty-four. Hoping to catch lightning in a bottle, the Cubs usually found that bottle empty.

The only noteworthy Cub of the pre-expansion era to wear #20 (besides **Stan Hack**, better known for wearing #6) was **Don Johnson** (1943–48). Johnson toiled in the minors for years and reached the majors at the fairly advanced age of thirty-one after the big leagues had been thinned by the military draft in 1943. The Chicago native became the regular second baseman and was an All-Star in 1944 and 1945, scoring 94 runs as the Cubs won the pennant. After the veterans returned from the war, Johnson was relegated to platoon and part-time status.

MOST OBSCURE CUB TO WEAR #20: **Rick Bladt** (1969) was called up briefly on June 15, 1969 at age twenty-two when Billy Williams, then in the middle of his consecutive-game playing streak, suffered a minor injury. Williams couldn't do anything but pinch-hit for a few days, which he did to keep his streak alive, so Bladt was used as a defensive replacement and actually got to start four games in center field, all of which the Cubs won. But after he went 0-for-3 in a win over the Pirates on June 26, he was returned to the minors, never again to wear a Cubs uniform. Six years later he resurfaced and played fifty-two games for the Yankees.

GUY YOU NEVER THOUGHT OF AS A CUB WHO WORE #20: **Howard Johnson** (1995). Neither a motel nor a restaurant, Johnson had been an All-Star with the Mets in the late 1980s and early 1990s, joining the 30–30 club three times and finishing as high as fifth in MVP voting twice. Naturally, by the time the Cubs signed him just before the strike-shortened 1995 season began, he was thirty-four years old and four years removed from his last good year. He hit .195 with seven homers in eighty-seven games and never played again. Despite what he showed in Chicago, HoJo always knew how to hit and became hitting coach for the Mets.

Stolen

The Cubs aren't generally known for stealing bases, but put a #20 on a Cub and he'll steal you blind, at least relatively. Bob Dernier (119) and Corey Patterson (86) lead the way, with Felix Pie's first career stolen base in 2007 pushing #20 into the top spot. (Though #20 barely surpasses the total of the all-time leader, the Peerless Leader—and numberless first baseman—Frank Chance, who had 400.) Ryne Sandberg put #23 in position to win this competition among numbers, but he was so good he insured that #23 would forever be stuck at 397 as it was retired in his honor. Sandberg had 344 steals, the most by any Cub whose career began after the nineteenth century.

Uni #	SB	Uni #	SB
20	408	24	146
23	397	25	146
21	337	2	144
11	331	17	134
12	291	5	120
1	284	4	117
7	277	9	113
18	186	15	113
10	184	8	112
6	182		

#21: SAMMY

Just who was **Sammy Sosa**? Was he "Selfish Sammy," the guy who walked around with the gold chains and the Jheri curls his first few years with the Cubs, striking out hundreds of times while pounding the occasional home run? The guy who refused to move down in the lineup in 2004 when it was becoming clear that his talent was declining, and then walked out on the team on the last day of the season after they collapsed and he learned he wasn't playing that day?

Or, was he "Smiling Sammy", the only major league player to have three 60-homer seasons (and he didn't win the homer title in any of them, losing twice to Mark McGwire and once to Barry Bonds)? The guy who set, besides his Cubs team record of 66, the record for the most homers hit in any calendar month with 20 in June 1998? The guy who'd run out to right field and hear cheers and chants and who'd give kisses to the TV cameras every time he'd hit a homer?

The answer probably lies somewhere in between. Up until 1997, Sammy was an enigma; he spent much of his first two seasons with the Cubs on the DL, and in 1996, when he seemed on pace for a 50-homer season, his year ended on August 20 when he was hit in the hand by a pitch from the Marlins' Mark Hutton, just after he had reached the 40-homer, 100-RBI mark the day before. He regressed in '97, hitting only .253 and striking out a team-record 174 times, even while smacking 37 dingers.

But that offseason, the Cubs hired Jeff Pentland as their hitting coach and he worked hard with Sammy, getting him to lay off the low outside pitches he'd often flail at. The results were staggering—even though his strikeouts remained high, his walk totals doubled; in 2001, he walked 116 times, tying Richie Ashburn's 1960 total for the most any Cub had walked in a season since 1912. Sammy's 2001 season, in which he hit 64 homers, drove in 160 runs (second most in Cubs history, behind Hack Wilson's team and major league record 191 in 1930), and slugged .737 (second in the NL), is arguably the single best offensive season in Cubs history, and one of the best in National League history.

The questions, though, will remain: was Sosa's five-season explosion (1998–2002), in which he *averaged* 58 homers and 141 RBI per year, tainted? Did Sammy use performance-enhancing drugs? We simply do not know, and no accusations are made here. But it is clear, even only five years after Sammy's disgraced exit from the team, in which he left the clubhouse early on the season's last day, was caught doing so on a security camera, and then lied about it, that home run totals are down, and that Sosa and McGwire, whose smiles and laughs highlighted the marvelous 1998 season, may have accomplished their mighty feats using artificial enhancements. Sammy was also suspended for seven games in 2003 for getting caught using a corked bat in a game; he claimed it was a one-time accident and his bats in the Hall of Fame were X-rayed and found to be cork free.

The numbers are what they are. They look spectacular on paper, but it will be up to future generations to ultimately decide what they mean.

The man who wore #21 the longest, apart from Sammy, was **George Altman,** one of the fine African-American prospects brought to the Cubs by scout Buck O'Neil. Altman, a little older than Billy Williams, with whom he debuted in 1959, played about two-thirds of the time in the Cubs' outfield in '59 and '60 and then got the full-time gig in right field in '61, having two fine years. His 27 homers, 96 RBI, .303 batting average and a league-best 12 triples earned him a spot on the 1961 National League All-Star team, and his .318 batting average was sixth-best in the National League in 1962.

And then, as seemed common in those days, the Cubs decided to dump a popular and productive player. The trade of Altman to the Cardinals was useful—it brought Lindy McDaniel, a fine reliever, and Larry Jackson, a solid starter, to the North Side—but Altman seemed to have a broken heart. Years later, he told writers that he still followed the Cubs, and his year in St. Louis perhaps proved it out—he hit only nine homers, though his age (thirty) might have also had something to do with his decline. After another year in exile from Wrigley with the Mets, Altman was reacquired on January 19, 1965, but, much of his talent gone, he was relegated to backup duty.

There were several other Cubs who wore #21 for more than two seasons and had some impact on their clubs. **Lennie Merullo** (1943–47) was a semi-regular shortstop for the wartime Cubs, though when it came time for World Series playing time in 1945, the shortstop job went to Roy Hughes, who started six of the seven games. **Eddie Miksis** (1951–56) was acquired in an eight-player deal with the Dodgers on the then-trading deadline of June 15, 1951, and was the Cubs' semi-regular if underwhelming second baseman for the next five-plus seasons. After committing 23 errors in 92 games at second base in 1952, the errors got so numerous that he was, by 1955, switched to the outfield.

Al Spangler (1967–69) was a useful pinch hitter and spare outfielder who became popular among bleacher fans, so much so that some used to insert his name when singing a certain part of the National Anthem ("O say does that *Al Spangler* banner yet wave . . . "). After Spangler became a coach in 1971, **Gene Hiser** (1972–75) took his place on the roster, at first wearing #16 and then switching to #21 in '72, but his production (.202 lifetime average) didn't match his promise. His only career home run, though, was memorable: on June 29, 1973, Hiser came up with two outs in the bottom of the ninth and homered to tie a game with the Mets that the Cubs eventually won in extra innings.

Jay Johnstone (1982–84) had been a wacky character with several teams (Angels, White Sox, A's, Phillies, Yankees, Padres, Dodgers) before joining the Cubs; he produced well enough as a spare-part outfielder, and also continued his zany ways. One day a local TV station hired him to fill in for their regular sportscaster and he did his sports report live from the upper deck of Wrigley Field, in uniform, while the game was still in progress in extra innings. And a kid who dominated Chicago suburban high school sports, both baseball and basketball, before being drafted by the Expos, **Scott Sanderson** (1985–89), came to his hometown team in 1984. Sanderson originally took #24 because his Expos number, #21, was taken by Johnstone, then switched to #21 in '85. Injured much of the time he was in Chicago, he was still a contributor to two NL East title teams, in 1984 and 1989, but he didn't become a big winner until after he left the Cubs for Oakland, for whom he won seventeen games in their pennant-winning season of 1990.

Part-timers and ne'er-do-wells round out the #21s: **Steve Mesner** (1938); **Frank Jelincich** (1941); **Bob Bowman** (1942); **Dick Errick-son** (1942); **Dave Hillman** (1958); light-hitting outfielder **Ellis Burton** (1963–64); **Jack Hiatt** (1970), the only postwar catcher to wear #21; **Mike Adams** (1976), whose father Bobby had worn #7 and #16 during his time with the Cubs from 1957–59—Mike became a number-switcher too, donning #30 in 1977 when pinch hitter extraordinaire **Greg Gross** (1977–78) joined the Cubs and asked for his old Phillies number; **Lenny Randle** (1980), who, later in his career while with

ELLIS BURTON   outfielder

the Mariners actually laid down near the third base line and attempted to blow a slow-rolling ball foul; and **Ty Waller** (1981–82), who wasn't much of a player (.255 in 92 Cubs at bats), but who has been a long-time base coach for the Padres and A's over the last two decades.

When **Jason Marquis** joined the Cubs before the 2007 season, he requested his old Cardinals number: 21. While you'd think that a player who produced as many homers and thrills as Sammy Sosa did would have his number taken out of circulation, at the very least, management didn't hesitate to grant Marquis's request. It remains to be seen whether #21 will eventually be retired, joining the famous names on the flagpoles at Wrigley Field. Of course, two of the four retired numbers (10 and 26) did have other wearers before they were finally honored by the Cubs.

MOST OBSCURE CUB TO WEAR #21: **Sal Madrid** (1947). Neither from Spain nor any of the Latin American countries, Madrid was born in El Paso, Texas, in 1920 and recalled for eight September games in which he hit .125 (3-for-24). Returned to the Texas League after the season, he never returned to the majors. Or Spain. He died in Ft. Wayne, Indiana, in 1977.

GUY YOU NEVER THOUGHT OF AS A CUB WHO WORE #21: **Burleigh Grimes** (1933). Grimes, the last legal spitballer, was acquired when the Cubs were forced to dump Hack Wilson only a year after his then club record 56-homer, 191-RBI season in 1930. The Cardinals were willing to take on the troubled Wilson (then flipped him to the Dodgers before the 1932 season even started), and sent the thirty-seven-year-old Grimes to the Cubs. He had a rocky '32 (6–11 during the season and a 23.43 ERA in the World Series) wearing #16, and then switched to #21 for '33; when he went 3–6 in 17 games, the Cubs released him.

Swing and a Drive . . . Swing and a Miss

It doesn't take a baseball savant to tell you that hitting home runs is harder than striking out. Most fans can tell you, though, that hitters who swing for the fences often wind up walking back to the dugout after not hitting anything. Plenty of others don't even try for home runs and come up dry. In the land of the K and the HR, #7—the leader in most hitting categories when stats are broken down by uniform number—plays second fiddle (fifth fiddle when it comes to homers). Sammy Sosa is the all-time Cubs leader in both home runs and in strikeouts; his #21 followed him up the ladder in both categories. No matter what Slammin' Sammy's legacy turns out to be as time passes, that guy could pile up whiffs and wallops. He accounted for 74 percent of the home runs (545) hit by #21's; K-wise, he had more help, with Sosa's 1,845 strikeouts contributing 54 percent of the overall whiff total for #21. He outhomered all but five of the numbers on this list, while ten cumulative numbers had more whiffs then Sammy all on his lonesome.

Uni#	Home Runs	Uni #	Strikeouts
21	736	21	3,305
10	644	7	3,008
9	568	11	2,951
8	537	9	2,943
7	535	10	2,679
14	518	12	2,240
26	413	8	2,196
6	360	20	2,091
23	342	6	2,044
17	339	18	2,008
12	333	23	1,870
11	305	24	1,841
18	303	16	1,790
25	302	25	1,661
16	278	17	1,637
2	260		
28	234		
43	231		
24	208		
20	202		

#22: WHAT MIGHT HAVE BEEN

"For of all sad words of tongue or pen the saddest are these: 'It might have been.'"

The above words are from the great poet John Greenleaf Whittier (1807–92), not to be confused with the fleet outfielder **Rondell Bernard White** (2000–01). White is the baseball embodiment of Whittier's poem, especially as they relate to #22 and Wrigley Field. White's knee problems prevented him from playing more than two full seasons out of fifteen big league years. Acquired at the 2000 trading deadline from Montreal, White appeared to be hitting his stride with the '01 Cubs, smacking 13 homers and posting a .302 average in 73 games in the first half. Then he got hurt again and didn't return until September.

The tale of #22 has been one with so many "might haves" for the Cubs, dating all the way back to one of its earliest wearers, **Dizzy Dean.** The Cardinals great, facing Earl Averill in the 1937 All-Star Game, had his toe broken by a line drive. Dean changed his pitching motion while trying to come back too soon, and he hurt his arm. The Cubs paid a then-record $185,000—plus three nondescript players—to get him from the Cardinals before the 1938 season. Though he could only pitch in thirteen games, he

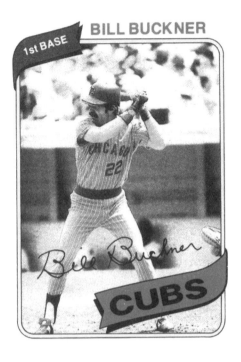

BILL BUCKNER

1st BASE

CUBS

went 7–1 with a 1.81 ERA and helped lead the Cubs to the pennant. But the arm damage sustained was too great, and he pitched in only thirty-one games over the next three seasons before retiring to become a coach, and later a broadcaster for several clubs whose malaprops ("He slud into third") became legendary. Sadly, his pitching for the Cubs wasn't.

Fast forward to 1977, and Cubs fans were again scratching their heads over the acquisition of an injured player: **Bill Buckner,** who'd been acquired from the Dodgers for the popular Rick Monday. (Ivan DeJesus was thrown into the deal and became the starting Cubs shortstop after having played in only eighty-seven games, hitting .183, for L.A. over the previous three years.) At first, Buckner's ankles and knees were so bad that he spent large swaths of time early in the '77 season either reduced to pinch-hitting or being pulled from games late. Finally healthy by the second half of '77, it seemed that the worse the Cubs were, the more Billy Buck shone. In 1980, a season in which the Cubs supplanted the Mets in the NL East basement, Buckner won the batting title with a .324 average. He was even better during the miserable '81 strike year. He made his lone All-Star team and led the NL in both doubles and games played. He finished in the top ten of the NL MVP voting in both '81 and '82. "There's nothing wrong with this team that more pitching, more fielding, and more hitting couldn't help," Buckner deadpanned.

And yes, he was a good defensive first baseman. He never won any Gold Gloves in Chicago, but Keith Hernandez had that award wrapped up eleven years running. Billy Buck's bad ankles eventually made him into a statue at first with the Red Sox, but he could still field most balls hit near him, as evidenced by his major league record 184 assists in '85. Even before Mookie Wilson's famed grounder eluded his glove, Buckner was dealt a cruel blow when, after seven seasons as the brightest spot in a dim Cubs lineup, he was replaced at first by Leon Durham and traded (for Dennis Eckersley and Mike Brumley) during the Wrigley renaissance of '84. Buckner, who didn't want to come to the Cubs in '77, feeling he "bled Dodger blue," wept at the press conference when he left the Cubs. It's ironic that the man who took Billy Buck's bag made the same glaring postseason error that would later become synonymous with Buckner's name.

Half a decade later, another pitcher donned #22 and the Cubs had great hopes for **Mike Harkey,** their top pick in 1987. He finished fifth in the NL Rookie of the Year voting after posting a 12–6, 3.26 performance and Cubs fans had high hopes for him. But Harkey broke down the next spring and had shoulder surgery. Although he came back to the rotation by 1993, his 10–10 record was marred by an ugly 5.26 ERA. After the '93 season he signed as a free agent with the Rockies, not the place to go for a rehabbing pitcher, and his ERA jumped again, to 5.74. After three more tries with the A's, Angels, and Dodgers, respectively, he was done at age thirty.

But the "saddest of words" could also apply to **Mark Prior** (2002–06). Prior, drafted in 2001 out of USC after being termed by some "the best college pitcher ever," received a five-year, major league contract and was in Chicago only a year after signing. He posted a respectable 6–6, 3.32 mark with 147 strikeouts in 116 innings at age twenty-one, finishing seventh in the 2002 NL Rookie of the Year balloting despite spending only three months in the majors. The next year Prior dazzled, going 18–6, 2.43, and finished second in the NL to teammate Kerry Wood in strikeouts with 245 as the Cubs won the NL Central. Even then, a crack began to appear in the façade. On July 11, 2003, after drawing a walk, Prior collided with Braves second baseman Marcus

Giles while running. He missed a month, and though he came back strong, some observers worried that this might change his pitching motion. Those fears came to pass at the start of the next year—Prior spent two months on the DL and wasn't strong until September. It was in his last 2004 outing, on September 30, that the Cubs, desperately trying to hold on to the wild card lead, received what was arguably Prior's greatest start. He threw nine innings, allowed just three hits and one run, and struck out sixteen Reds. But the Cubs lost in extra innings and lost their playoff spot.

The next year, Prior suffered a horrifying freak injury on May 27 when a line drive off the bat of the Rockies' Brad Hawpe hit him in the elbow, breaking a bone. At first it seemed season-ending, if not career-threatening, but Prior was back in the rotation four weeks later, throwing six one-hit innings against the White Sox. He went a mediocre 7–6, 4.07 the rest of the year and started 2006 on the DL.

In coming back too soon, he may have suffered Dizzy Dean's fate. It's possible that hurrying back from the broken elbow altered Prior's motion. In his return on June 18, 2006, he gave up four homers to the Tigers and wound up finishing 1–6 with a 7.21 ERA; his last appearance on a major league mound to date was a three-inning, five-earned-run loss to the Brewers on August 10, 2006. Prior's departure from the Cubs was as unpleasant as his arrival was ballyhooed—asked to go to the minors in 2007, Prior responded by saying, "I'm just an employee." He never actually took the mound in 2007, and signed with the Padres in 2008, but he never threw a pitch that year, either. The "best college pitcher ever" has instead been one of the great "might haves" with his career in severe doubt at age twenty-eight.

Twenty-six Cubs donned #22 before the NL expanded in 1962; only seventeen have worn it since. And other than in the pages of this book, it's not likely anyone will remember **Marv Gudat** (94 Cubs at bats in 1932), **Bud Tinning** (1933–34), **Roy Henshaw** (1934–36), **Curt Davis** (1937, sent to St. Louis in the Dizzy Dean deal), **Emil Kush** (one game wearing #22 in 1942, three more years wearing #28 from 1946–49), **Charlie Gilbert** (1943, 1946), **Stu Martin** (.220 in 1943), **Bill Schuster** (1944–45, who got one at bat in the '45 World Series and scored the

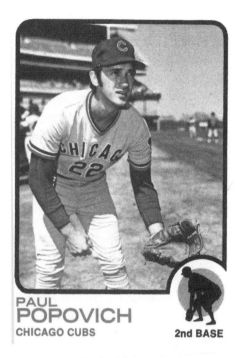

PAUL POPOVICH
CHICAGO CUBS   2nd BASE

winning run in Game 6 as a pinch runner in the twelfth inning), **Cecil "Rabbit" Garriott** (0-for-5 in 1946), **Doyle Lade** (1947), **Ralph Hamner** (1947), **Clarence Maddern** (1948–49), **Herm Reich** (1949), **Bob Borkowski** (1950–51), **Jim Davis** (1954–56), **Freddy Rodriguez** (seven games, 7.36 ERA in 1958), or **Gordon Massa** (1958). So we memorialize them here.

Other than Buckner, Harkey, and Prior, the best-known and perhaps best-loved Cub to wear #22 was infielder **Paul Popovich,** who had two separate stints with the Cubs. "Popo" came up through the Cubs farm system alongside Don Kessinger, and when Kess and Glenn Beckert became the Cubs' double play combination in 1965, Paul was relegated to backup duty. Never a strong hitter, he was sent to the Dodgers in the Jim Hickman/Phil Regan deal in November 1967. His .232 average for the '68 Dodgers, splitting time between shortstop and second base, may not sound like much today, but keep in mind that the Dodgers hit .230 as a team that year and the entire NL, in the "Year of the Pitcher," batted only .243! Reacquired from L.A. on June 11, 1969, Popovich spent four years playing slick defense backing up both Beckert and Kessinger, hitting .254—again, a decent average for a middle infielder in that era—filling in as the starter for the rest of the season when Beckert went down with an injury in August 1973.

And the rest of the #22s are the usual suspects: **Ron Dunn** (1975), a power-hitting prospect whose power never surfaced in Chicago (3 long balls in 112 Cub at bats); **Wayne Tyrone** (1976), who followed his brother Jim (1972, 1974–75) into a Cubs uniform, and hit only a little better (.228 to Jim's .181 in blue pinstripes); **Billy Hatcher** (1984–85), who had stellar moments in the postseason—for other teams (a dramatic home run in the 1986 NLCS for the Astros, and a .750 average in the 1990 World Series for the Reds); **Jerry Mumphrey** (1986–88), who had two fine years (.304 in 1986 and .333 in 1987) as the (mostly) regular left fielder, but who sulked when relegated to pinch-hitting duty in '88 and slumped to a 9-for-66 finish; and **Eddie Zambrano** (1994), the Cubs' second-best Zambrano, who hit six homers in part-time duty as a spare outfielder/first baseman.

MOST OBSCURE CUB TO WEAR #22: **Tarrik Brock** (2000). The second-best Cub to be named "Brock," Tarrik was a beneficiary of MLB's policy allowing the Cubs and Mets to take some extra players on the active roster to Japan for their season-opening series in 2000. He got a hit in his first major league at bat on March 29 in Tokyo, but only one more hit in eleven further AB through April 22, at which time he was returned to the minors. The Cubs released him at the end of the 2000 season and he never again reached the majors.

GUY YOU NEVER THOUGHT OF AS A CUB WHO WORE #22: **Catfish Metkovich** (1954). George Michael Metkovich, who supposedly got his nickname from stepping on a catfish and cutting his foot while on a fishing trip, played for the AL champion 1946 Red Sox, was sold to Cleveland, and wound up playing for the Oakland Oaks of the Pacific Coast League in 1948, one of the minors' greatest teams ever, earning PCL MVP honors in 1950. He moved on to the White Sox and Pirates, and then came to the Cubs in the ten-player deal that brought Ralph Kiner and Joe Garagiola to Chicago, hit .234 in sixty-one games, and was sold to the Milwaukee Braves in the offseason.

Streaking

Yes, they call it the streak, but it's not what you think. This streak concerns what Cubs uniform number has been in use the most consecutive years. No Cubs uniform number has been in use consecutively since 1932, but one number did make it fifty-seven consecutive years. That was #22, which was worn by Marv Gudat during his one and only season as a Cub for the '32 pennant winners, and #22 was in use every year until Jerry Mumphrey wore it in his final major league game in 1988. Below is a list of all streaks of at least fifteen consecutive years.

For a list of the longest current streaks and how many consecutive years each number on the 2008 Cubs has seen active duty, see chapter 24.

All-Time Longest Streaks

Uni #	Number of consecutive years used	Year streak started	Last year of streak
22	57	1932	1988
18	53	1948	2000
7	48	1945	1992
24	39	1970	2008
5	35	1974	2008
6	35	1974	2008
20	33	1976	2008
11	32	1977	2008
3	30	1966	1995
20	30	1943	1972
36	30	1979	2008
33	29	1941	1969
9	26	1966	1991
12	26	1983	2008
27	25	1962	1986
30	25	1948	1972
2	24	1966	1989

Uni #	Number of consecutive years used	Year streak started	Last year of streak
11	24	1932	1955
1	23	1971	1993
4	23	1972	1994
34	22	1972	1993
48	22	1967	1988
6	21	1945	1965
14	21	1953	1973
21	21	1958	1978
25	21	1978	1998
36	21	1957	1977
38	21	1988	2008
11	19	1957	1975
19	19	1960	1978
19	19	1981	1999
41	19	1977	1995
46	19	1990	2008
51	19	1988	2006
2	18	1991	2008
40	18	1984	2001
10	17	1958	1974
10	17	1977	1993
12	17	1964	1980
12	16	1932	1947
17	16	1946	1961
8	15	1978	1992
23	15	1980	1994
27	15	1990	2004
34	15	1956	1970
42	15	1955	1969

#23: RYNO!

What can we say about **Ryne Sandberg** that you don't already know? All-American boy, matinee-idol good looks, high school quarterback who had every intention of playing for his home-state school, Washington State (and with his size, he'd probably have made a pretty good NFL quarterback), until the Phillies waved enough money under his nose to get him to sign and ride the low-minors buses.

And he stagnated there—his minor-league numbers were nothing special—until Dallas Green, who had been the Phillies farm director when

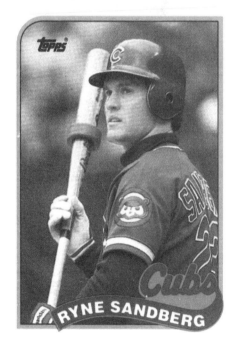

Sandberg was drafted, decided that there was no DeJesus-for-Bowa deal unless the skinny shortstop was included.

This was just after Sandberg, wearing #37 in red-and-white

pinstripes, had his only hit in a Phillies uniform, a bloopy little single to right off Mike Krukow in Wrigley Field on the final day of a bleak season for the Cubs, September 27, 1981. In the bottom of the sixth, with the Phillies trailing 13-0, Green, then the Phils' field boss, sent Sandberg out to play shortstop and two innings later, he got his first major league hit.

There would be 2,385 more hits to come for Sandberg, all while wearing Cubs blue. Perhaps the most notable of those hits came in what has since been dubbed "The Sandberg Game" (June 23, 1984) where two home runs he hit against ex-Cubs closer Bruce Sutter helped win a key game against the arch-rival Cardinals. There was also an MVP award (1984), two playoff appearances, and a league-leading 40-homer season in 1990. A hand broken by a pitch from the Giants' Mike Jackson in spring training 1993, robbed Sandberg of much of his power and prompted a hasty early retirement when he wasn't hitting in June of the following season (it happened the same morning that the Nicole Brown Simpson/Ron Goldman murders were breaking news. Chicago may have been the only city where the Sandberg retirement story was bigger); and then a curtain-call sort of return for two seasons, 1996 and 1997. He did put up one more power salvo (25 homers, 92 RBI in '96) before retiring for good, tearfully, in front of a grateful sellout crowd at Wrigley on September 21, 1997 (he played six more road games after that, but got a terrific sendoff when he singled to left in that last home game and was taken out for a pinch runner, to a tremendous ovation). And then it was off to the Hall of Fame.

But even in retirement Sandberg wasn't done influencing baseball and the Cubs; in his Hall induction speech in 2005, he made a point of saying he had played the game "the right way," perhaps a veiled slam at the steroid-enhanced sluggers who came along just after he retired. Two years later he took a job managing in the low minors in the Cubs organization, perhaps planning a return to the major leagues as a coach or manager sometime in the future. He is the best-loved Cub of his generation and one of the finest to ever wear the blue pinstripes. His #23 was retired on August 28, 2005, joining #10, #14, and #26 on flags flying above the Wrigley Field foul poles.

Besides Sandberg, only one other player wore #23 for more than three seasons: **Carmen Fanzone** (1971–74). Originally signed by the Red Sox, he was acquired in a minor all-Italian deal for infielder Phil Gagliano on December 3, 1970. Fanzone had some power, blasting 22 career homers in about a full season's worth of at bats (588), but he couldn't hit for average (.224) and wasn't a very good fielder (at third base, he had a career fielding average of .896). His best talent was playing the trumpet. Fanzone has enjoyed a long career as a musician in California following his departure from baseball, and he has played the National Anthem before games at Wrigley Field.

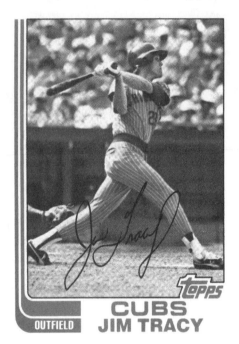

CUBS
OUTFIELD JIM TRACY

The answer to the trivia question: "Who was the last Cub to wear #23 before Ryne Sandberg?" is **Jim Tracy,** who at one time appeared to be a pretty good outfield prospect. He played in eighty-seven games for the awful 1980 and 1981 Cubs, hit .249 with three home runs, and was traded to the Astros after the '81 season ended, never to play again in the major leagues. Tracy eventually returned to the bigs, though, managing the Los Angeles Dodgers from 2001–05 (winning the NL West in 2004) and the Pirates from 2006–07.

Many of the rest of the #23s are players who also wore other numbers: **Leroy Herrmann** (1932, switched to #21 in '33); **Roy Joiner** (1935; took over Herrmann's #21 in '34); **Phil Cavarretta** (1937–38, far more famous as #44); **Doyle Lade** (1947–50; Lade wore #19 and #22 before settling in at #23); **Andy Varga** (1951); **Bubba Church** (1954–55); **Jerry Kindall** (1956–58); **Jim Brosnan** (1958); **Moe Thacker** (1958; Moe was a multinumber guy, also wearing #8, #19, #22 and #25 in various Cubs stints); **Art Schult** (1960); **Don Young** (1965), whose fame, or more accurately infamy, came while wearing #29 in 1969; and **Ron Campbell** (1966), who wore a different number in each of his three Cubs seasons (#7 in 1964, #15 in 1965, and #23 in 1966; hitting .272, .000, and .217, respectively).

MOST OBSCURE CUB TO WEAR #23: **Manny Jimenez** (1969). Jimenez had a fine rookie year with the Kansas City A's in 1962, hitting .301 with 11 homers in 479 at bats for a team that lost ninety games. They proceeded to make him a part-time player and he never hit well again (although he did have 12 homers in 204 AB in 1964). For some inexplicable reason, Cubs management thought it prudent to trade not one, but two, players (Joe Campbell, who had had three major league at bats, and a useful relief pitcher, Chuck Hartenstein) to the Pirates for Jimenez before the 1969 season. He made the Opening Day roster, but Leo Durocher nailed him to the bench. He had six at bats, all as a pinch hitter, with one hit, before vanishing from the major league scene forever.

GUY YOU NEVER THOUGHT OF AS A CUB WHO WORE #23: **John Buzhardt** (1958). Buzhardt wore #23 as a September call up in 1958 and threw pretty well (1.85 ERA) in six games. The next year he switched to #38 and threw . . . not so well (4.97 ERA in 31 games, 10 of which were starts). He was then traded to the Phillies in a four-player deal, the centerpiece of which was Richie Ashburn coming to the Cubs. Buzhardt later had two good years as part of a pretty good rotation for the 1964 and 1965 White Sox.

Gold Standard

The Cubs have won thirty-four Gold Gloves since that award for fielding excellence was established in 1957. Ernie Banks was the first Cub to win it, one of thirteen Cubs to receive the award. The Cubs have had six players win the award multiple times. The Cubs also have the bases covered, winning an award at each position on the diamond (outfielders are recognized as playing one position).

Gold Glove Player	#	Year	Position
Jody Davis	7	1986	C
Total for #7 - 1			
Andre Dawson	8	1987	OF
Andre Dawson	8	1988	OF
Total for #8 - 2			
Randy Hundley	9	1967	C
Total for #9 - 1			
Ron Santo	10	1964	3B
Ron Santo	10	1965	
Ron Santo	10	1966	
Ron Santo	10	1967	
Ron Santo	10	1968	
Total for #10 - 5			
Don Kessinger	11	1969	SS
Don Kessinger	11	1970	
Total for #11 - 2			
Ernie Banks	14	1960	SS
Total for #14 - 1			
Ken Hubbs	16	1962	2B
Total for #16 - 1			
Mark Grace	17	1992	1B
Mark Grace	17	1993	

Gold Glove Player	#	Year	Position
Mark Grace	17	1995	
Mark Grace	17	1996	
Total for #17 - 4			
Glenn Beckert	18	1968	2B
Total for #18 - 1			
Bobby Dernier	20	1984	OF
Total for #20 - 1			
Ryne Sandberg	23	1983	2B
Ryne Sandberg	23	1984	
Ryne Sandberg	23	1985	
Ryne Sandberg	23	1986	
Ryne Sandberg	23	1987	
Ryne Sandberg	23	1988	
Ryne Sandberg	23	1989	
Ryne Sandberg	23	1990	
Ryne Sandberg	23	1991	
Total for #23 - 9			
Derrek Lee	25	2007	1B
Total for #25 - 1			
Greg Maddux	31	1990	P
Greg Maddux	31	1991	
Greg Maddux	31	1992	
Greg Maddux	31	2004	
Greg Maddux	31	2005	
Total for #31 - 5			

#24: FABIAN, LaCOCK, AND A GUY NAMED BROCK

Lou Brock (1961–64) is perhaps the greatest might-have-been in Cubs history. The Cubs had been lucky to get Brock in the first place. The Cardinals scout who coveted Brock was out of town when the outfielder traveled to St. Louis, so Brock got on the bus to Chicago and signed for a $30,000 bonus on August 22, 1960. A little more than a year later, he singled off Robin Roberts in his first major league at bat. He made two errors in the game, though, and his fielding soon inspired Cubs fans to say, "Brock as in Rock." In 1962 he became one of three players to ever homer into the distant center field bleachers at the Polo Grounds (Hank Aaron and Joe Adcock being the others), but he fanned frequently—he K'ed 122 times in '62, the first of nine triple-digit-strikeout seasons by Brock—and he didn't walk much until late in his career. The Cubs should have been more patient with him, but they jumped at the chance to get established pitching.

They sent Brock and two others to the Cardinals for Ernie Broglio and Bobby Shantz. They knew Shantz, thirty-nine, was at the end of the line, but Broglio was twenty-eight and coming off an 18–8 season, and he'd won twenty-one games in 1960. Besides, the Cards threw in out-fielder Doug Clemens, who was the same age as Brock. To top it off, the Cardinals players were furious they'd given up Broglio. Brock had a difficult adjustment period, but manager Johnny Keane told Brock he needed to run. Brock took off and so did the Cardinals, who passed the Phillies and won the pennant. The Cubs slid all the way to eighth.

Until Rickey Henderson came along, Brock held the post-1900 record for single-season and career steals. Stolen bases can be overrated, but a comparison of steal totals for Brock and Cubs for the decade after the trade shows a dimension missing from the Cubs. Between 1965 and 1974 Brock stole 100 more bases than the entire Cubs team (670-570). He finished first in the category eight times while the Cubs were last in steals four times. Never mind Brock's 3,023 hits and 1,610 runs. The Cardinals also won three pennants and two world championships behind the play of their Hall of Fame left fielder.

Beyond Brock, #24 has been mostly worn by journeymen Cubs. The longest tenure in the jersey is seven years, by **Paul Minner** (1950–56), a mainstay of the Cubs rotation in the early and mid 1950s. Minner's best year was 1952, when he went 14–9, 3.74, finishing ninth in the NL in wins for the only Cubs team between 1946 and 1963 not to have a losing record (they finished exactly .500 at 77–77, though a distant 19.5 games out of first place). Another pitcher who had some success wearing #24 was **Scott Sanderson** (1984), who went 8–5 for the NL East champions. Sanderson switched to #21, the number he had worn in his Montreal Expos days, the following year and stayed with that number for the rest of his tenure in Chicago, through 1989. Of the fourteen Cubs who have worn #24 since Sanderson—including **Henry Blanco** (2005–08)—none has been a pitcher.

One of those non-pitchers was outfielder **Brian Dayett** (1985–87), who was acquired from the Yankees in a six-player deal after the 1984 season. He began the '85 season on the roster but barely played—starting only two games and pinch-hitting in fifteen others. One of those pinch-hitting appearances was particularly memorable. In the bottom of the sixth inning on May 22, 1985, Dayett was sent up to bat for starting pitcher Dennis Eckersley with the bases loaded and the Cubs trailing, 4-2. He hit a grand slam off the Reds' Tom Browning, leading the Cubs to a 7-4 win. The four RBI were the only runs he drove in the entire season (granted, 26 at bats isn't much of a "season"). Browning, who became famous in Cubs lore later in his career when he appeared in uniform on a rooftop across from Wrigley Field *during a game*, was said to have placed a baseball card of Dayett's in his locker to remind himself to never take any major league hitter for granted.

Ralph Pierre "Pete" LaCock (1972) began his Cubs career wearing #24. He switched to #25 on his promotion to the majors in September 1973 because **Cleo James,** who had worn #24 two years earlier, was also recalled and reclaimed it on the basis of seniority, and then wore #23 when recalled in 1974 and for the rest of his time with the Cubs, because **Jerry Morales** had claimed his San Diego number, 24. LaCock was a child of the sixties, with flowing blond locks cascading below his cap. He looked the part of a seventies ballplayer, but he never hit much for the Cubs. His main claim to fame was his Hollywood father, Ralph Pierre LaCock, Sr., who is

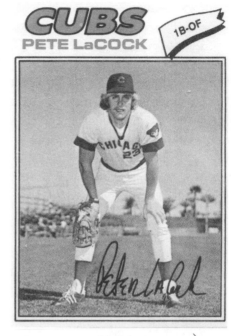

CLEO JAMES

better known as Peter Marshall, most famous for hosting the TV game show *Hollywood Squares.* "Circle gets the square."

As for Morales (1974–77, 1981–83), his bushy mustache made him one of the most popular Cubs with female fans during his two tours of duty on the North Side. A fine center fielder, he was having one of his best seasons in 1977, hitting .331 at the All-Star break and being selected to the NL All-Star team. He entered the game in the sixth inning and in the eighth, an errant Sparky Lyle pitch hit him in the knee. That injury, plus back problems, derailed his career; after '77 he was traded away, had some poor years in St. Louis, New York, and Detroit, then was later reacquired and became a capable backup for those early eighties Cub squads.

Steve Buechele (1992–95) was the team's regular third baseman for nearly four seasons after the Cubs were able to dump Danny Jackson's contract on the Pirates in exchange. Buechele—whose name was pronounced like an old carpet company (Boushelle) that used to

advertise on Chicago TV, and so that ad jingle was played when he came to the plate—was a competent hitter with a bit of power (15 homers in 133 games in 1993). But he was slow-footed and a statue in the field. This lack of speed came into play when, on July 28, 1992, Buechele had doubled, tripled, and homered and came up to bat in the bottom of the eighth against the Pirates at Wrigley Field in a game the Cubs were winning 10-1. On a grounder to deep short, Buechele was called out by first-base umpire Terry Tata; a faster runner might have been given the benefit of the doubt, and thus, a cycle. Buechele had to settle for a 3-for-5 day, his best as a Cub.

There were varying degrees of success for other wearers of #24. One provided a memorable moment: **Tom Goodwin** (2003) produced a cushion-increasing, RBI-double in the top of the ninth inning in Game 5 of the 2003 Division Series that acted as a final sign that the Cubs really were going to win their first postseason series since the Roosevelt (Teddy) Administration. Goodwin led the '03 Cubs with 19 steals and a .345 average as a pinch hitter. And his first homer as a Cub was a game-winner in the ninth at Pittsburgh on May 22, 2003. Goodwin also sported #5 during his Cubs tenure.

Who was the last Cub to hit .400 for a season in more than ten at bats? Why, **Todd Haney** (1995–96), of course. This reserve infielder took a .192 career average in two seasons with the Expos and Cubs into 1995, when he hit .411 in 73 at bats. He also drew seven walks to bulge his on-base percentage to .462. Only three other players since Ted Williams in 1941 had batted .400 in fifty or more at bats. Haney broke his thumb sliding in September, and the Cubs re-signed the free agent, but it was over. He got more playing time in '96 and hit just .134.

Other #24s, however, never even saw that ray of sun. The career of **Bob Raudman** (1967) was a controlled experiment in Wrigley Field. "Shorty"—caring lab partners pointed to his 5-foot-8 frame—played eight games and batted 29 times in 1967 producing a .241 average, a walk, and four strikeouts. In 26 at bats over eight games the next year, he posted a paltry .154 average with a walk and four strikeouts. Professor Durocher terminated the experiment.

Future Phillies manager **John Felske** (1968) made his major league debut with his hometown Cubs on July 26, 1968. Playing in only four games with two at bats (no hits), he eventually was acquired by the Brewers in the minor league draft, where he found a home for his .135 career average. Later in 1968 the Cubs tried the fun new way to learn mathematics—the **Jimmy McMath** way! It's easy! Here's a sample problem: Take number 24, add 1968; now take two from the hit column and divide by 14 in the at bat column. You get .143. And there's no career remainder!

Switch-hitting outfielder **Ken Henderson** (1979–80) spent the final two seasons of his sixteen-year career on the Cubs bench, in yet another failed attempt by the Wrigley-era management to squeeze more home runs out of a former star. The Iowa native had nearly as many hits as walks in Chicago, but he wasn't potent as a pinch hitter.

Shane Andrews (2000) was another reclamation project; he had hit 69 home runs in four-plus seasons in Montreal, but with alarmingly low batting averages. It was thought that installing him as the regular third baseman at Wrigley Field would allow his natural power to come through. That thought, as so many over the years, didn't work. Andrews did smash 19 HR in 259 AB as a Cub, but he hit only .236. He does have the distinction of hitting the first home run by a U.S.-based major league player in an official game in Japan, smacking a two-run blast off Mets' reliever Dennis Cook on March 29, 2000.

In the early days, the Cubs apparently considered #24 the uniform to give to players with unusual names: **Fabian Kowalik** (1935–36), whose primary career distinction is that he is one of only two major leaguers in history with that given name (if you must know, Fabian Gaffke, a backup outfielder for the Red Sox and Indians from 1936–42 is the other); **Greek George** (1941), so nicknamed due to his ancestry— though maybe the native Georgian with three first names, Charles Peter George, was into fraternities as a Stormy Petrel at Oglethorpe U.—and in any event he was sent packing to the minors after hitting .156 in 64 at bats in Chicago; **Heinz Becker** (1943), who was wearing a different number (7) when he played for the pennant-winning 1945 Cubs; and **Ox Miller** (1947), whom the Cubs somehow thought could help them after he had gone 1–3, 6.88 and been released by a woeful St. Louis Browns team after the 1946 season. The Browns had the right idea: Miller started four games for the '47 Cubs, went 1–2 with a 10.13 ERA, and then was let go.

MOST OBSCURE CUB TO WEAR #24: If those last few names didn't do it for you, here are two more to try: **Bill "Gabe" Gabler** and **Gene Fodge**, both Class of 1958. Gabler appeared in three September games in '58, pinch-hitting in all three and striking out each time. Fodge had worn #24 earlier in the '58 season (from April through July), making four starts and twelve relief appearances and posting a 4.76 ERA while the team went 3–13 in games in which he appeared. Gabler gets the nod because not only did he appear in fewer games, but almost no one saw him—the total attendance for those three games, one in Philadelphia and two at Wrigley Field, was only 19,965, and since Gabler never appeared before the seventh inning, you'd have to figure that many of those people had left the ballparks by then. So for anyone reading this who remembers seeing him in person, we salute you, and for the masses of you who didn't, now you know who he is.

GUY YOU NEVER THOUGHT OF AS A CUB WHO WORE #24: **Tommy Davis** (1972). Davis's career could be termed "Guy You Never Thought Of As (Fill In The Blank)." After eight years with the Dodgers, during which he won two batting titles (1962 and 1963, finishing third in MVP voting in '62), Davis began an odyssey that had him playing for: the Mets, the White Sox, the Pilots (yes, the Pilots), the Astros, the A's, the Cubs, the A's again, the Cubs again, the Orioles, the Angels, and the Royals. As was the Cubs' typical M.O. in the fifties, sixites, and seventies, they picked up Davis, a former star, hoping he'd catch fire and help a struggling team back into contention. The 1970 Cubs were a team desperately trying to claw into the playoffs in a weak division; with only two weeks left in the season they purchased Davis from Oakland; he went 11-for-42 (.262) with 2 HR, but the Cubs finished second. Two years later, they did it again; Davis had been released at the end of spring training by the A's (where he had returned when the Cubs let him go after '70), and remained unsigned until the Cubs inked him on July 6. He went 7-for-26 in fifteen games before the Cubs shipped him to Baltimore for Elrod Hendricks on August 18. Later, the designated hitter rule saved Tommy's career. He put up three decent years as a DH for the Orioles in 1973, 1974, and 1975.

More Streaking

While no uniform number has been in use for every year since the inception of Cubs numbers in 1932, #24 holds the spot for the longest current streak at thirty-nine seasons—from Cleo James in 1970 to 2008 Cub Henry Blanco. The list below includes all numbers worn by the '08 Cubs and how many consecutive years that number has been in service.

To see the numbers that have the longest streak for consecutive years in use, go to chapter 22.

Current Streak

Uni #	Number of consecutive years used	Year streak started	Uni #	Number of consecutive years used	Year streak started
24	39	1970	17	7	2002
5	35	1974	43	7	2002
6	35	1974	53	7	2002
20	33	1976	7	6	2003
11	32	1977	40	6	2003
36	30	1979	50	6	2003
12	26	1983	39	5	2004
38	21	1988	49	5	2004
46	19	1990	35	4	2005
2	18	1991	45	4	2005
9	14	1995	47	4	2005
15	14	1995	58	4	2005
3	12	1997	30	3	2006
8	12	1997	57	3	2006
41	12	1997	62	3	2006
48	12	1997	18	2	2007
4	11	1998	21	2	2007
28	11	1998	42	2	2007
16	10	1999	63	2	2007
29	10	1999	1	1	2008
32	10	1999	22	1	2008
25	9	2000	33	1	2008
34	9	2000	44	1	2008
19	8	2001			

#25: RAFFY, CANDY, D-LEE, AND TWO GUYS NAMED MOE

Over the last four decades, the overwhelming majority of the players who have worn #25 for the Cubs have been outfielders. So wouldn't you know it, the current occupant of the jersey is probably the best player who's ever worn it, and he's a first baseman: **Derrek Lee** (2004–08).

Affectionately known as D-Lee to Cubs fans, and nephew of former major league outfielder Leron Lee, he was acquired in a salary-dump trade from the Marlins right after . . . well, you know what happened in 2003 . . . in exchange for formerly hot Cubs first base prospect Hee Seop Choi. Solid and consistent in Florida, where he had hit at least 21 homers for four consecutive years, Lee improved on that with a 32 HR, 98 RBI season in 2004, his first on the North Side, both career highs. He followed that up with a superlative season in 2005, smashing 46 homers, driving in 107 runs, leading the NL in doubles with 50, winning the batting title with a .335 average and finishing third in the MVP balloting. He missed a season of 200 hits and 100 extra-base hits by just one extra-base hit.

DERREK LEE

In an April 2006 game at Dodger Stadium, D-Lee suffered a broken wrist in a collision at first base with LA's Rafael Furcal. With Lee out of the lineup, the Cubs suffered one of their worst seasons ever. He attempted a couple of comebacks, but with the Cubs in last place he shut down for the season on September 14 (save for a token appearance on September 30 at home in a long extra-inning game against the Rockies), in part due to the injury and also because of the diagnosis in his daughter Jada of the rare eye disease Leber's Congenital Amaurosis (LCA), which causes blindness. D-Lee has created a foundation, Project 3000, to raise money to find a cure for LCA. His charitable work and classy demeanor on the field have made him among the most popular Cubs of his era.

Several all-time memorable moments in Cubs history have been provided by #25s. **Willie Smith** (1968–70) was a pitcher who converted to the outfield. The Cubs acquired him in a deal for Lou Johnson on June 28, 1968 (he even pitched in one game for the Cubs after they got him). The following year, on Opening Day, April 8, after the Cubs had blown a 5-2 ninth-inning lead to the Phillies and then fell behind 6-5 in the eleventh, Smith was sent up to pinch-hit for Jim Hickman with a runner on base and one out. He promptly hit a two-run walkoff homer, even though they weren't called "walkoffs" forty years ago. It sent the sellout crowd of 40,796 into a frenzy, which lasted . . . well, about a month shorter than it should have. And on another Opening Day, April 4, 1994, **Karl "Tuffy" Rhodes** (1993–95) hit three home runs off the Mets' Doc Gooden. In keeping with the tone of that strike-bound season, where the Cubs wound up with a league-worst 49–64 record: all three of the roundtrippers were solo jobs . . . and the Cubs lost that game, 12-8. Rhodes hit only five more the rest of the season (in 265 more AB), though he later became a home run hero in Japan. And finally, **Orlando Merced** (1998) wore Cubs blue in only twelve games in September 1998, managing just three hits in twelve pinch-hitting appearances. One of those hits, however, was one of the most dramatic walkoff home runs in Cub history. On September 12, 1998, Merced's only homer in a Cubs uniform—a three-run job in the bottom of the ninth—climaxed a comeback against the Brewers, turning a 10-2 deficit into a 15-12 triumph.

Walker Cooper (1954–55) was an All-Star eight times with four different teams. None of those teams was the Cubs. He played parts of two years in Chicago and did fine—he batted .310 in 57 games in 1954—but Wrigley in the fifties was littered with former stars playing out the string with the Cubs. Another Cub #25 who had his best seasons elsewhere was **Luis Gonzalez** (1995–96), who was acquired by trade for Scott Servais in the middle of the 1995 season, played well enough, but left via free agency when the Cubs wouldn't meet his contract demands. At the time that seemed reasonable, but later Gonzalez had four All-Star seasons for the Diamondbacks and was a key part of their 2001 world championship team, delivering the series-winning hit off of Yankee closer Mariano Rivera.

Another Cub who left too soon was **Rafael Palmeiro** (1986–88). He was a slick-fielding first baseman, but with the Cubs' luck, they had one of those in Mark Grace. Palmeiro hit .307 in 152 games for the Cubs in 1988, but Grace came up from Iowa in May and quickly claimed ownership of first base. Palmeiro played outfield 212 times as a Cub and never stood in the pasture for another major league inning as he went on to become a charter member of the 500-homer, 3,000-hit, Congressional fibber club. The Palmeiro trade also netted—with Jamie Moyer sent to Texas in the same deal—"Wild Thing" Mitch Williams, who was instrumental in the Cubs winning their last NL East title in '89.

Three Cubs managers wore #25: **Bob Scheffing** (1957–59), **Jim Marshall** (1974–76), and **Don Baylor** (2000–02). Scheffing's three seasons were full years, and both Marshall and Baylor managed two full years and part of a third, so that's just about eight full seasons worth of games with #25 at the helm. Only one of those years (2001 under Baylor) produced a winning record, and the combined won-lost total under managers wearing #25 is 570–692, a winning percentage of .452. We provide this information as a public service for future Cubs managers, who might want to choose a different uniform number.

Two guys named **Moe** (**Thacker** and **Morhardt**) both wore #25 in 1961, Thacker from April through July and Morhardt in September. Neither was very good (Thacker, a backup catcher, hit .171 and Morhardt, a first baseman, was 5-for-18). **Johnny Pramesa** spent 22 games in uniform #25 in 1952, one of which was in Brooklyn on May 18. This otherwise ordinary 7-2 Cubs loss wouldn't be worth mentioning fifty-seven years later, except that in the fourth inning, Jackie Robinson stole home, with a diving Pramesa, who caught only 17 games in a Cubs uniform, just missing the tag on the artful Dodger. A photo of this steal has become an iconic baseball image, turned into a popular poster.

Others who spent brief times in jersey #25 include **Jim Hughes** (1–3, 5.16 in 1956); **Chris Krug** (.203 in 71 games in 1965 and 1966; Krug's given name was "Everett," but he was nicknamed "Chris" because he was born on December 25); **Don Bryant** (13 games in 1966); **Hal Breeden** (23 games, .139 in 1971); **Adrian Garrett** (.222 in 1973 after having been acquired from Atlanta in the 1969–70 offseason, sent to Oakland in 1971 and then reacquired a year later); **Candy Maldonado** (ballyhooed as a power-hitting outfielder upon his 1992–93 offseason acquisition after hitting twenty HR the year before in Toronto, he hit .186 with three HR in seventy games before being dumped to Cleveland in August); and **Derrick White** (1-for-10 in 1998, but that one hit was a memorable one—a home run in an interleague game against the White Sox at Wrigley Field that the Cubs wound up winning, 7-6).

And then there was **Gary Scott** (1991–92). Scott, despite never having played above Class A, had a spectacular spring training in 1991 and impressed manager Don Zimmer enough that Zim plugged him in as the Opening Day third baseman. Scott was supposed to end the revolving door of third basemen that had plagued the Cubs since Ron Santo was sent away after 1973. He got off to a horrendous start—his average never getting over .200—and by mid-May was back in the minors after posting a miserable .165 major league batting average. Under a new manager, Jim Lefebvre, the Cubs tried him again in '92, but he hit even worse (.156) and was shuttled back and forth to the minor leagues before being traded to the Marlins in the offseason. He did have one shining moment as a Cub, though, hitting a grand slam (one of only three home runs he hit in the majors) off the Phillies' Kyle Abbott on April 20, 1992, helping lead the Cubs to an 8-3 victory. That homer accounted for one-quarter of all of Scott's major league RBI.

MOST OBSCURE CUB TO WEAR #25: **Joe Campbell** (1967), who played one game in the majors, on May 3, 1967. On that date he started in right field, saw no chances, and struck out in all three at bats in a 4-0 shutout at the hands of the Braves. You say, "Hey, I could have done that." The difference is, Joe Campbell *did* do it. Campbell never even got to wear the home pinstripes in a game, as his only appearance was in Atlanta.

GUY YOU NEVER THOUGHT OF AS A CUB WHO WORE #25: Though **Eddie Stanky** (1943–44) and **Frank Thomas** (1960–61) certainly qualify, this one goes to **Bobby Bonds** (1981). The excited voice of Jack Brickhouse came on the air on the night of June 4, 1981 from Pittsburgh, where the Cubs were already seventeen games out of first place with an execrable 10–35 record. He told the audience that the Cubs had acquired a "big name player" who was going to recapture the terrific years of his youth on the North Side and turn things around for that woeful club. Thus were we introduced to Barry's father, whose best years were seven years gone, and who had played for eight different teams in those seven years. Before we could even get accustomed to him wearing #25, he made a diving attempt on a sinking liner off the bat of the Pirates' Tim Foli (who was the second batter of the game) and landed hard on the turf at Three Rivers Stadium, breaking a finger. Foli's ball went for a triple and Bonds didn't play again until August. He hit .215 with six HR in 45 games in a Cubs uniform and retired at the end of the 1981 season.

Numbers Game

Finally, a reasonable theory as to why #7 leads nearly every offensive statistical category based on uniform number: it's simply been worn in more games than any number in Cubs history. You have to go back to World War II to find the last time #7 wasn't worn for consecutive years by a Cubs player or a coach. And it's only been worn by coaches for six seasons since numbers were first broken out at Wrigley in 1932, whereas several other single-digit numbers have been taken by coaches for years at a time, preventing players from accruing statistics while wearing them. Even when #7 belonged to a manager, it was during Charlie Grimm's tenure as a player-manager in the 1930s.

Yet, truth be told, this theory of constant use, which sounds rational enough, is only plausible of late; #7 didn't become the most oft-worn Cubs jersey until 2008, when Mark DeRosa appeared in 149 games for the second straight year. And #11, the previous leader, was vacant in '08 following Jacque Jones's move to Detroit. After interpreting uni numbers and stats over and over again, the only theory that actually works is this: It's random, but given the Cubs' long and colorful history, it's interesting to know.

Uni#	Games
7	6,814
11	6,734
17	6,062
9	5,809
21	5,559
6	5,297
18	5,232
10	5,042
8	4,814
12	4,625
20	4,231
24	3,995
16	3,860
23	3,727
22	3,719
25	3,698
28	3,634
15	3,556
19	3,490
1	3,356

#26: BILLY WILLIAMS EVERY DAY

While many baby-boomer era Cubs fans idolized Ernie Banks for his production and sunny personality, or Ron Santo for his passion for the game and great play at third base, Sweet Swingin' **Billy Williams** got far less notice while putting up a Hall of Fame career.

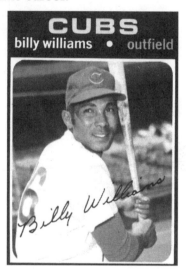

He went about his job quietly, consistently producing year in and year out while playing in 1,117 consecutive games from 1963 through 1970. He played in 150 or more games for twelve straight seasons, 1962-73, and, along with Santo, is the co-club record holder for games in a season, 164 (all the decisions plus two tie games in 1965).

Billy was installed as the regular left fielder in 1961, at the age of twenty-three. The Cubs were terrible—they finished 64–90 and would have finished last if not for the even more awful Phillies—but Billy blossomed. He hit .278/.338/.484 with 25 homers and 86 RBI, and was named National League Rookie of the Year, the first of two straight Cubs to win the award (the late Kenny Hubbs following in 1962).

The following year Billy began a remarkable streak—no, not his consecutive game streak, which would come later, but a series of twelve straight years in which he would drive in no fewer than 84 runs, and in ten of those years (all except 1967 and 1973) he had 90 or more. He began the streak during the worst period for offense since before World War I.

He was primarily a left fielder, although in 1965 and 1966 he played mostly in right field. He didn't really have the arm or the range to cover right—he played there mostly because the other options, guys like Doug Clemens, Don Landrum, and Byron Browne were even worse— so in '67 he moved back to left field, to stay there until an ill-advised attempt to make him a first baseman in 1974.

On September 21, 1963, Billy sat out an otherwise ordinary 4-0 loss to the Braves. Warren Spahn was pitching, so perhaps head coach Bob Kennedy sat him against "a tough lefty." It would be the last game he would miss for nearly seven years. The next day, Billy began a consecutive-game playing streak that lasted until September 3, 1970, when Billy told manager Leo Durocher he wanted to end the streak. It had gotten too big for him, he thought, and he didn't want the added pressure as he approached what was then the second-longest streak in history, Everett Scott's 1,307 games (and after his streak had been kept going the previous year in mid-June with three token pinch-hitting appearances after he had suffered a minor injury in Cincinnati). Billy's National League record was broken by Steve Garvey on April 16, 1983. Interesting note: had Williams not skipped that September 21, 1963 game, his streak would have been 166 games longer (1,283), as he had played in all 155 previous games that year, and the final eleven games of 1962.

One of Billy's biggest disappointments was never winning an MVP award, even in his two biggest years, 1970 and 1972. In 1970, a hitters' year, he hit .322/.391/.586, with 42 home runs and 129 RBI. He led the National League in runs, hits (tied with Pete Rose), and total bases, but lost the MVP to Johnny Bench, who had a spectacular year for the eventual pennant-winning Reds. Two years later, Billy won the batting title, with a .333 average, becoming the first Cub to do so since Phil Cavarretta in 1945. The rest of his line included a .398 on base percentage, a .606 slugging percentage, and finishing second in RBI (by two) and third in homers (by three), but Bench again won the MVP for the NL champions. That's about as close as anyone has come to winning the Triple Crown in the last forty years. Billy also led the league in 1972 in total bases, slugging percentage, OPS, and extra-base hits. During one twelve-game stretch in mid-July 1972, he went 28-for-53 (.528) with six homers and seventeen RBI.

Seven years after he retired, Billy was invited to play in a pre All-Star Game event, an AL against NL Old-Timer's game, at the old Comiskey Park, celebrating the fiftieth anniversary of the first All-Star game in 1933. At age forty-four, still in playing-shape trim, he was one of the youngest players in that game. And early in that three-inning affair, he came up to bat against Hoyt Wilhelm and promptly hit a monstrous home run into the right-field upper deck.

Wilhelm, a Hall of Famer in his own right, was nearly sixty-one years old at the time, but Billy's home run became the talk of many national sportswriters covering the event. It also got people remembering how good a hitter Billy was, and some of the writers who subsequently voted for him for the Hall of Fame said it was a factor in their votes and his eventual election. His Hall vote totals—23 percent in 1982 and 40 percent in 1983—steadily climbed after that, and he was elected to Cooperstown in 1987 (after missing by only four votes in 1986). On August 13, 1987 the Cubs retired #26 in Billy's honor. Though underrated for most of his career—and often an afterthought compared to NL outfielders Aaron, Mays, and Clemente (he only was chosen to play in seven All-Star Games for the NL; that trio was selected a total of sixty-three times!)—Billy got support at the perfect time.

Billy coached for the Cubs in varying capacities (mainly as first base and bench coach) for fifteen seasons after his retirement, also spending three years in Oakland as coach with the A's in the mid-1980s. (He had played his last two seasons as a DH for Oakland, appearing in his lone postseason series and, sadly, going hitless as the A's were swept in the last ALCS of their dynasty.) The thirty-one seasons in which he wore the Cubs uniform exceed that of any other single individual; Billy participated in over 5,000 Cubs games as a player or coach. And in each and every one of them, he conducted himself with class, dignity, and grace.

In the Wrigley era, Cubs ownership and management didn't believe in retiring numbers, though they never reissued Ernie Banks's #14 after his retirement in 1971. Strangely, Williams's #26 didn't get the same treatment—possibly because he didn't finish his career as a Cub, as Banks did. Two years after Billy was traded to the A's, #26 was issued to **Larry Biittner** (1976–79). The man with the strangely spelled surname was a capable fourth outfielder/backup first baseman, but it was still odd to see Billy's #26 worn by this total stranger to Cubs fans. Biittner became a familiar face at Wrigley, even if his two main claims to fame as a Cub came in incidents he'd probably wish be forgotten. On July 4, 1977, in the first game of a doubleheader at Wrigley Field against his former team, the Cubs trailed 11-2 in the top of the eighth inning. Manager Herman Franks, trying to save his bullpen with the temperature approaching 100 degrees, sent Larry in to pitch with two out and a runner on second. Let's just say he wasn't very good: Biittner allowed five hits, a walk, three home runs, and was warned by plate umpire Terry Tata for supposedly throwing at the head of Expos outfielder Del Unser. Biittner threw up his arms as if to say, "Throwing at him? Me? I couldn't get the ball near the plate if I tried!" He did register three strikeouts and the eternal memories of Cubs fans, who were treated to this WGN-TV graphic upon his entry to the game: LARRY BIITTNER: PIITCHING.

Two years later, on September 26, 1979, Biittner was playing right field, in a meaningless game between the fifth-place Cubs and the sixth-place Mets. In the fourth inning, Mets outfielder Bruce Boisclair hit a ball to right and Biittner took off after it, his cap flying off as he pursued the flying sphere, which dropped in for a double—and promptly landed under the cap. He frantically looked around for it as bleacher fans yelled at him, "Hat! Hat!" Biittner located the ball and threw Boisclair out trying for third base.

When Billy Williams returned to the Cubs as a coach in 1980, Biittner switched to #33.

Many years before either Williams or Biittner donned #26, **Hank Borowy** (1945–48) sported the number. The Cubs bought Borowy, who had World Series experience, from the Yankees on July 27, 1945, and he went 11–2 down the stretch to lead the Cubs to the pennant. Borowy, who finished sixth in the 1945 NL MVP voting, teamed with Claude Passeau, Hank Wyse, and Ray Prim to form the league's top rotation. Borowy became the first pitcher to have a twenty-win season split between the two leagues, a feat later matched by Rick Sutcliffe in the Cubs' 1984 NL East title year. In the World Series, Borowy shut out the Tigers in the opener but did not pitch again until Game 5, which he lost. He tossed the last three innings in relief the next day as the Cubs won in twelve innings. Although worn out, Borowy started Game 7 two days later. He was knocked out in the first inning. You couldn't blame him. (Some would fault manager Charlie Grimm.) The Cubs hoped that the twenty-nine-year-old Borowy would remain a solid starter for them for years to come, but he developed arm trouble and lasted only three more years in Chicago before bouncing around to the Phillies and Tigers.

MOST OBSCURE CUB TO WEAR #26: **Fritzie Connally** (1983). In addition to the fact that "Fritzie" isn't a very good name for a baseball player, Connally wasn't a very good baseball player. The last Cub to wear #26 before it was rightfully given to Billy Williams for good, he went hitless in ten at bats wearing the number. Connally was part of the multiteam deal after the 1983 season which helped bring Scott Sanderson to the Cubs.

GUY YOU NEVER THOUGHT OF AS A CUB WHO WORE #26: **Moe Drabowsky** (1956–58), one of only four major leaguers born in Poland, was a bonus baby who became the Cubs' top pitcher in his first full season at age twenty-one. Drabowsky led the 1957 Cubs in starts, complete games, innings, strikeouts, and ERA. But he had a reputation as a practical joker, and so the straight-laced 1950s era Cubs, never known for letting baseball talent interfere with getting rid of players who didn't fit the mold, sent him to the Milwaukee Braves with Seth Morehead for Andre Rodgers and infielder Daryl Robertson on March 31, 1961. This began an odyssey that saw Drabowsky play for eight organizations, including Baltimore twice, where he became a solid reliever and a key contributor to two Orioles world champion teams in 1966 and 1970, plus stints with both the Kansas City A's and Royals. Drabowsky also donned #39 for the Cubs in 1959 and 1960.

The Best-hitting Cubs Number

#7s big lead in all-time Cub at bats (22,304) and hits (6,019) leaves an opening for other numbers that have seen a little less action to snatch away the best batting average, just as Rick Monday grabbed that flag away from those two seditious punks who would have burned it in the Dodger Stadium outfield back in 1976. Nothing quite as serious here, though it is kind of ironic that Monday wore #7.

Anyway, without further ado, the best-hitting Cubs number ever is . . . #62. What? Yes, #62 is the owner of a .500 average earned in just two at bats with one hit, by a pitcher, no less: Bob Howry. In 2006, Howry singled; he struck out his only other time up, in '08. You won't find it on the list below, though. Nor will you find #58—a number with only 117 at bats (and a splendid .291 average) which is dominated by the call up years of Geovany Soto. His .426 average in September 2007 helped him win a starting job behind the plate and a uniform number forty digits to the south in the fifth-best all-time hitting slot at #18. On the other end, the worst-hitting Cubs number is #54, at a robust .073 in 110 at bats. That number has been occupied by pitchers, plus three hitless at bats by outfielder Clarence Maddern in 1946.

To keep it fair, we've held the minimum to 10,000 at bats for a uniform number to qualify for this list. (That's about 130 at bats per year since the Cubs started wearing uniform numbers in 1932.) The payoff is that #26 takes the top all-time spot at .288. It's fitting that the classy Billy Williams, who owns 82 percent of the career at bats for #26, gets this honor. For those who are still biitter that Larry Biittner was assigned the number after Williams left, #26 wouldn't have reached 10,000 at bats without the ex-Expo. And .288 for #26 may forever hold the top honor since the number is now retired for Williams. It also makes up for the somewhat random results that follow. The next two spots are owned by #2 and #6, with Billy Herman and Stan Hack, respectively, as the most consistent stars to wear those numbers (with Herman wearing #2 for not even half his Chicago tenure and Hack owning a few other numbers as well). Well, no one ever said being a Cubs fan was going to be logical.

Uni #	AB	H	Avg
26	10,325	2971	.28875
2	11,437	3219	.28145
6	17,331	4862	.28054
17	12,825	3547	.27657
18	15,714	4328	.27542
10	16,389	4453	.27171
7	22,304	6019	.26986
14	10,295	2764	.26848
23	12,052	3232	.26817
1	10,444	2792	.26733
16	11,115	2937	.26424
25	10,052	2654	.26403
21	17,454	4590	.26298
8	15,155	3962	.26143
9	19,025	4946	.25997
12	14,198	3686	.25961
11	22,210	5666	.25511
24	10,623	2704	.25454
20	12,187	3086	.25322

#27: THE VULTURE AND THE TOOTHPICK

It is one of the saddest moments in modern Cubs history. On September 7, 1969, the Cubs, having lost three in a row but still maintaining a 3½ game lead in the NL East, led the Pirates 5-4 in the ninth inning at Wrigley Field. A win would have stanched the losing streak and righted what many worried was a sinking ship. But on a two-out, two-strike pitch, Pittsburgh's Willie Stargell launched a ball onto Sheffield Avenue, tying the game, and the Cubs eventually lost, 7-5 in eleven innings. The losing streak reached eight and the Cubs fell out of first place, never to return. The homer was hit off closer **Phil Regan** (1968–72). Regan was acquired in early 1968 from the Dodgers, where he had picked up the nickname "The Vulture" for "vulturing" wins—four in 1966 alone—by coming into games with leads, blowing them, and then having the Dodgers come back and get him a win. Regan, unlike modern closers, was a workhorse, throwing 127 innings in his first Cubs season and posting 10 wins, 25 saves (leading the NL), and a 2.20 ERA. In '69, however, gassed from overuse, his ERA ballooned to 3.70. His walks were up and strikeouts down and the Stargell HR led to him being virtually booed out of town, or at least the North Side of town, as he was eventually sold to the White Sox in 1972.

Later, he became a college baseball coach and a respected pitching coach for several teams, including the Cubs in 1997 and 1998, serving as Kerry Wood's first major league pitching coach.

Phil Regan | PITCHER

Besides Regan, only one Cub—**Derrick May**—wore #27 for as many as five seasons (in May's case, two September call ups and three full years, 1992–94). May, son of former big leaguer Dave May and a highly touted first-round draft pick, looked the part of the power prospect: tall and imposing at 6-foot-4, 225. It didn't take long for the Cubs to recognize that May couldn't hit left-handed pitching, however, and he was relegated to platoon status. His best Cubs season came in 1993, when he drove in 77 runs, but even then he hit only ten homers. His lackadaisical performance in the outfield led some fans to nickname him "Derelict May." He left the Cubs after 1994 and drifted through five more seasons with five more teams: the Brewers, Astros, Phillies, Expos, and Orioles, the same number of clubs his dad played for as a spare outfielder.

In the early years, #27 was a number given to many forgettable players. It began with **Bobo Newsom,** who later became famous for having several different stints with bad AL teams in St. Louis, Philadelphia, and Washington (all three of which moved, but not because of Bobo). He won 211 major league games, but none of them as a Cub, for whom he threw only one inning in 1932. Several others wore #27 briefly in the 1930s, 1940s, and 1950s, some becoming more famous wearing other numbers: **Gene Lillard** (1939), **Eddie Waitkus** (1941—#36 later on), **Lennie Merullo** (1941—five years wearing #21), **Russ Meers** (1941), **Walter Signer** (1945), **Al Glossop** (1946), **John Ostrowski** (1946), **Dutch McCall** (1948), **Bill Serena** (1949—six seasons in #6), **Cal McLish** (1951) and **Jim Brosnan** (1954). Brosnan also wore two future retired numbers, #23 and #42, and, as did many Cubs in that era, had several better seasons elsewhere, in his case in Cincinnati, where he helped the Reds to the NL pennant in 1961 and wrote about the experience in *Pennant Race*, the follow up to his landmark book, *The Long Season*.

Sam Jones (1955–56) was sort of like a young Nolan Ryan. "Toothpick Sam," so named because of his build (6-foot-4, 200), threw really hard; he just didn't always know where it was going. In 1955, his first full major league season, he struck out 198, leading the NL (by 38), but he also walked 185, leading the league (by 77). On May 12, 1955, he threw one of the sloppiest no-hitters in baseball history (and the first by a Cub in thirty-eight years), walking the bases loaded in the ninth inning and then striking out the side. The Cubs tired of Jones's wildness, and flicked the Toothpick to the Cardinals in an eight-player deal involving no one of lasting baseball significance. Naturally, Jones enjoyed some success in St. Louis, winning twenty-one games and finishing second in the 1959 Cy Young voting.

Danny Murphy became the youngest Cub since the nineteenth century when he debuted at age seventeen on June 18, 1960, wearing #42. He was just past his eighteenth birthday when he became the youngest Cub to collect a homer, in an 8-6 loss to Cincinnati on September 13. The next year, switching to #27, he became the youngest in club history to make the Opening Day roster, but his promise as an outfielder faded. It wasn't until '69 that he reappeared in the bigs, on the other side of town, as a pitcher. He went 4-4 with a 4.66 ERA over two seasons as a White Sox reliever.

After that, various and sundry outfielders wore #27 through the 1970s and 1980s. **Champ Summers** (1975–76) had a great baseball name but not that much of a career; his first major league homer was perhaps his most memorable—a pinch-hit grand slam on August 23, 1975. The Cubs had back-to-back six-run innings that day, but lost to Houston, 14-12. Sigh. The rumba line continues: **Joe Wallis** (1977); **Mike Vail** (1978–80); **Hector Cruz** (1981); **Mel Hall** (1982–84), who did have promise and a decent major league career, but his best contribution to the Cubs was being included in the Rick Sutcliffe trade; **Thad Bosley** (1984–86), better known after his baseball career as a gospel singer; and **Rolando Roomes** (1988), one of only four major leaguers born in Jamaica (Chili Davis, Devon White, and Justin Masterson are the others, if you want some good bar-bet trivia).

Recent years have seen catchers, "more famous under other number" guys, and pedestrian pitchers sport #27: **Willie Banks** (1995), **Doug Jones** (1996), **Scott Sanders** (1999; no one could confuse him with former Cub Scott Sanderson, either by number—Sanderson wore #21 and #24—or by performance; Sanders put up a 5.52 ERA in sixty-seven games), **Corey Patterson** (2000, better known as a #20, this was his first Cubs number), **Joe Girardi** (2001–02, this was Joe's second go-around with the Cubs—he wore #7 the first time); **Damian Miller** (2003, the glue of the NL Central champs that year); **David Kelton** (2004); **Craig Monroe** (2007); and **Casey McGehee** (2008), of whom we can say only: his name is pronounced "McGee."

MOST OBSCURE CUB TO WEAR #27: **George Hennessey** (1945). Hennessey pitched in five games for the 1937 St. Louis Browns, who went 46–108; five more for the 1942 Phillies, who went 42–109, and then, for some reason, the 1945 pennant-bound Cubs decided to sign him at age thirty-seven. He pitched in two games and was shipped to the minors on June 13, never to return. We know there was a war on, but geez, no other 4-Fs were around? Now you know he wore a Cubs uniform in a pennant-winning year—and not many players have.

GUY YOU NEVER THOUGHT OF AS A CUB WHO WORE #27: **Todd Zeile** (1995). Zeile could win the "Guy You Never Thought of As" award for quite a few teams. After hitting 75 homers over six years in St. Louis, he was traded to the Cubs on June 16, 1995, in a year when the Cubs thought that adding just one more power hitter might help them to the postseason. Zeile hit just .227 with nine dingers and made his disdain for Cubdom well known. He was allowed to depart as a free agent, and over the next nine years his baseball odyssey took him to the Phillies, Orioles, Dodgers, Marlins, Rangers, Mets, Rockies, Yankees, Expos and finally back to the Mets for a curtain call (he homered in his last at bat). Eleven teams played for is more than any modern player except one: Mike Morgan—the guy the Cubs traded to get Zeile.

Numbers Off to the Triple

While #7 has collected more triples than any other uniform number in Cubs history, the bearers of that number aren't in the same ballpark with the unnumbered sluggers of days gone by who made the triple their own. Before uniform numbers, when ballparks were bigger and no one posed to watch their deep drives, the triple was the power stat of the day. The four Cubs on the career list with triple-digit triples—Jimmy Ryan (142), Cap Anson (124), Frank "Wildfire" Schulte (117), and Bill Dahlen (106)—collected just one triple among them while calling Wrigley Field home. Schulte, an outfielder in the Cubs' glory days of the early twentieth century, outlasted Tinker, Evers, and Chance, playing at Wrigley the year the Cubs moved in, in 1916. That was still sixteen years shy of the introduction of uniform numbers at Wrigley. With numbers, it doesn't quite add up. Ernie Banks had 90 of the 94 triples at #14, keeping it way down on this list; Phil Cavarreta had 99 three-baggers, but the total is split among four numbers (#3, #4, #43, #44), with only one of those numbers making the list.

Uni#	Triples
7	183
11	162
10	144
6	127
18	122
9	121
4	110
21	109
23	105
8	104
17	101
12	100
2	98
14	94
26	93
1	91
20	90

#28: CLOSING TIME

Of the thirty-three players and one coach who have worn #28 for the Cubs, only seven—**Jack Russell, Russ Meyer, Jim Willis, Glen Hobbie, Lee Gregory, Mitch Williams,** and **Randy Myers**—have been moundsmen. But between Williams and Myers, they posted 164 saves wearing the blue pinstripes.

Myers's 53 saves in 1993 established a National League record that stood until John Smoltz broke it with 55 in 2002, and Williams's 36 saves in 1989 helped the Cubs win the NL East title. Those totals still rank first and fifth on the all-time Cubs single season list.

Mitch Williams was known as "The Wild Thing" because his antics and his penchant for throwing pitches with an unknown destination were similar to Charlie Sheen's character Rick "Wild Thing" Vaughn in *Major League,* which came out the year Williams came to the Cubs. Williams came from the Rangers in the eight-player deal that sent Rafael Palmeiro to Texas. Palmeiro, a singles hitter at the time (he had hit only eight home runs in nearly 600 at bats in 1988), put up ten thirty-homer seasons after leaving the Cubs and before becoming discredited for testing positive for steroids. Without Williams's flamboyance and baseball smarts (on September 11, 1989, he picked off Expos rookie Jeff Huson to end a Cubs victory, getting a save without throwing a pitch), they wouldn't have won the division. In the NLCS, Williams gave up the series-winning, two-run single to Will Clark, an eerie precursor to his serving up the World Series-winning homer to Joe Carter four years later as a Phillie.

The Cubs dealt Williams to Philadelphia the day before Opening Day 1991, for middle-of-the-road relievers Bob Scanlan and Chuck McElroy. But Cubs fans will always remember the man who was described by his teammate Mark Grace as "pitching like his hair was on fire."

Randy Myers had been best known in Cubs history for serving up the first walkoff of Mark Grace's career on July 30, 1989, in a key game in that playoff year, while Myers was a Met. The next year, Myers became one of Lou Piniella's "Nasty Boys" with the world champion Reds. Signed as a free agent by the Cubs before the 1993 season, Myers paid immediate dividends in Chicago by setting the NL record for saves, 53, although that Cubs team finished far out of playoff contention. It was on August 15 of that year that the Cubs marketing department

arranged to give fans posters of the then-popular Myers. Unfortunately, Myers chose that day to give up homers to Barry Bonds and Matt Williams, breaking a 7-7 tie in the eleventh inning. Bleacher fans littered the field with the posters, prompting the Cubs, for several years afterward, to not give out promotional items in the bleachers until after the game.

Myers was involved in another weird brouhaha in the second-to-last game he pitched in a Cubs uniform. On September 28, 1995, with the Cubs desperately trying to hold on in the very first wild-card race, Myers gave up a crucial eighth-inning longball to James Mouton of the Astros. As manager Jim Riggleman was taking Myers out of the game, a disgruntled fan ran out on the field. Myers responded with what shortstop Shawon Dunston later termed "one of those martial arts moves," and pinned the assailant to the turf until authorities hauled him away. This incident did have a happy ending—the Cubs wound up bailing Myers out by winning the game, coming from behind in the eighth, tenth and eleventh innings—but the Cubs still failed to capture the wild card.

Only one other Cub wore #28 for more than four seasons, and his gentle nature was quite the opposite of the volatile Williams and the hard-throwing Myers. **Jim Hickman**, known as "Gentleman Jim," had crossed paths with the Cubs in a memorable way while a Met in 1963. Mets pitcher Roger Craig had lost eighteen consecutive games, then an NL record, but on August 9, Hickman hit a walkoff grand slam at the Polo Grounds off Cubs reliever Lindy McDaniel, winning the game for Craig and the Mets, 7-3. After a stint with the Dodgers, he was dealt to the Cubs on April 23, 1968 (along with reliever Phil Regan). Hickman sat mainly on the bench until Leo Durocher made him the team's primary rightfielder in spring training of 1969. He hit a then-career high of 21 homers in 338 at bats, tying Billy Williams for third best on the club, although Williams batted nearly twice as many times.

The following year, playing every day splitting time between first base and the outfield, Hickman had a career year, hitting .315 with 32 homers and 115 RBI. This performance earned him his first and only invitation to the All-Star team, and an eighth place finish in the NL MVP voting. In that All-Star Game, Hickman played a role in one of the Midsummer Classic's most memorable moments, as his single drove in the winning run in the twelfth inning. That runner was Pete Rose, whose full-speed crash into Indians catcher Ray Fosse sent the latter to the hospital and perhaps ruined a career.

From **Jack "Not A Terrier, A Pitcher" Russell** (1938–39) to **Bobby Sturgeon** (1940–42) to **Russ Meyer** (1947–48) to **Jim Willis** (1953–54) to **Hal Rice** (1954) to **Lloyd Merriman** (1955) to **Glen Hobbie** (1957–58) to **Bob "No Relation To George" Will** (1960–63), the early years of Cub #28s were forgettable, though Hobbie did have two sixteen-win seasons wearing #40 in 1959 and 1960.

In the years post-Hickman, #28 was mostly an outfielder's number, with the notable exceptions of Williams and Myers. This list of outfielders, though, would frighten no one, except perhaps a Cubs manager trying to make out a lineup card: **Ron Dunn** (1974), **Joe Wallis** (1975–76), **Jerry Martin** (1979–80), **Steve Henderson** (1981–82), **Henry Cotto** (1984), **Mitch Webster** (1988), **Ced Landrum** (1991), **Pedro Valdes** (1996, 1998), **Roosevelt Brown** (1999–01), **David Kelton** (2003), **Todd Hollandsworth** (2004–05), and **Michael Restovich** (2006); Restovich was considered for the "obscure" nod, because he had had a great spring training and was pushed by GM Jim Hendry as a possible right field platoon partner for Jacque Jones, who never could hit lefties. But Dusty Baker refused to play him; Restovich appeared in ten games but never started, and eventually he was sent back to the minors.

One infielder of note who wore #28 was **Mark Bellhorn**, who came over from Oakland in a deal for a minor leaguer. Never showing power in his A's days, in 2002 Bellhorn hit 27 home runs. Two of those 27 round-trippers came on August 29, when Bellhorn connected from both sides of the plate in the fourth inning of a 13–10 Cubs win over the Brewers, becoming only the second player in history to perform that feat. He also drew 76 walks that year, but drove in just 56 runs and fanned 144 times. He was traded to Colorado in 2003, but he emerged on the national scene a year later playing in his native Boston. Mahk Bellhown played a pivotal role in helping the Red Saux win the 2004 World Series.

There is one final #28 note: **Mark Grace's** #17 is still worn by fans who bought his jersey when he was a Cub for thirteen seasons from 1988 to 2001. But Grace was issued #28 when he was called up on May 2, 1988 and wore it for a three-game series in San Diego. Grace switched to #17 when the Cubs returned home on May 6 in honor of his first base idol, Keith Hernandez. Grace didn't win eleven straight Gold Gloves like his hero did, but he did receive the award four times in five years and had a Hernandez-esque, built-for-doubles swing that made him an idol at his park.

MOST OBSCURE CUB TO WEAR #28: **Lee Gregory** (1964). Gregory, acquired before the 1964 season for another obscure reliever, Dick LeMay, pitched briefly for the Cubs in April, and returned in late July, generally performing mop-up duty in blowouts. He appeared in eleven games, all losses, and the Cubs lost those eleven games by a combined score of 94-30. The Fresno State graduate left the majors and returned to Fresno, where he still lives.

GUY YOU NEVER THOUGHT OF AS A CUB WHO WORE #28: **Kal Daniels** (1992). Daniels, whose real given name was **Kalvoski,** had hit 100 homers by age twenty-eight when, on June 27, 1992, he was acquired by the Cubs from the Dodgers for a minor leaguer. Management hoped his left-handed power would solidify Chicago's left-field problem for years to come. Instead, Daniels moped because he wasn't starting every day; he played in forty-eight games, starting only twenty-eight of them, hitting four homers before being released at the end of the 1992 season, his last in the majors.

North Side, South Side

There have been 129 players who have worn numbers for both the Cubs and White Sox during their careers, from 1932 through 2008. Many have seen distinguished service with the Cubs and had short stays on the South Side—Ron Santo comes to mind, regrettably. Others have worn the Pale Hose for several years and stopped in at Wrigley Field for a brief appearance. Both Hall of Famers on this list—Hoyt Wilhelm and Rich Gossage (both also on the short list of relievers in Cooperstown)—fit this latter category. There are far more who had short stays on both sides of town.

Player Name	Cubs Uniform #(s)	Years Played With Cubs	Years Played With White Sox
David Aardsma	54	2006	2007
Bobby Adams	7,16	1957–59	1955
Paul Assenmacher	45	1989–93	1994
Earl Averill	6	1959–60	1960
Frank Baumann	48	1965	1960–64
George Bell	11	1991	1992–93
Jason Bere	46	2001–02	1993–98
Hi Bithorn	17,35	1942–46	1947
Bobby Bonds	25	1981	1978
Zeke Bonura	25	1940	1934–37
Thad Bosley	18	1983–86	1978–80

Player Name	Cubs Uniform #(s)	Years Played With Cubs	Years Played With White Sox
Jim Brosnan	27,42,23	1954–58	1963
Warren Brusstar	41	1983–85	1982
Smoky Burgess	4,8,11	1949–51	1964–67
John Buzhardt	23,38	1958–59	1962–67
Johnny Callison	6	1970–71	1958–59
Larry Casian	55	1995–97	1998
Phil Cavarretta	43,23,3,44	1934–53	1954–55
Steve Christmas	18	1986–86	1984
Loyd Christopher	32	1945	1947
Neal Cotts	48	2007–08	2003–06
Wes Covington	43	1966	1961
Dick Culler	7	1948	1943
Tommy Davis	29,24	1970–72	1968
Mike Diaz	15	1983	1988
Steve Dillard	15	1979–81	1982
Miguel Dilone	32	1979	1983
Jess Dobernic	17	1948–49	1939
Moe Drabowsky	26,39	1956–60	1972
Vallie Eaves	41,14	1941–42	1939–40
Hank Edwards	16	1949–50	1952
Lee Elia	19	1968	1966
Scott Eyre	47	2006–08	1997–2000
Scott Fletcher	20	1981–82	1983–91
Ken Frailing	47	1974–76	1972–73
Oscar Gamble	20	1969	1977–85
Ross Gload	6	2000	2004–06
Tom Gordon	45	2001–02	2003
Rich Gossage	54	1988	1972–76
Warren Hacker	17,18	1948–56	1961
Steve Hamilton	37	1972	1970
Ralph Hamner	22,35	1947–49	1946
Ron Hassey	15	1984	1986–87
Grady Hatton	20	1960	1954
Bill Heath	19	1969	1965
Ken Henderson	24	1979–80	1973–75
Greg Hibbard	37	1993	1989–92
Guy Hoffman	50	1986	1979–83
Bob Howry	62	2006–08	1998–2002
Jim Hughes	25	1956	1957

Player Name	Cubs Uniform #(s)	Years Played With Cubs	Years Played With White Sox
Darrin Jackson	30	1985–89	1994–99
Lance Johnson	1	1997–99	1988–95
Jay Johnstone	21	1982–84	1971–72
Matt Karchner	52	1998–2000	1995–98
Don Kessinger	11	1964–75	1977–79
Bruce Kimm	7	1979	1980
Jim King	20	1955–56	1967
Fabian Kowalik	24	1935–36	1932
Ken Kravec	37	1981–82	1975–80
Jack Lamabe	40	1968	1966–67
Dennis Lamp	47	1977–80	1981–83
Don Larsen	40	1967	1961
Vance Law	2	1988–89	1982–84
Dave Lemonds	48	1969	1972
Darren Lewis	6	2002	1996–97
Dick Littlefield	34	1957	1951
Bob Locker	36	1973–75	1965–69
Kenny Lofton	1,7	2003	2002
Bill Long	37	1990	1985–90
Andrew Lorraine	55	1999–2000	1995
Jay Loviglio	17	1983	1981–82
Turk Lown	35,31	1951–58	1958–62
Robert Machado	29,72	2001–02	1996–98
J. C. Martin	12,6	1970–72	1959–67
Morrie Martin	45	1959	1954–56
Dave Martinez	1	1986–2000	1995–97
Randy Martz	34	1980–82	1983
Jim McAnany	20,22	1961–62	1958–60
Chuck McElroy	35	1991–93	1997
Lynn McGlothen	40	1978–81	1981
Cal McLish	12,27	1949–51	1961
Lloyd Merriman	28	1955	1955
Catfish Metkovich	22	1953	1949
Bob Miller	45	1970–71	1970
Bob Molinaro	29	1982	1977–81
Danny Murphy	20,42,27	1960–62	1969–70
Jaime Navarro	38	1995–96	1997–99
Wayne Nordhagen	20	1983	1976–81
Ron Northey	10	1950–52	1955–57

Player Name	Cubs Uniform #(s)	Years Played With Cubs	Years Played With White Sox
Emmett O'Neill	19	1946	1946
Jose Ortiz	20	1971	1969–70
Johnny Ostrowski	47,50,27	1943–46	1949–50
Donn Pall	47	1994	1988–93
Ken Patterson	34	1992	1988–91
Reggie Patterson	52	1983–85	1981
Josh Paul	29	2003	1999–2003
Taylor Phillips	29,41	1958–59	1963
Juan Pizarro	46	1970–73	1961–66
Whitey Platt	48	1942–43	1946
Howie Pollet	16	1953–55	1956
Mike Proly	36	1982–83	1978–80
Jim Qualls	42	1969	1972
Phil Regan	27	1968–72	1972
Steve Renko	50	1976–77	1977
Carl Reynolds	43	1937–39	1927–31
Marv Rickert	46,35	1942–47	1950
Bob Rush	30,17	1948–57	1960
Luis Salazar	11,10	1989–92	1985–86
Scott Sanderson	24,21	1984–89	1994
Ron Santo	15,10	1960–73	1974
Carl Sawatski	18,11,15	1948–53	1954
Jimmie Schaffer	5	1963–64	1965
Bob Shaw	33	1967	1958–61
Clyde Shoun	23,21	1935–37	1949
Charley Smith	19	1969	1962–64
Eddie Solomon	40	1975	1982
Sammy Sosa	21	1992–2004	1989–91
Joe Stephenson	50	1944	1947
Jimmy Stewart	19	1963–67	1967
Tim Stoddard	49	1984	1975
Steve Stone	30	1974–76	1973–78
Tanyon Sturtze	34	1995–96	1999–2000
Kevin Tapani	36	1997–2001	1996
Bennie Tate	11	1934	1930–32
Dick Tidrow	41	1979–82	1983
Steve Trout	34	1983–87	1978–82
Vito Valentinetti	57	1956–57	1954
Hoyt Wilhelm	39	1970	1963–68
Rick Wrona	1	1988–90	1993

#29: INFIELDERS AND OUTFIELDERS TO GO, PLEASE

ALL-TIME #29 ROSTER:

Player	Year
Bobby Mattick	1938
Kirby Higbe	1938
Barney Olsen	1941
Emil Kush	1946–49
Preston Ward	1950, 1953
Ray Blades (coach)	1953
John Andre	1955
Tom Poholsky	1957
Taylor Phillips	1958
Harry Bright	1965
Byron Browne	1965–67
George Altman	1967
Clarence Jones	1968
Don Young	1969
Tommy Davis	1970
Brock Davis	1970–71
Al Montreuil	1972
Dave Rosello	1973–74
Jim Tyrone	1975
Mike Sember	1978
Steve Davis	1979
Scot Thompson	1981
Bobby Molinaro	1982
Ty Waller	1982
Tom Veryzer	1983–84
Steve Lake	1986
Chico Walker	1986–87
Doug Dascenzo	1988–92
Jose Guzman	1993–94
Robin Jennings	1997, 1999
Jeff Huson	2000
Robert Machado	2001
Fred McGriff	2001–02
Lenny Harris	2003
Josh Paul	2003
Andy Pratt	2004
Rey Ordonez	2004
Ben Grieve	2004
Mike Fontenot	2005
Angel Pagan	2006–07
Jeff Samardzija	2008

Twenty-nine is an odd number. OK, you're saying, that's obvious. But we don't mean mathematically. It's "odd" in that it's not a "special" number, not divisible by 5 or 10, not a double digit number like 44, not having any particular quality that would make anyone really desire to wear it.

As a result, only two Cubs have worn the number for more than three seasons. The player who wore it in exactly three seasons—**Byron Browne** (1965–67)—played only one full year, 1966, and had 5 and 19 at bats in '65 and '67, respectively. Browne is more notable for being part of one of the landmark events in baseball history. And it doesn't have anything to do with the outfielder's three years as a Cub, or his seasons as an Astro or a Cardinal. On October 7, 1969, a transaction involving seven players (eventually nine) sent Tim McCarver, Joe Hoerner, and Browne from St. Louis to Philadelphia for Dick Allen, Jerry Johnson, and Cookie Rojas. One other player involved in the trade refused to change teams. Curt Flood sued MLB to eliminate the reserve clause that had forever bound a player to the team that held his contract. Flood lost the case, and his career, but it paved the way for arbitration, free agency, and massive multiyear contracts. Browne played in Philadelphia with little complaint, but flashy Willie Montanez, sent to Philly to take Flood's place in the deal, ate up a lot of Browne's playing time. Browne ended his career in Philadelphia in '72.

Emil Kush wore #29 for four years, but in his brief appearances for his hometown Cubs before heading off to war for three years, he wore #20 and #22. When he returned from World War II, Kush went 9-2 in 1946 and 8-3 in '47. He had a 3.48 career ERA in 150 Cubs games, primarily in relief.

The Cub who wore #29 the longest was **Doug Dascenzo,** who sported it for parts of five seasons from 1988–92. Dascenzo was only 5-foot-8, 160, had no power (three homers in 1,070 at bats as a Cub), but he played competent defense and could steal a base now and again (47 steals in the blue pinstripes). Yet his biggest claim to fame as a North Sider was his four pitching appearances in 1990 and 1991, in games the Cubs lost 19-8, 13-5, 14-6, and 13-4. Little Doug had a nice breaking pitch and allowed no runs in a career total of five innings, giving up three hits—all singles—walking two, and striking out two. He almost made you wonder how he might pitch in games where the Cubs *weren't* trailing by eight runs or more.

Over the long history of uniform numbers worn by Cubs, no one else has worn #29 for more than two seasons. The most notoriety gained by a #29 was probably garnered by **Don Young,** who wore #23 in a brief call up at age nineteen in 1965, and then was handed #29 and the starting center fielder's job in 1969 when Adolfo Phillips flopped. Young wasn't much of a hitter—.218 lifetime—and his forte was supposed to be his defense. But on July 8, 1969, in the ninth inning of a game against the Mets in front of 37,278 at Shea Stadium, Young let two fly balls—a bloop by Ken Boswell and a long fly by Donn Clendenon—drop; he wasn't charged with any errors, but had he caught the balls, the Cubs would have won, 3-1. Instead, the Mets won, 4-3, and after the game Young was publicly reamed out by his manager, Leo Durocher, and third baseman Ron Santo. The reserved young man took it to heart, would play only 32 games the second half of the year, and virtually vanished from public view after that. Cubs fans wanting complete team autographed balls from the star-crossed '69 team eventually located him working as a building custodian in Colorado.

Apart from these players, #29 was mostly assigned to the "last guy on the roster," players such as **Taylor Phillips** (1958); **Harry Bright** (1965); **Mike Sember** (1978); **Steve Davis** (1979); **Bobby Molinaro** (1982); **Ty Waller** (1982); **Robin Jennings** (1997, 1999); **Jeff Huson** (2000); **Robert Machado** (2001), who later became the only Cub #72; **Josh Paul** (2003); and **Andy Pratt** (2004). The number also went to veteran players acquired in-season: **George Altman** (1967); **Clarence Jones** (1968), who had worn #27 in 1967 but found it taken by Phil Regan upon his '68 recall; **Tommy Davis** (1970); **Steve Lake** (1986), like Jones, losing a number (#16, to future Red Sox manager Terry Francona) when recalled from a minor league stint; **Rey Ordonez** (2004); and **Ben Grieve** (2004).

After **Angel Pagan** (2006–07) returned to the Mets from whence he came, #29 wasn't issued at the beginning of the 2008 season. It was claimed by former Notre Dame wide receiver **Jeff Samardzija,** now a hard-throwing relief pitcher, because his original #50 (worn in spring training) had been taken by pitching coach Larry Rothschild after Rich Harden had requisitioned Rothschild's #40, the number Harden had worn in Oakland. If Samardzija had thought about #45, his number on the Notre Dame baseball team, Sean Marshall already had that. No one would have faulted the Valparaiso, Indiana product if he'd gone with #83, his wide receiver number with the Fighting Irish. Perhaps in time, Samardzija might make #29 a memorable Cubs number.

MOST OBSCURE CUB TO WEAR #29: **Al Montreuil** (1972). As a Cajun from Louisiana, Montreuil should have had his name pronounced "Mon-TROY" (or a reasonable facsimile thereof), but beloved Cubs TV announcer Jack Brickhouse insisted that the second baseman's name was pronounced "Montréal," like the Canadian city. It made no sense, yet it wasn't a question for long. Montreuil, at 5-foot-5, 128 pounds, one of the smallest players in Cubs history, went 1-for-11 in his five-game (three starts) Cubs career.

GUY YOU NEVER THOUGHT OF AS A CUB WHO WORE #29: **Fred McGriff** (2001–02). After Mark Grace left under less-than-ideal circumstances following the 2000 season, the Cubs thought Hee Seop Choi would be ready to take over first base. He wasn't. So they went into the season with Matt Stairs, Ron Coomer, and Julio Zuleta manning the position. When they were suddenly thrust into contention, management set its sights on the longtime Brave and Padre McGriff, then playing for his hometown team in Tampa. He let it be known he wasn't sure if he wanted to leave his family (leading some fans to dub him "The Family Man"), and it took until nearly the non-waiver deadline to finish the deal. Taking the field to a standing ovation at Wrigley on July 29, he had an RBI single in his Cubs debut against St. Louis, but otherwise McGriff was underwhelming as the Cubs faded and finished third. McGriff complained about all the day games, leading to yet another fan nickname: "The Prince of Darkness." His uninspiring manner and poor 2002 season turned most fans against him, especially when it was learned that interim manager Bruce Kimm was continuing to play him—retarding the development of Choi—solely so McGriff could post another 30 HR, 100 RBI season. After he accomplished that with a two-run homer on September 22, 2002, he sat out the final six games except for one token pinch-hit appearance, and then slinked off to Los Angeles (so much for being "close to home"). McGriff is one of the least-liked Cubs of the last half century.

Scoring by the Number

Baseball has enough theories and statistics to make the game seem utterly complicated, but really, the only thing a team needs to do to win is to simply score more runs than their opponent. Touch home plate, win game. That's the simplest theory there is. While driving in the runs is the center of a lot of attention in baseball, getting on base and scoring the runs sometimes gets overlooked. Not here. Nothing proves that it's a team game more than the distribution of runs. The three Cubs who have scored the most runs in the last century are Ryne Sandberg (1,316), Billy Williams (1,306), and Ernie Banks (1,305). It couldn't be much closer. But look on this list and the respective numbers they wore rank eleventh (#23), fourteenth (#26), and eighteenth (#14). None of those three numbers will ever rank any higher as all three are retired. (Though Williams scored four of those runs while wearing #41.) It doesn't matter what number the ducks on the pond are, as long as they come home.

Uni#	Runs
7	2,968
11	2,651
21	2,483
6	2,308
9	2,247
10	2,198
17	2,069
18	2,065
8	1,826
12	1,755
23	1,752
20	1,592
2	1,575
26	1,517
1	1,437
16	1,391
25	1,384
14	1,369
24	1,304
4	1,280

#30: CAN YOU PITCH? HAVE WE GOT A NUMBER FOR YOU!

ALL-TIME #30 ROSTER:

Player	Year
Jim Asbell	1938
Bill Fleming	1942
Jesse Flores	1942
Paul Derringer	1943–45
Bob Rush	1948–49
Frank Hiller	1950–51
Vern Fear	1952
Willie Ramsdell	1952
Duke Simpson	1953
Vern Morgan	1954
Jim Bolger	1955
Pete Whisenant	1956
Cal Neeman	1957
John Briggs	1958
Dick Drott	1959–61
George Gerberman	1962
Dick LeMay	1963
Wayne Schurr	1964
Kenny Holtzman	1965–71, 1978–79
Dan McGinn	1972
Steve Stone	1974–76
Mike Adams	1977
Carlos Lezcano	1980–81
Hector Cruz	1982
Chuck Rainey	1983–84
Chico Walker	1985
Darrin Jackson	1985, 1987–89
Dave Clark	1990
Bob Scanlan	1991–93
Ozzie Timmons	1995–96
Jeremi Gonzalez	1998
Mark Guthrie	1999–00
Raul Gonzalez	2000
Matt Stairs	2001
Matt Clement	2002–04
Buck Coats	2006
Ted Lilly	2007–08

Of the thirty-seven Cubs who have worn #30, more than half—twenty-one—have been moundsmen. There were exceptions, of course, and once the players began to make more money and flex their muscles with management in the 1980s, this pattern shifted somewhat. But once **Dick Drott** (1959–61, also wore #18 in 1957–58) was issued #30 in 1959, a parade of pitchers donned this number, some well-known, others not.

Ken Holtzman | PITCHER

Perhaps the best-known was **Kenny Holtzman** (1965–71, 1978–79), who was the greatest Cubs left-hander since Hippo Vaughn, more than fifty years earlier. Holtzman is the only

Cubs pitcher since the 1880s to toss two no-hitters and he holds the team marks since 1900 for starts and strikeouts in a season by a lefty. Taken in the fourth round of the first-ever amateur draft in 1965, the University of Illinois product made the major leagues at age nineteen before that season even ended, and was likened to Sandy Koufax—an unfair comparison for any pitcher in the 1960s—because Holtzman fit the profile: he was left-handed, Jewish, and as a rookie he beat Koufax, 2-1, in the only meeting between the two pitchers. In that memorable game at Wrigley Field, Holtzman took a no-hitter into the ninth inning, a portent of things to come, before giving up a hit and a run. The next year Holtzman went 9-0 in twelve starts while fulfilling his military obligation. He pitched—and won—when he could get a pass.

Holtzman thrived under heavy use in 1969. He won seventeen times, including six shutouts, and tossed his first no-hitter on August 19. The no-hitter was famously saved by Billy Williams, who caught a long drive off the bat of Hank Aaron which, seemingly destined to land on Waveland Avenue, was blown back by a stiff wind and snagged at the wall. It was the first no-no without a strikeout in the majors since 1892, which was strange for a power pitcher. Holtzman fanned 176 in '69 and 202 the next year. In '71 he pitched his second no-hitter on June 3 in Cincinnati, but his 9–15 record and 4.38 ERA soured him on the Cubs and the Cubs front office on him, and he was dealt to Oakland for Rick Monday.

As in Chicago, where he was overshadowed by future Hall of Famer Fergie Jenkins, Holtzman pitched in the wake of the A's Catfish Hunter. Vida Blue, the reigning AL MVP, cast a big shadow, too. No matter, Holtzman completed a dominating staff. The mustachioed A's won three straight world championships. Holtzman won 77 games in four years, and posted a 4-1 mark and a .333 batting average in World Series play. He also won the decisive Game 7 of the '73 Series against the Mets.

Holtzman pitched for the Orioles and Yankees before returning to the Cubs in 1978. Holtzman no longer had No. 2—or No. 3—stuff; in those energy-conscious days, some fans used to call his fastball the "Ecology Pitch," since it seemingly couldn't go faster than 55 MPH. While his uniform still said 30, he was now thirty-two. He had no wins in twenty-three appearances in '78, mostly in relief. He came back in '79 as a starter and went 6–9, giving him an 80–82 mark and 988 strikeouts in nine years of service as a Cub. Before he left he gave us one final reminder of what might have been—a three-hit shutout of the Astros on July 7, 1979, his final major league victory.

In keeping with the Jewish theme, the principal occupant of uniform #30 in between Holtzman's two Cubs stints was **Steve Stone** (1974–76). Stone, one of three players acquired from the White Sox for Ron Santo after the 1973 season, had by far the best Cubs career of that trio. As a full-time starter for three Cubs teams that went a combined 216–270, Stone posted a 23–20 mark with a respectable 4.04 ERA. He missed much of the 1976 season with injuries and after that year left to sign as a free agent with the crosstown White Sox, and later won a Cy Young Award with the Orioles. Upon his retirement he went into broadcasting and was for more than twenty years the color analyst on Cubs TV broadcasts, and currently serves that role for the White Sox. Another White Sox broadcast analyst who wore #30 for the Cubs is **Darrin Jackson** (1985, 1987–89). After a brief call up at age twenty-two due to an injury to Bob Dernier, in which Jackson looked totally overmatched, he became a backup outfielder two years later. As was the case for many Cubs, Jackson had his best years elsewhere (in San Diego and on the South Side of Chicago, where he hit .312 in 1994).

Prewar, #30 wasn't issued until 1938, and worn by no one of significance: **Jim "I Got the Nickname 'Big Train' for Hitting .182" Asbell** (1938); **Bill "Not the Sports Announcer" Fleming** (1942), and **Jesse "The First Cub Born in Mexico" Flores** (1942). After Flores was sold to the Athletics following the '42 season, #30 was taken over by **Paul Derringer** (1943–45), better known as a Cardinal and Red; Derringer had helped lead Cincinnati to two pennants in 1939 and 1940. He had enough left in the tank at age thirty-eight to post a fine 16-11, 3.45 record in 1945, helping lead the Cubs to the pennant. Unfortunately, his 6.75 ERA in the '45 World Series wasn't very good and he retired after the season.

In the 1980s, 1990s, and 2000s, #30 was worn by a number of outfielders, none of whom had any meaningful impact: **Carlos "Not as Good as My Cousin Sixto" Lezcano** (1980–81); **Hector "Not as Good as My Brother Jose" Cruz** (1982); **Chico "I Don't Have Any Baseball-playing Relatives" Walker** (1985); **Dave "Shouldn't I Have Worn #5?" Clark** (1990); **Ozzie "I Don't Have a Clever Nickname" Timmons** (1995–96); **Raul "0-for-2 as a Cub" Gonzalez** (2000); and **Buck "Great Baseball Name, No Baseball Talent" Coats** (2006) . . . and a number of no-impact pitchers: **Chuck "I Took a No-Hitter to Two Outs in the Ninth" Rainey** (1983–84); **Bob "I Was Acquired for Mitch Williams" Scanlan** (1991–93); **Jeremi "Someone Anglicized My Name from Geremis" Gonzalez** (1998); and **Mark "I'm Left-handed" Guthrie** (1999–2000).

No coaches need apply: #30 is one of only seven numbers that has never been worn by a Cubs coach or manager (13, 17, 21, 23, 24, and 32 are the others). But there have been numerous sightings of coaches and managers on the mound to talk with high-maintenance pitchers wearing #30, such as **Matt Clement** (2002–04) and **Ted Lilly** (2007–08) in recent years.

MOST OBSCURE CUB TO WEAR #30: **George Gerberman** (1962), who at age twenty was called up from the minors to start one of the 1960s' most meaningless games, a September 23 tilt between the 99-loss Cubs and the 116-loss Mets. Gerberman pitched 5.1 innings, allowed three hits and five walks, but only one run. He popped up and walked in his only plate appearances, and then left the game, never to pitch in the majors again. The Mets won the game, 2-1, dealing the Cubs their 100th loss of the year, the first of only two times the Cubs have ever hit the century mark in that dubious category (1966 is the other).

GUY YOU NEVER THOUGHT OF AS A CUB WHO WORE #30: **Matt Stairs** (2001). You probably think of Stairs mostly as a DH-type, although that's a misconception—he's played more outfield in his career than DH. Mostly an AL player, he was traded to the Cubs for minor leaguer Eric Ireland in the 2000–01 offseason and quickly became a clubhouse leader who was also known for knocking down a few beers after games with fans at bars near Wrigley Field. (His hometown in New Brunswick is where Canadian lager Moosehead is brewed.) He wasn't particular about his number, either; originally issued #24, when Michael Tucker was acquired on July 20, 2001 and expressed interest in wearing that number, Stairs readily gave it up and switched to #30 for the rest of the season, before leaving the Cubs that offseason via free agency. The vagabond Stairs finally made (and won) the World Series in 2008 with his eleventh team, the Phillies.

The Chain

When Kenny Holtzman—he of the two no-hitters (plus two near misses) and eighty wins as a Cub—demanded and received a trade after irreconcilable differences with manager Leo Durocher, it marked the beginning of the breakup of the 1969 Cubs. The November 29, 1971 transaction also begat a sequence of trades that would bring the Cubs top-notch players stretching more than thirty years and culminating with a Hall of Famer whose number was retired on the North Side.

Holtzman, a Cub from 1965 to 1971, was sent to Oakland in return for slugging center fielder Rick Monday, who in 1965 had become the first player ever chosen in the amateur player draft. Monday had five good seasons in Chicago (1972–76) before he was dealt to the Dodgers for Bill Buckner and Ivan DeJesus, both of whom were solid regulars and Wrigley favorites. Buckner (1977–84) was then traded for Dennis Eckersley (1984–86), who helped lead the Cubs to the '84 NL East title. Let's just say that the trade of uber-closer-to-be Eck to Oakland in 1987 for three players who never played in the majors was the one weak link in the chain. (Mark Leonette, one of three returned from Oakland, put on a Cubs uniform without appearing in a game, but that is a story for Chapter #32.)

But the chain had already proved that it would hold. DeJesus (1977–81) went to the Phillies for Larry Bowa (1982–85) . . . and a skinny kid shortstop named Ryne Sandberg, who moved to second base and filled out a Cubs uniform from 1982 to 1997 (with a brief retirement that coincided with the strike years). The chain ended with Ryno flying his #23 over Wrigley.

#31: FERGIE AND MAD DOG

The Cubs have, through 2008, worn numbers on their backs for seventy-seven seasons. And for twenty of those seventy-seven, #31 has been worn by a Hall of Fame pitcher. (Yes, we know one of them isn't yet in the Hall, but he will be.)

FERGIE
JENKINS
CHICAGO CUBS

PITCHER

And neither one of them, when first coming to the Cubs, appeared to be anything special at all. When, on April 21, 1966 the Cubs acquired **Ferguson Jenkins**, John Herrnstein, and Adolfo Phillips from the Phillies for veteran pitchers **Bob Buhl** (whose number Fergie took) and Larry Jackson, the Cubs were initially more excited about Phillips. Jenkins made a couple of spot starts early in '66 and was finally moved into the rotation to stay on August 25; that's when his talent started to shine. In nine late-season starts in '66 he went 4-2 with a 2.13 ERA, capped by a four-hit shutout of the pennant-winning Dodgers on September 25.

You know what happened next. Six straight twenty-win seasons, topped off with a Cy Young Award in 1971 when he won 24 games (and hit six home runs, a team record for pitchers that was equaled by Carlos Zambrano in 2006). His 20–15 mark in 1968, the noted "Year of the Pitcher," should have been better: he lost five 1-0 games and was taken out of another tie after throwing ten shutout innings.

But it all started to sour in 1973, along with the rest of the bunch that never did win; Fergie fell to 14–16 and after the season was traded to the Rangers, for whom he won 25 games in '74. Despite spending two years with the Red Sox in between Rangers stints, he never did play in the postseason, and when granted free agency by Texas after the 1981 season, he was contacted by Dallas Green to see if he had anything left in the tank at age thirty-nine.

He did, though it didn't help the Cubs finish higher than fifth. Jenkins went 14–15 but with a fine 3.15 ERA that ranked eleventh in the NL. The next year age caught up with him and his ERA jumped to 4.30, and though he was in training camp with the eventual 1984 NL East champion Cubs, he showed nothing in several spring appearances and was released.

That very summer, a skinny high school kid from Las Vegas was the Cubs' second-round pick in the amateur draft. **Greg Maddux** didn't look like a ballplayer (in fact, he barely looked old enough to go to high school, much less have graduated; the picture taken of him for his first Cub spring training camp made him look so young that some fans jokingly dubbed it "his Bar Mitzvah photo"), but he blazed through the Cubs farm system and was in the major leagues two years later, making his debut as, of all things, a pinch runner in the eighteenth inning of a game suspended on September 2, 1986, finished the next day. He remained in the game to pitch and gave up a game-winning homer to Houston's Billy Hatcher, who had a knack for delivering clutch hits.

That was one of the few low moments Greg Maddux had as a Cub. Put in the rotation the next year at age twenty-one, his numbers were poor (6–13, 5.87) but his bulldog attitude began to show, and the best example of this occurred on July 7. San Diego's Eric Show hit Andre Dawson in the face with a pitch that day, sparking a brawl in a game Maddux had started. The next inning, Maddux struck out the first two batters and then hit Benito Santiago—giving the hint that he felt Santiago was responsible for calling the pitch that hit Dawson.

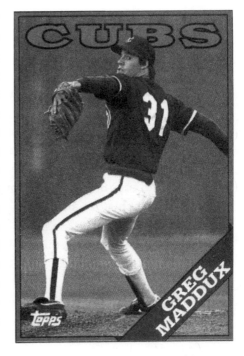

The next year Maddux exploded onto the national scene by going 18–8 and making his first All-Star team. He helped the Cubs to the 1989 NL East title by winning nineteen games, but he got pounded in the NLCS; it took him until the mid-nineties and several tries with Atlanta before he pitched well in the postseason.

Cubs fans will never forget or forgive then-GM Larry Himes for letting Maddux walk via free agency after the 1992 season, when he won the first of his four consecutive Cy Youngs. He wanted to stay, but the Cubs tried to lowball him on a contract and he went to the Braves, having his finest years there, before returning to the Cubs for a curtain call in 2004. Maddux, not the pitcher he once was, went 16–11 with a 4.02 ERA. He was supposed to be a key cog in the Cubs repeating as a postseason team but that didn't work out, as they blew a certain wild-card berth in the season's final week. Two years later, Maddux threw six five-hit, one-run, no-walk innings against the Cardinals at Wrigley Field on July 29, 2006, leaving the field to one of the loudest ovations ever at the old ballyard; two days later he was sent to the Dodgers, helping L.A. achieve a postseason berth. After a stint with the Padres, he wound up back with the Dodgers in 2008, and pitched against the Cubs in the Division Series with 355 regular season wins in his pocket at age forty-two. He announced his retirement from baseball on December 8, 2008.

You have to believe #31 will be retired by the Cubs when Maddux is inducted into the Hall of Fame; the retirement will honor both Jenkins and Maddux in the same manner that the Yankees retired #8 for both Bill Dickey and Yogi Berra. Maddux and Jenkins are two of the greatest pitchers in Cubs history and the flag will fly forever at Wrigley Field, honoring them both.

The honor wasn't given to either after they left the Cubs. The uniform was won by six other players after Fergie's departure: **Tom Dettore** (1975–76), who on April 14, 1976 was responsible for allowing what is generally considered to be the longest home run in Wrigley Field history, an estimated 600-foot shot hit by Dave Kingman, then of the Mets (Dettore would pitch only three more major league games before being released); **Joe Coleman** (1976); **Jim Todd** (1977); **Davey Johnson** (1978), the only non-pitcher to wear #31 after Jenkins; and **Ray Fontenot** (1985–86), the Cubs' second-best Fontenot. Six others: **Kevin Foster** (1994, 1997–98), **Bobby Ayala** (1999), **Brad Woodall** (1999), **Mike Fyhrie** (2001), **Donovan Osborne** (2002), and **Mark Guthrie** (2003) sported it in the Maddux interregnum between 1992 and 2004.

Before the arrival of Fergie, there were only three players to wear #31 for more than two seasons, all pitchers: **Bob Chipman** (1944–49), a swingman who both started and relieved and who is one of the few pre-1960 Cubs to wear a single number for his entire tenure with the team; **Turk Lown** (1956–58), who also wore #35 in his first stint for the Cubs from 1951–54; and **Bob Buhl** (1962–66). Buhl had helped lead the Milwaukee Braves to the 1957 NL pennant with an 18–7 season, but he was a .500 pitcher (51–52) in his four full Cubs seasons (plus one game in 1966). His most notable accomplishment in a Cubs uniform was a negative one: he went 0-for-70 as a hitter in 1962, the most at bats by anyone in a season in major league history without registering a single hit.

MOST OBSCURE CUB TO WEAR #31: **John Goetz** (1960). Taking advantage of an early 1960s roster rule allowing teams to carry a few extra players in the season's first month, the Cubs gave Goetz the only four appearances of his major league career in April. They probably wish they hadn't. He was pretty bad, allowing four runs in an 18-2 loss to the Giants, and five in a 16-6 loss to the Cardinals, upon which he was sent back to the minors. Goetz hailed from a town that must have had something to do with his family: Goetzville, Michigan.

GUY YOU NEVER THOUGHT OF AS A CUB WHO WORE #31: **Davey Johnson** (1978). Five years after he set a record for homers by a second baseman (43, with the Braves in 1973), the Cubs acquired Johnson from the Phillies, hoping he could recapture some of that power. His '73 season proved to be one of the biggest flukes in baseball history though, as Johnson never hit more than 18 homers in any other season. He did, however, hit 26 home runs for the Tokyo Giants in 1976 before coming back stateside and enjoying a bounceback season for the Phillies. He came to Chicago in August 1978 and hit well enough in brief duty with the Cubs—.306 in 49 at bats—but after the season he retired and soon embarked on a long managing career.

Here's to the Winners

If you have one game you need to win and you could pick any Cub throughout history to pitch it, who would you choose? Mordecai "Three Finger" Brown is a pretty good call. Maybe Orval Overall? They each won twice in the last World Series in which the Cubs emerged victorious, but that might be going back too far. Besides, they didn't wear numbers. If you need a Cub on the hill for a must-win game, that's got to be #31. Between Fergie Jenkins and Greg Maddux, they combined for exactly 300 wins in a Cubs uniform: 167 for Fergie, 133 for Mad Dog. This pair of aces at #31 makes that uniform number dominate just about every pitching category. Even if they took #31 out of circulation permanently—a pretty enlightened idea considering how no number has yet been retired by the Cubs for a pitcher (much less two)—it would still take Ted Lilly and whoever follows him at runner up #30 almost a decade of twenty-win seasons to catch them.

Uniform #	Wins
31	472
30	280
32	279
34	262
36	245
17	236
49	221
46	211
33	209
38	204
48	201
37	194
40	194
22	170
13	153
18	138
39	135
16	123
45	118
14	112

#32: ALMOST FAMOUS

Saturday, September 2, 1972 dawned gloomy and rainy in Chicago, and as a result only 11,144 fans came out to Wrigley Field that day to see the Cubs take on the Padres. The rain eventually stopped and **Milt Pappas** (1970–73) threw a no-hitter, an 8-0 victory that absolutely, positively, beyond a shadow of a Bruce Froemming doubt, should have been a perfect game.

Froemming, who was then in his second year as a major league umpire, swears to this day that the 3-2 pitch on Larry Stahl was outside. But the game had long since been decided (the Cubs had a

4-0 lead after three innings and padded it to 8-0 in the bottom of the eighth), and you've got a chance to make baseball history, and the pitch is borderline (which all replays showed it was), what do you do? Of course you ring up the pinch hitter.

But Froemming didn't, and Pappas had to retire the next hitter—ironically, an ex-Cub, Garry Jestadt—on a ground ball, to preserve his no-hitter.

Pappas had been a solid pitcher for the Orioles, and Reds, but he had fallen out of favor in Cincinnati due to clashes with popular Reds pitcher turned broadcaster Joe Nuxhall. Pappas was dumped to the Braves, and, in 1970, off to a 2-2, 6.06 ERA start and relegated to the Atlanta bullpen, he was sold to the Cubs on June 23.

That change of scenery rejuvenated Milt. He went 10–8, 2.68 in twenty starts, and he followed that up with back-to-back seventeen-victory seasons in 1971 and 1972. As he was still only thirty-three years old, the Cubs could have been forgiven if they thought they could get perhaps three or four more seasons out of him.

It was not to be. In 1973, his fastball nearly gone (though he was never a big strikeout pitcher, his 48 strikeouts while walking 40 in 162 innings was alarming), Pappas fell to 7–12 with a 4.28 ERA. He came to spring training in 1974 hoping to make the ballclub for a number of reasons, not the least of which was that he needed only one more victory to become only the third pitcher in major league history to win 100 games in each league. At that time the only other two were thought to be Cy Young and Jim Bunning. Later research showed that turn of the twentieth century pitcher Al Orth also had accomplished the feat, and since then Fergie Jenkins, Nolan Ryan, Randy Johnson, Dennis Martinez, Kevin Brown, and Gaylord Perry have won 100 games in each league.

Pappas never got the chance. On April 1, 1974, just days before the season began, the Cubs, who had "backed up the truck" in the offseason and traded many of the late sixties regulars, gave Milt his unconditional release.

Pitching has been the mission of #32s at Wrigley Field. Of the forty-five players who have worn it, position players have numbered a

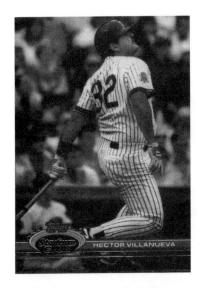

baker's dozen: **Coaker Triplett** (1938), **Newt Kimball** (1938), **Cy Block** (1942), **Loyd Christopher** (1945), **Ted Pawelek** (1946), **Harry Chiti** (1950-52, 1955-56), **Rodney Scott** (1978), **Miguel Dilone** (1979), **Sam Mejias** (1979), **Mel Hall** (1981), **Hector Villanueva** (1990, though calling him a "position" player is a stretch—Hector could hit but not field), **Eric Karros** (2003), and **Daryle Ward** (2007). Rodney Scott was perhaps one of the fastest players ever to wear a Cubs uniform; he stole 27 bases in only 78 games and had a .403 OBP in '78, but the Cubs didn't like his demeanor and shipped him to Montreal, where he managed the feat of 63 steals with a .307 OBP in 1980. Karros's one season in a Cubs uniform was memorable, as he helped them to the 2003 NL Central title; he took a personal video camera and chronicled the last few weeks of the season, but only his close friends and family have ever seen it. After the Cubs lost the NLCS, Karros spent more than $80,000 to take out a full-page ad in the *Chicago Tribune* thanking Cubs fans for making his year so memorable and was quoted as saying, "Every major leaguer should spend at least one year as a Cub."

One player most Cubs fans wish had never spent even one day in a Cubs uniform was **Ernie Broglio** (1964–66). The circumstances of his acquisition are well-known and lamented to this day. But at the time, sportswriters almost unanimously thought the Cubs had fleeced the Cardinals, who only really got question mark Lou Brock in the six-player deal; Broglio had won eighteen games the year before and as he was only twenty-eight, it was thought he had many years left. Instead, all he had was arm trouble; he won only seven games in a Cubs uniform and was done by age thirty in July 1966.

Rich Nye (1966–69), a southpaw who inherited Broglio's #32 as a September call up in 1966, burst on the scene a year later when he won thirteen games as a twenty-two-year-old. Unfortunately, he appeared to inherit Broglio's arm woes, too. When injuries cut his baseball career short, he went on to veterinary school. After getting his degree, he began a veterinary practice in the Chicago area, which eventually became the Midwest Bird & Exotic Animal Hospital, where Dr. Nye practices to this day.

Jon Lieber (1999–2002, 2008) became what Broglio might have been—a solid starter for the Cubs for several years, including a twenty-win season in 2001, the last twenty-win season to date for a Cub. Injured in 2002, he was allowed to depart via free agency because the Yankees were willing to give the injured pitcher a guaranteed contract. He returned to Chicago in 2008, but was disappointed when he didn't make the starting rotation.

Other pitchers who wore #32 included **Jim Cosman** (1970); **Jim Dunegan** (1970), who pinch-ran three times and briefly considered a comeback as an outfielder after his pitching career failed; **Tom Dettore** (1974), who switched to #31 in 1975 and 1976 when **Darold Knowles** (1975–76), who had been a postseason stud for the A's, came to the team and requested his Oakland number. Knowles is still the only man to ever pitch in all seven games of a single World Series (1973), but after posting a 5.81 ERA in the Cubs bullpen in 1975, Knowles became known to many fans as "The Torch" (as opposed to the "fireman" who would come in to put out rallies). That brings us to **Calvin Schiraldi** (1988–89), whose World Series failures for the Red Sox seemed to scar him for the rest of his baseball life. Schiraldi had been a college teammate of Roger Clemens's and was considered a better prospect by some, but by the time he got to the Cubs he couldn't pitch well anymore. The Cubs tried him as a starter and reliever, but he failed in both roles and was eventually traded to the Padres.

In the 1990s, more pitchers modeled #32: **Danny Jackson** (1991–92), a big-money free agent who signed with the Cubs, flopped in Chicago, and followed it with two good seasons for the Phillies; **Jessie Hollins** (1992); **Dan Plesac** (1993), a former Brewers closer whose Cubs playing career was much shorter than his Comcast SportsNet Cubs broadcasting career; **Chuck Crim** (1994); and **Kevin Foster** (1995-96).

MOST OBSCURE CUB TO WEAR #32: **Loyd Christopher** (1945), not to be confused with actor Christopher Lloyd of *Taxi* and *Back to the Future* fame, played one game as a Cub for the 1945 pennant winners, standing briefly on the outfield grass without fielding a ball. He did play before and after his Wrigley stint in Sox both Red and White, but it amounted to just fifteen other appearances in the bigs. His brother Russ had a seven-year career as a pitcher.

GUY YOU NEVER THOUGHT OF AS A CUB WHO WORE #32: **Larry Gura** (1985). This may seem an odd choice, as Gura came up through the Cubs farm system, but he had only three of his 126 career wins in the blue pinstripes. After being up and down for four years (wearing #40), the Cubs shipped him to the Rangers for yet another pitcher who never had any impact, Mike Paul. He never played a game for Texas; they traded him to the Yankees, who traded him to Kansas City, where he had several outstanding seasons. He finished in the top ten in the Cy Young voting three times and pitched in the 1980 World Series. Only when he was washed up and released—the same year, ironically, that the Royals would finally win a World Series after a decade of trying with Gura—did the Cubs bring him back, and only because of injuries to the pitching staff. After posting an 8.41 ERA in five appearances wearing #32, he was let go by the Cubs, ending his career.

Obscurity, Thy Name Is Leonette

Mark Leonette is unique in Cubs history. He was acquired by the Cubs on April 3, 1987, along with two other minor leaguers, Brian Guinn and Dave Wilder, from Oakland for Dennis Eckersley (one of the worst deals the Cubs ever made). Neither Guinn nor Wilder ever played in the major leagues. Leonette came as close as you can get. He was recalled from Iowa on July 3, 1987 and handed #32 as a replacement for the injured Dickie Noles. On July 11, Scott Sanderson was activated from the DL and Leonette was returned to Iowa. You won't find Leonette in any encyclopedia because—though he did warm up once at Wrigley—he never appeared in a game.

Leonette is the only Cub and one of a very short list of people in major league history to have the dubious distinction of being on an active roster during the time of the twenty-five-man roster limit yet never appearing in a game. There are other Cubs who were on the twenty-five-man roster and didn't appear in that particular season but did later appear for a major league team at some point. Leonette *never* appeared. Thus, we remember him as perhaps the most obscure Cub of all.

#33: A WYSE MAN ONCE SAID . . .

. . . don't take Cubs uniform #33.

In the more than three-quarters of a century that the Cubs have taken the field bearing numbers on their backs, only two players have worn #33 for more than three seasons:

Hank Wyse, the best player to wear it, donned it for a pennant winner during his five-year stint as #33 (1943–47) after starting his Cubs career in late '42 wearing #45, and **Bill Bonham,** the player who wore it the longest (1971–77).

That's it. The rest of 'em are completely forgettable (even the only coach to wear #33, former Dodgers and Giants stalwart, **"Fat" Freddie Fitzsimmons,** couldn't hold it for more than three seasons), which is why we'll briefly remember them here, but first a few words about the Wyse man.

Hank Wyse, nicknamed "Hooks" for his sweeping curveball, moved into the Cubs rotation in 1944 after a good year as a swingman in '43 (38 appearances, 15 starts, 2.94 ERA). He won 16 games in '44 and then burst onto the national scene in 1945 when he won 22 games, finishing second in the league in wins, fourth in ERA, making his only All-Star team, and placing seventh in the MVP balloting. On April 28, 1945, he took a no-hitter into the eighth inning against the Pirates,

only to have it broken up by Bill Salkeld with one out. He pitched the ninth inning of the Cubs' 9-3 loss in Game 7 of the 1945 World Series, for sixty-three years the last Cub to pitch in a World Series game. To his dying day, Wyse maintained that had manager Charlie Grimm started him instead of Hank Borowy, the Cubs would have won the game and the Series.

Wyse suffered a back injury in an accident working in a war plant that prevented him from serving in World War II, but even with the back injury he could still pitch, sometimes wearing a corset. The back finally forced him to the sidelines and minors—he eventually resurfaced with the Philadelphia A's in 1950, after two years away from the majors, but he wasn't nearly the same pitcher.

Unlike Wyse, Bonham was a fireballer who worked his way into a veteran Cubs rotation in the early 1970s slowly—he didn't make it fully until after two September call ups (1971 and 1972); he made 15 starts and 29 relief appearances in 1973, with a fine 3.02 ERA. The next year, with veterans Fergie Jenkins and Bill Hands both gone, Bonham became the "ace" of a 96-loss team's rotation. Despite having a decent 3.86 ERA, Bonham went 11–22; he is the last Cub to have reached that loss threshold (and probably will wear that mantle forever, as most modern managers won't let pitchers stay in the rotation long enough to lose that many games games). He threw hard (his 191 Ks in 1974 ranked sixth in the league) but he was also wild (109 walks that same year ranked fifth in the NL). As a lasting testimony to the wild Bonham heat, on July 31 of that year he also became the ninth National League pitcher—and third Cub (after Orval Overall and Jim Davis)—to fan four batters in one inning, accomplishing the rare feat in the second inning of the first game of a doubleheader. The batter who reached base was the opposing pitcher, Montreal's Mike Torrez, who did so on a passed ball.

Bonham never fulfilled the potential fans and management saw in him, and in October of 1977 he was traded to the Reds in a mystifying deal that brought veteran starter Woodie Fryman (who had to be coaxed out of retirement to play, and then got dumped after less than half a season) and then-minor leaguer Bill Caudill to the North Side. Bonham slid in behind Tom Seaver in Cincy's rotation and enjoyed consecutive winning seasons, something he was never able to do in Chicago.

And the rest? Well, there are the guys who were more recognizable wearing other numbers: **Andy Pafko** (1943, better known at #48), **Ken Hubbs** (1961, #16 later on), **Larry Biittner** (1980; he had worn #26 but ceded it back to Billy Williams when Billy returned as a coach in '80), **Mitch Webster** (1989; he had sported #28 but Mitch Williams claimed it when he was acquired before the '89 season—two Mitches enter, one Mitch leaves), **Terry Adams** (1997; he had given his old #51 to big-ticket closer Mel Rojas, only to take it back right after Rojas, who had stunk all year, was dumped to the Mets), and **Daryle Ward** (2008; he gave Jon Lieber his old #32 back when Lieber returned to the Cubs).

There are the guys who went on to more fame with other teams: **Gene Mauch** (1948–49), better known as a longtime major league manager, winning 1,902 games with four teams in the 1960s, 1970s, and 1980s; **Lou Johnson** (1960), who became a solid outfielder for two Dodgers World Series teams before a brief and unsuccessful return to the Cubs in '68; **Joe Carter** (1983), whose departure to hit 396 homers with other teams is a bit palatable because he brought the club Rick Sutcliffe and the 1984 NL East title; and **Bill Mueller** (2001–02), a class act who suffered a serious knee injury crashing into an advertising sign in St. Louis and who eventually got a World Series ring with the 2004 Red Sox.

There are pitchers worth forgetting for their terrible outings, but we remember them here: **George Riley** (1979), nick-named "Heat" for a fastball whose location was often a mystery; **Allen "Not The Talented Mr." Ripley** (1982); **Porfi Altamirano** (1984), the only major leaguer ever named "Porfi"; **Yorkis Perez** (1991), the only major league "Yorkis" and a distant relation to all the others in the pitching Perez family (Pascual, Carlos, Melido), but with none of their ability; **Tom Edens** (1995), who was not the man the Chicago-area expressway was named after; **Ramon Morel** (1997), not possessed of mushrooming talent; **Don Wengert** (1998); **Brian McNichol** (1999); and former Twins top draft pick **Dan Serafini** (1999).

Another first-round pick who wore #33 and whose potential is lamented to this day was **Lance Dickson** (1990). Two months after he was drafted from the University of Arizona, Dickson was in the major leagues, with a big looping curveball that was as good as any in the game. He began with two mediocre outings and in the third inning of his third start, something popped in his left elbow. He spent four more years trying to make it back to the majors, but he never made it past Iowa.

We'll give the final words here to **Bob Hendley** (1965–67), a left-hander of ho-hum talent who had been acquired from the Giants on May 29, 1965, the only player of any real use to either team in a trade that brought old-timers Ed Bailey and Harvey Kuenn to the Cubs, and sent Dick Bertell and Len Gabrielson to San Francisco. A little more than two months later, Hendley carved himself a permanent footnote in baseball history when he one-hit the Dodgers, allowing only one unearned run. The date was September 9, 1965 and Hendley, for whom that was his best game as a Cub, had the misfortune of pitching against Sandy Koufax the night he threw his perfect game. It still ranks as the lowest-combined-hit game in major league history.

MOST OBSCURE CUB TO WEAR #33: **Phil Mudrock** (1963). Just the name makes Mudrock worthy of recognition here. At first you'd think it was M-U-R-D-O-C-K, but no, he really was named "Mudrock," like a character out of *The Flintstones*. Originally signed by the Yankees, in whose organization he threw a no-hitter for Kearney in the Nebraska State League in 1956, the Cubs acquired Phil in the minor league draft in 1960. On the roster at the start of 1963, Mudrock came in to pitch the eighth inning on April 19 in San Francisco with the Cubs losing, 4-1. He allowed two hits and a run, committed a balk, and never again appeared in the majors.

GUY YOU NEVER THOUGHT OF AS A CUB WHO WORE #33: **Lew Burdette** (1964-65). Burdette, no relation to 1962–64 Cub Freddie Burdette (maybe the Cubs thought they were getting Lew's little brother when they signed him), was the hero and MVP of the 1957 World Series with three complete-game wins against the Yankees for the Milwaukee Braves. He won twenty for the Braves in '58 and finished third in the Cy Young voting. Burdette was the winning pitcher on May 26, 1959 when Pittsburgh's Harvey Haddix threw twelve perfect innings but lost in the thirteenth on a run-scoring hit by Joe Adcock. Burdette threw a no-hitter of his own against the Phillies on May 18, 1960. But the workload caught up with him. He was traded to the Cardinals in 1963 and to the Cubs a year later for Glen Hobbie. A shell of his former self, he was a Cub for just less than one full year: from June 2, 1964 to May 30, 1965, putting up a 9–11, 4.94 mark in thirty-five games (twenty starts). Sold to the Phillies, he had one final good year out of the bullpen for the Angels in 1966 at age thirty-nine.

One from Column A, One from Column B . . .

A total of 349 Cubs have worn more than one number during their tenure with the club. We present here the twenty-five most indecisive; those who have worn four or more different numbers during their tenure with the team. There are many different reasons for number changes; in the early days, numbers didn't seem to have the meaning they do now, so even as great a player as Stan Hack wore eight different ones, the most of any Cub.

In more recent times, number changes were dictated by different stints with the team, a player being acquired "outranking" another and forcing a number change, or simply someone wanting to change his luck.

Three players deserve special note here, because they wore three different numbers in the same season: Wimpy Quinn (4, 16, and 18 in 1941), Roberto Pena (7, 28, and 41 in 1965), and Ryan Theriot (3, 7, and 55 in 2006).

Player	Uniform Number Changes	Uniform Numbers
Stan Hack	8	6,20,25,31,34,39,49,54
Charlie Grimm	7	1,6,7,8,38,40,50
Charlie Root	6	4,12,14,17,19,49
Lon Warneke	6	12,16,17,19,32,36
Bill Lee	5	11,15,19,24,31
Clyde McCullough	5	5,8,9,10,21
Moe Thacker	5	8,19,22,23,25
Bobby Adams	4	2,7,16,51
Phil Cavarretta	4	3,23,43,44
Billy Connors	4	3,4,38,45
Red Corriden	4	19,41,51,56
Bill Fleming	4	30,32,36,46
Adrian Garrett	4	5,23,25,28
Billy Jurges	4	5,8,11,45
Pete LaCock	4	22,23,24,25
Peanuts Lowrey	4	2,7,43,47
Jim Marshall	4	2,12,25,27
Lou Novikoff	4	14,19,26,45
Will Ohman	4	13,35,45,50
Pete Reiser	4	6,7,27,46
Larry Rothschild	4	40,41,47,50
Bob Scheffing	4	10,25,33,46
El Tappe	4	2,10,52,55
Ryan Theriot	4	2,3,7,55
Jack Warner	4	33,34,38,40

#34: WE GOT WOOD

Legend.

That's what **Kerry Wood** could have been by now, after ten major league seasons, had his career not been derailed by injuries. The buzz around Kerry started even before he threw a single professional pitch. He was a high school phenom, going 12–0 with a 0.77 ERA his senior year, resulting in his being made the fourth overall selection in the 1995 amateur draft by the Cubs. Blessed with great size for a pitcher, great talent, and a great baseball name, Wood rocketed through the Cubs farm system. In the spring of 1998, Wood was clearly the best pitcher for the Cubs during training camp, but at age twenty it was felt he needed more time in Triple-A. That prompted a comment from then-Angels manager Terry Collins, who was asked shortly after Wood was reassigned to Iowa who he thought would win the World Series that year. When Collins said, "The Cubs," he was asked why. His answer: "If the Cubs have five pitchers better than Kerry Wood, they'll definitely win the World Series."

Wood's 1998 stay in Iowa lasted exactly one start—a five-inning, one-hit, eleven-strikeout performance. He was quickly recalled to make his major league debut, facing the Expos in Montreal on April 12, 1998, but his performance was less than spectacular. In four-plus innings, Wood walked three, allowing four hits and four runs in a 4-1 Cub loss.

One more bad start and two good ones later, Wood took to the mound to face the Houston Astros at Wrigley Field on on May 6, 1998. On what otherwise would have been a forgettable, mild but drizzly Wednesday afternoon, Wood's twenty-strikeout, one-hit shutout win was arguably the most dominating pitching performance in Cubs history. The only hit allowed was an infield single in the third inning by future Cub Ricky Gutierrez, which was muffed by third baseman Kevin Orie. Had a similar play occurred in the later innings, it likely would have been ruled an error by the official scorer. The only other baserunner Wood allowed was Craig Biggio, who he hit with a pitch in the sixth; it's no disgrace drilling the all-time HBP leader. When Wood later spoke to his high school coach about this game, the fact that he walked nobody was what he was most proud of, and rightfully so. Wood's masterpiece was one of the most dominating performances ever, calling to mind Sandy Koufax's fourteen-strikeout perfect game against the Cubs on September 9, 1965.

But injuries dogged Kerry even before that Rookie of the Year season ended. He missed a month, came back and threw well in the NLDS against the Braves in a series-ending loss, and then blew out his elbow with one of the first pitches he threw in spring training 1999. He had Tommy John surgery and missed the entire season—and when he returned on May 2, 2000, he not only threw six scoreless innings, but homered in his first at bat.

He could have won nineteen games in 2002 if the Cubs had a better bullpen—the pen blew seven games that Wood left in the seventh inning or later with a lead—and then he and Mark Prior dominated the NL up to the very cusp of the 2003 World Series. Wood failed in Game 7 of the NLCS, and, crying at his locker, took the blame himself. It was just another example of his leadership abilities.

Two more years filled with injuries had Kerry about to retire in mid-2007, but suddenly his arm felt better and his fastball returned. He threw well in a set-up role and was anointed the Cubs' closer to begin 2008; he had a 34 saves—a fitting number—after never having one before in his career. His one scoreless inning of relief in a Game 2 loss to the Dodgers in the 2008 division series made Wood the first Cub since Charlie Root to play in four postseasons for the team. Despite the solid performance Wood had in his first year as closer, the Cubs allowed him to leave via free agency for Cleveland at the end of the 2008 season.

Apart from Kerry Wood, there are only three other Cubs players who have sported #34 for more than four seasons, all pitchers with promise who ultimately failed. **Cal Koonce** (1962–67) made a spectacular debut in 1962, less than a year after signing a professional contract, going 10–10, 3.97 at age twenty-one. That may not sound "spectacular," but consider that the team lost 103 games, and Koonce was the only pitcher among the top five starters (who accounted for 147 of the 162 starts) without a losing record. Injuries and constant shuttles between the minors and majors befuddled him, and after never winning more than seven games in four and a half more seasons with the Cubs, Koonce was sold to the Mets, where he became an important bullpen cog in their 1969 World Series team.

After a couple of September call up years, **Ray Burris** (1973–79) burst on the scene in 1975, at age twenty-four, posting a 15-win season for a 75-victory team. When he won 15 again the next season and lowered his ERA to 3.11, hopes were high for Burris to become a solid part of the rotation for years to come. But he regressed in 1977 even as the team became, briefly, a contender; he dropped to 7–13, with a 4.76 ERA. The next year he started out in the bullpen, posting a 6.23 ERA before being traded to the Yankees for Dick Tidrow. Three years later, after a disastrous stint with the Mets, he landed in Montreal, resurrecting his career with a fine 9–7, 3.05 season for the Expos. He was in line to be the winning pitcher in the deciding game in the 1981 NLCS had the Expos managed to score one more run and had Steve Rogers not given up the winning home run to another former Cub, Rick Monday.

Steve Trout (1983–87), whose father, Dizzy, had a 0.66 ERA in two starts against the Cubs in the 1945 World Series for the Tigers, was acquired in a multiplayer deal with the White Sox before the 1983 season. Steve had a 13-win season for the 1984 NL East champions, but his carefree attitude toward playing (he was nicknamed "Rainbow," and it fit) got him traded to the Yankees just after throwing back-to-back shutouts in 1987. He was, as it turned out, almost done: he won only eight more major league games between bouts of sheer wildness.

Meanwhile, #34 was worn by quite a number of players who had seen better days elsewhere. **Mort Cooper** (1949), a three-time 20-game winner for the Cardinals earlier in the 1940s, signed with the Cubs before the 1949 season. He appeared in one game, on May 7. He walked the first batter he faced, threw a wild pitch, then gave up a single and a three-run homer. Six days later he was released. **Russ "Not the Valley of the Dolls Director" Meyer** (1956), returning to the Cubs after successful seasons in Philadelphia and Brooklyn, pitched in twenty games with a 6.32 ERA before being waived. **Dick Littlefield** (1957) was the very definition of "journeyman." The Cubs were his ninth stop on a nine-year, ten-city major league tour. **Frank Thomas** (1966), the well-traveled, 286-homer first baseman was reacquired (he had an earlier Cub tour of duty in 1960 and 1961) in an attempt to recapture the past; five at bats later he was done. **Hank Aguirre** (1969–70), formerly a fine starter for the Tigers, pitched in 58 rather pointless games in relief for the Cubs at age thirty-eight and thirty-nine.

Other #34s had only temporary stays: **Jim Ellis** (1967) pitched in just eight games as a Cub, but he did contribute to the team as part of the trade that brought Jim Hickman and Phil Regan to the North Side; **Clint Compton** (1972) had a great baseball name but only one appearance, giving up two runs in an 11-1 loss to the Phillies on October 3, 1972. **Ken Patterson** (1992) was involved, unintentionally, in one of the funniest moments in Wrigley Field history. Scheduled to start the second game of a doubleheader against the Cardinals on September 19, 1992, Patterson had to wait until film director Daniel Stern shot a scene for his movie *Rookie of the Year* between games. If you are not familiar with this film, it involves a twelve-year-old boy who suddenly develops a 100 MPH fastball following an accident. The scene featured the boy, Henry Rowengartner (played by Thomas Ian Nicholas), coming in from the bullpen for his first appearance. Stern, who also played the insane Cubs pitching coach in the film, asked the crowd to chant "Henry! Henry! Henry!" He did a couple of takes and was satisfied. When the second game began, the Cardinals hit Patterson all over the yard, upon which the crowd chanted, "Henry! Henry! Henry!" to general laughter. **Tanyon Sturtze** (1995–96) had one of the more unusual names in baseball history, but only a short Cubs career: eight appearances with a 9.00 ERA. His lone shining moment as a Cub was a four-inning shutout relief appearance on July 7, 1996, gaining him a win as the Cubs beat the Reds, 7-6, in thirteen innings.

MOST OBSCURE CUB TO WEAR #34: **John Pyecha** (1954). Pyecha got into only one major league game, against the Reds in the season's sixth game on April 24. After pitching two scoreless innings, protecting a 5-3 Cubs lead, he gave up a three-run walkoff homer to Wally Post and was shortly after sent back to the minors, never to return. Bye-cha.

GUY YOU NEVER THOUGHT OF AS A CUB WHO WORE #34: **Johnny Vander Meer** (1950). Twelve years after his back-to-back no-hitters for the Reds, the thirty-five-year-old Vander Meer was purchased by the Cubs, who, as was very typical for the 1950s, tried to squeeze lemonade out of an old lemon. Nothing remained to be squeezed. Vander Meer went 3–4, 3.79 in 32 appearances (six starts) for an 89-loss Cubs team, and the southpaw was released at the end of the season.

Da Bears and Da Little Bears

The Bears and Cubs share a species, a city, and, for half a century, shared Wrigley Field. They also have a few numbers in common. Here's a look at the thirteen retired Bears numbers—the most by any NFL team—and a looksee as to the most noteworthy Cub who wore the corresponding number. The Bears dominate the line of scrimmage from the opening whistle on this one.

Papa Bear George Halas, who briefly played major league baseball for the Yankees in 1919 before founding and starring for the Bears—or the Decatur Staleys as they were then known—was perhaps the main reason the NFL survived the Depression and thrived in the decades that followed. Two of his greatest players—Pro Football Hall of Famers #66 (Clyde "Bulldog" Turner, 1940-52) and #77 (Red Grange, 1925, 1929-34)—had numbers that have never been worn by a Cub.

For kicks, a few 2008 Bears and Cubs are included to continue the comparison for those who may not be up on their old-time Bears (and shame on you if you call yourself a Bears fan and don't know your foreBears). The Cubs have the upper hand in the present day numerical battle, though some of the best Bears don't line up against the Cubs.

#	Bears Great	Years	Best Cub to Wear Number
3	Bronko Nagurski*	1930–37, 1943	Kiki Cuyler*
5	George McAfee*	1940–41, 1945–50	Nomar Garciaparra
7	George Halas*	1920–28	Gabby Hartnett*
28	Willie Galimore	1957–63	Jim Hickman
34	Walter Payton*	1975–87	Kerry Wood
40	Gale Sayers*	1965–71	Larry Gura
41	Brian Piccolo	1966–69	Fred Norman
42	Sid Luckman*	1939–50	Bruce Sutter*
51	Dick Butkus*	1965–73	Terry Adams
56	Bill Hewitt*	1932–36	Brian McRae
61	Bill George*	1952–65	Babe Phelps
#	2008 Bear	2008 Cub	
8	Rex Grossman	Mike Quade (coach)	
9	Robbie Gould	Reed Johnson	
12	Caleb Hanie	Alfonso Soriano	
18	Kyle Orton	Geovany Soto	
22	Matt Forte	Kevin Hart	
23	Devin Hester	Not in Use, Retired for Ryne Sandberg*	
31	Nathan Vasher	Not in Use	
54	Brian Urlacher	Not in Use	
55	Lance Briggs	Not in Use	

* designates player as Hall of Famer in either Canton or Cooperstown.

#35: HI, HY, BUDDY, BO, AND TURK

It says a lot about a number when the best Cub to wear it was a coach. The great **Rogers Hornsby** wore #35 in 1958–59, returning to the Cubs more than a quarter century after being canned as player-manager (while wearing #9). In fact, #35 has endured so much mediocrity, **Chris Speier**, a .246-hitting three-time All-Star shortstop with the 1970s Giants, a reserve with the mid-1980s Cubs (wearing #28), and a coach for the last two years of the Dusty Baker regime as #35, is the most recognizable name on this list next to Rajah's. No Cub has worn #35 for more than four seasons, and that wearer, **Turk Lown** (1951–54), last wore it more than fifty years ago.

Lown pitched his first six seasons in a Cubs uniform, the first four of them wearing #35. After being a less-than effective spot starter (16–27, 4.96) his first three years, Lown spent part of '54 in the bullpen. After spending the 1955 season in the Pacific Coast League (going 12-5), Lown returned to Chicago in '56 wearing #31. He had two effective seasons as a reliever, recording 13 saves in '56 and 12 in '57, which would have ranked third both years in the NL had saves been invented then (they weren't until 1960; save totals before then have been retroactively calculated). Naturally, Lown's success got him traded away from the Cubs. He was sent to the Reds for Hersh Freeman, who pitched nine games for the Cubs before leaving baseball. Lown, meanwhile, helped lead the White Sox into the 1959 World Series, leading the AL with 15 saves.

And apart from that, #35 has been most well-known for the odd, cute, or funny names that its wearers owned. **Hi Bithorn,** who also wore #17 and #25, was the first major leaguer born in Puerto Rico; **Hy Vandenberg** (1944–45) was an effective spot starter (7–3, 3.49) for the '45 NL champs; **Buddy Schultz** (1975–76), no relation to ex-Cub Barney Schultz, put up a 6.14 ERA in 35 Cubs appearances and eventually wound up with Barney's old team, the Cardinals; and **Bo Porter,** who went 5-for-26 for the 1999 Cubs and is now the third-base coach for the Florida Marlins.

Others have worn #35 for only one season: **Jon Perlman** was the Cubs' first draft pick in 1979. He spent six years in the minors and six games in a Cubs uniform, posting an 11.42 ERA before being released. **Willie Banks** had a good year for the Twins in 1993, so naturally, that got Cubs management interested in dealing for him. He went 8–12, 5.40 for the Cubs in 1994 and switched to #27 in 1995. He is the second-best Banks in Cubs history.

And in 2000, four players wore #35, though none of them memorably. **Danny Young,** a left-hander who threw hard, made the team by having a good spring training largely because the Cubs were permitted to have an expanded roster for their Opening Day trip to Japan. Young threw three innings, walked six and struck out none and was gone by April 6. He is one of the lowest-round draft picks ever to make the majors, originally drafted in the eighty-third round by the Astros in 1991. In June 2000, **Brant Brown** was reacquired by the Cubs in a three-way trade and donned #35 for a three-game series vs. the White Sox at the Cell because his former number, 37, was then being worn by **Scott Downs.** When the Cubs returned home from their road trip to the South Side, Brown and Downs swapped shirts and Downs became the third player to wear #35 in the 97-loss 2000 season. Downs donned it for only seven starts before being traded to Montreal for Rondell White on July 31. Two weeks later it was worn by **Will Ohman,** but it would be five years before the southpaw stuck in the bigs and started racking up appearances like he would uniform numbers (#45, #50, #13).

The most fun anyone had in #35 must have been had by **Randall Simon** (2003). Acquired from the Pirates only a few weeks after a well-publicized incident in which he had "attacked" one of the Miller Park Racing Sausages in Milwaukee with his bat (he had meant it as a playful gesture, but the young woman playing the hot dog, Mandy Block, did fall over), Simon later autographed the bat for Block and, when returning to Milwaukee later that season as a member of the Cubs, bought Italian sausages for an entire section of the ballpark (many of them Cubs fans). Simon hit six homers in 33 games for the Cubs and batted .333 in 24 postseason at bats, but when the Cubs traded for Derrek Lee before the 2004 season, Simon, who could only play first base, was let go. He last appeared in the majors with Philadelphia in 2006.

MOST OBSCURE CUB TO WEAR #35: **Vicente Amor** (1955). Cubs fans didn't have very much time to "amor"—Spanish for "love"—the Cuban native, who had been acquired the previous offseason from the Oakland Oaks of the Pacific Coast League. He appeared in four games, pitching six innings and allowing three earned runs, and was then sent back to the minors. Two years later, he pitched in nine games for the Reds before vanishing from the majors forever.

GUY YOU NEVER THOUGHT OF AS A CUB WHO WORE #35: **Woodie Fryman** (1978). In a rather point-less exchange, Fryman, who had won 110 games in a dozen seasons for the Phillies, Pirates, Tigers, Expos, and Reds, was acquired on October 31, 1977 from Cincinnati in return for Bill Bonham, a hard-throwing right-hander who was supposed to be the Next Big Thing for the Cubs rotation. Bonham managed to last three years in Cincinnati before arm troubles forced him to retire at age thirty-one, but Fryman, who was already thirty-seven when the Cubs acquired him, lasted only two months in Chicago, going 2–4, 5.17 before being traded back to one of his former teams, the Expos, on June 9 for a player to be named later. The player later named on July 23 turned out to be Jerry White, who made one of the greatest catches in Wrigley Field history on August 2 against the Cardinals: a laid-out, diving grab that helped preserve a 3-2 win. Fryman, meanwhile, pitched effectively for Montreal for several more seasons including their lone playoff year in 1981, and White was also sent back to Canada, where he spent several years as a backup outfielder.

Strikeouts by the Bushel

With Fergie Jenkins as the all-time Cubs strikeout leader (2,038) and fellow #31 Greg Maddux fifth on the all-times Cubs rolls at 1,305, it only makes sense that the number leads all others in the art of fanning. With clubhouse manager Yosh Kawano favoring numbers in the thirties for pitchers, it's no wonder that the thirties dominate the list, with #35 the lone exception in the top twenty (it's a contact number, so to speak, with plenty of hitters mixed in with soft-throwing pitchers). Five numbers—again, all in the thirties—have reached the 3,000-K plateau. Another big year by Ryan Dempster and #46 could crash the party.

Uniform #	Strikeouts
31	5,071
30	3,269
32	3,216
34	3,062
36	3,034
46	2,836
49	2,632
38	2,431
37	2,379
40	2,332
48	2,320
33	2,277
17	1,845
39	1,680
22	1,585
44	1,534
43	1,516
45	1,476
18	1,287
47	1,286

#36: SARGE

Gary "Sarge" Matthews (1984–87) was among the most popular Cubs of his time, despite arriving on the scene late in his career, presumably washed-up, and initially viewed warily by Cubs fans who thought he was just another faded former Phillie brought over by Dallas Green for old times' sake.

Matthews, a speedster with mid-range power as a Giant and Brave in the 1970s, had declined to a .258 average with only ten home runs for the 1983 NL champion Phillies, and though he earned NLCS MVP honors that autumn with three homers against L.A., he hit only .250 as the Phillies dropped the World Series to the Orioles. So when Green came calling at the end of spring training in 1984, after the Cubs had lost thirteen straight exhibition games and were desperately seeking help, the Phillies were more than willing to send Matthews and Bob Dernier to Chicago for another faded former star, reliever Bill Campbell, and a minor leaguer, Mike Diaz, who never played in a game for Philadelphia.

The "Sarge" got his nickname from the salutes he gave to the left-field bleacherites who applauded him every time he came to his position; he arranged one day for painters' caps with sergeant stripes to be distributed in the bleachers. While that will certainly make a player popular at Wrigley, Matthews earned his stripes with his bat—he started fast with a .339 April average—and fans loved his aggressive play in the outfield and on the basepaths. He drew 103 walks—the most for a Cub since Richie Ashburn walked 116 times in 1960—and Matthews led the league in that category and in on-base percentage (.410). His 101 runs ranked fifth in the NL and he also finished fifth in MVP voting behind Ryne Sandberg, as the Cubs took the NL East title.

It was a final hurrah. Injured much of the next two years, his perform-ance tailed off and, some say, with it the Cubs' fortunes. Matthews was eventually shipped to Seattle for a minor leaguer, but we will never forget Sarge's wonderful 1984 season.

DON ELSTON   pitcher

Other than Matthews and **Koyie Hill,** who wore both #36 and #55 during his brief tenure with the club in 2007 (and who stuck with #55 when recalled in September 2008), #36 has been worn exclusively by pitchers since 1950, when **Johnny Klippstein** first donned it. Klippstein had some promise, putting up decent years for pretty bad teams from 1950 to 1953. But when he had a bad year in 1954, he was shipped to Cincinnati for three players who had little impact. Eventually Klippstein became a good middle reliever for several teams in the 1960s, pitching in two World Series (for the 1959 Dodgers and 1965 Twins). **Don Elston** wore Klippstein's #36 briefly at the end of the 1953 season under the "If the Shirt Fits, He Wears It" theory then in place for the Cubs. Klippstein didn't pitch after August 17 and Elston threw in two late-season games, but Elston got #36 back when he returned to the Cubs to stay in 1957. Elston had sev-eral seasons as a workhorse reliever and "closer" (before the current definition of the term), putting up 63 saves and having one All-Star appearance in eight Cubs seasons through 1964.

Bob Humphreys pitched most of his nine-year career for the Washington Senators, but his one year as a Cub (1965) was effective; his odd "side-saddle" pitching motion produced a 3.15 ERA in 41 appearances. Humphreys had been scheduled to wear #39 for the North Siders, but when the Cubs acquired Ted Abernathy the day before Opening Day in 1965, Abernathy claimed the number he had worn in Cleveland and Humphreys was reassigned #36.

Bill Stoneman (1967–68) threw two no-hitters as an Expo and later built a world championship team as Angels GM, but his two years in Chicago were pretty forgettable. **Joe Decker** (1969–71) was another prospect who never made it; he and Bill Hands were shipped to the Twins for Dave LaRoche after the 1972 season. Others who wore #36 with little distinction in the 1970s and 1980s were **Tom Phoebus** (1972); **Bob Locker** (1973, 1975)—yet another reliever who had his better years for other teams; **Horacio Pina** (1974); **Ramon Hernandez** (1976–77); **Bill Caudill** (1979–81), one of several relievers for the 1979 team who had success as a closer elsewhere (the Cubs did have this guy named Sutter); and **Mike Proly** (1982–83) rounds out this group.

Starting pitchers had more success wearing #36. After "The Sarge" departed, #36 returned to being a pitcher's number, and three starting pitchers wore it with some distinction. **Mike Bielecki** (1988–91), a former first-round draft pick of the Pirates who had never made it with them, was acquired by the Cubs for a minor leaguer before the 1988 season. After rusting in the bullpen that year, manager Don Zimmer put him in the rotation in 1989 and he responded with an eighteen-win season, helping lead the Cubs to the NL East title. Bielecki, a terrible hitter (.043, with 35 strikeouts in 70 at bats during the 1989 regular season), had a two-run single in the Cubs' six-run first inning in Game 2 of the 1989 NLCS vs. the Giants, but he couldn't last on the mound long enough to get the victory in that game, the only one the Cubs won in the series. He finished ninth in the Cy Young voting, but injuries and ineffectiveness made that his one year in the sun; he was dealt to Atlanta in 1991.

Mike Morgan, who set the major league record for most teams played for with twelve, had two stints with the Cubs; in his first, wearing #36 from 1992–95, he posted a 16–8, 2.55 season in '92. During that season he gave a nod to baseball history; on June 21 he was the Cubs starter in Philadelphia on a day when the Phillies were hosting a "Turn

Back the Clock" day. Wearing a Cubs uniform from the 1940s, Morgan threw his first pitch with an old-fashioned 1940s style windmill windup. Morgan's baseball odyssey brought him back to the Cubs in 1998; he had to wear #38 because **Kevin Tapani** (1997–2001) had claimed #36 the year before, when he was signed as a free agent. Injuries limited Tapani to just thirteen starts in 1997, but he went 9–3, 3.39, portending a better year in '98, and he delivered, although his 4.85 ERA was a bit unsightly. He won nineteen games, the most for a Cub since Greg Maddux won twenty in 1992, and he threw nine outstanding innings in Game 2 of the NLDS against the Braves. Unfortunately, the Cubs scored only once that night, and with one out in the ninth, Javy Lopez homered off Tapani to tie the game, which the Braves won in ten innings.

Of the old-time Cubs who wore #36, perhaps the best known is **Eddie Waitkus** (1946–48), who had three solid seasons as the Cubs' first baseman. Naturally, he was traded away to have his best years elsewhere. Looking at his career statistics, you might wonder why he played in only 54 games in his first season with the Phillies in 1949. He wasn't injured playing baseball—he was shot by a young Chicago woman, Ruth Ann Steinhagen, who had become obsessed with him when he played for the Cubs. She checked in to the Edgewater Beach Hotel, where visiting teams then stayed, when the Phillies first came to town in June 1949, and summoned Waitkus to her room on a ruse. She then shot him. Waitkus nearly died, but he eventually recovered and played several more seasons. The story—eerily similar to what happened to Cub Billy Jurges in 1932—served as the basis for Bernard Malamud's novel *The Natural*; naturally the names, teams and details were changed.

MOST OBSCURE CUB TO WEAR #36: **Jim Kirby** (1949). You're saying, "Who?" and so were we. Kirby appeared in three games, recording two at bats and one hit, a single. He never played in the field. He wore #36 from May 1–13, 1949. The contemporary newspaper statistics have him scoring a run, but baseball-reference.com doesn't. He was sent to a minor league club in Nashville on May 18 and was later optioned to Dallas; he was sold outright to that club on September 16 and never returned to the major leagues. And now you know everything there is to know about the obscure major league life of James Herschel Kirby.

GUY YOU NEVER THOUGHT OF AS A CUB WHO WORE #36: **Robin Roberts** (1966). Here's one you could win a bar bet with: The 1966 Cubs lost 103 games. How many Hall of Famers played for that team? The answer is "four," and most people are going to think you're including Ron Santo, who should be in but isn't. But if Santo finally does make it, that'll make *five* Hall enshrinees from a last-place team. The other four are Ernie Banks, Billy Williams, Fergie Jenkins, and Roberts, yet another faded star the Cubs attempted to re-shine. As recently as 1964, at age thirty-seven, Roberts had put together a fine 13–7, 2.91 year with the Orioles. But when the Cubs acquired him on July 13, 1966 following his release by Houston, he was thirty-nine and done. He appeared made nine starts as a Cub, went 2–3, and became the only pitcher in major league history to allow 500 home runs in a career (as the saying goes, "You have to be good to do that.") Ten years later he was enshrined in Cooperstown—NOT wearing a Cubs cap.

For Appearances' Sake

As we said in chapter 31, if you had a game to win and you were to call a Cubs number out to win it for you, it would be #31. It makes sense. Number 31 has the most wins by a landslide, so why wouldn't you call for that number with the game on the line? And if #31's already in the game and getting fatigued, the odds are you'd wave in #36. In might trot Kevin Tapani, Mike Bielecki, Mike Morgan, or Don Elston, who appeared in 448 games as a Cub, third most on the all-time club list and all while wearing #36. Or if #31 is Fergie Jenkins or Greg Maddux, you might want to stick with them for another batter.

Uniform #	Games
31	1,698
36	1,619
32	1,492
38	1,340
34	1,296
33	1,284
46	1,262
45	1,240
37	1,224
30	1,207
49	1,201
41	1,095
48	1,027
47	964
39	962
40	960
44	956
43	945
35	914
17	869

#37: ERICKSON AND ELLSWORTH

In 1963, a tall left-hander won 22 games, had an ERA of 2.11, and led his team in complete games and strikeouts. Sandy Koufax? No, **Dick Ellsworth** (1960–66), who just the year before had lost twenty for a horrid 103-loss Cubs team. But in '63, at age twenty-three, he burst on the national scene. There weren't separate NL/AL Cy Young Awards at the time (that wouldn't happen until 1967, and Koufax won the '63 CYA unanimously, but had there been second-place voting, it surely would have gone to Ellsworth). So the Cubs had their dominant lefty for a decade or more, right?

Unfortunately, wrong. Ellsworth's ERA increased to 3.75 in 1964, when he finished 14–18. By 1966 he was a twenty-game loser again (8–22, for yet another 103-loss team; Ellsworth and Cal Koonce were the only pitchers to throw a full season for both 103-loss Cubs teams). Six straight 200-plus inning seasons had taken a toll on Ellsworth's arm; the Cubs shipped him to Philadelphia after the '66 season for **Ray Culp** (8–11 as #37 in '67, his lone Cubs season). Ellsworth spent the rest of his baseball life as a spot starter/middle reliever, and was done at age thirty-one. After his retirement he returned to his hometown of Fresno, California, where he had a successful career in commercial real estate;

in 2005 he became a partner in the group that now owns the Fresno Grizzlies of the Pacific Coast League.

Apart from Ellsworth, #37 is another number that hasn't been worn by many successful Cubs players. The only other two to wear it for more than three years are **Paul Erickson** (1943–48), a good middle reliever/spot starter (seeing a pattern here?) for the 1945 NL champions, and **Gene Baker** (1953–57), the nearly-forgotten "second black player" for the Cubs, called up with Ernie Banks primarily because in the less-enlightened 1950s, African-American players had to be called up in pairs so that they'd have a roommate on the road. Baker had three good years as Banks's DP partner before he was sent to the Pirates along with Dee Fondy, for Lee Walls and Dale Long.

Most of the rest can be classified by two types. Retreads: **Dewey Adkins,** acquired in 1949, six years after his last major league stint in Washington at age thirty-one, posted a 5.68 ERA; **Steve Hamilton,** a 4.76 ERA in 22 appearances in 1972, long after his World Series days with the Yankees were over; and **Doug "Up The" Creek,** who posted a 10.50 ERA in three games in 1999. And never-weres: **Jack Cusick,** .177 in 64 games in 1951; **Vern Fear,** no fear from NL hitters for his 7.88 ERA in eight 1952 innings; **Earl Stephenson,** 4.43 in 16 games in 1971—at least he produced by being part of the deal that brought Jose Cardenal to Chicago; **Willie Prall,** who started three games at the end of the lost 1975 season with an 8.59 ERA; and **Bill Johnson,** another of Dallas Green's ex-Phillie pick ups, who posted a 3.59 ERA in 14 games in 1983 and 1984 and then vanished.

For a time it seemed as if #37 was reserved as the "Number Given to Former White Sox Players Who Became Cubs." In the 1980s and 1990s, no fewer than three former South Siders—**Ken Kravec, Bill Long,** and **Greg Hibbard**—all donned #37. Until Ted Lilly won 15 games in 2007 and 17 in 2008, Hibbard stood as the only Cubs left-hander to win that many games in a season since Kenny Holtzman had 17 wins in 1970. Chicago native **Erik Pappas,** one of the few non-pitchers to wear #37, went 3-for-17 in 1991. Pappas was later traded to the White Sox—by Kansas City—but he never played on the South Side. He is noted for being the second-best Pappas to wear a Cubs uniform.

Brant Brown, known to some as "the poor man's Mark Grace," burst on the scene with a walkoff homer against the White Sox on June 5, 1998. Later that year he was responsible for one of the dark moments of that wild-card winning year when, on September 23, he dropped what would have been a game-ending fly ball to cost the Cubs a game in Milwaukee, prompting broadcaster Ron Santo to utter the immortal words, "Oh, NOOOOOOOOOOOOO!" on the air. Brown hit 14 homers in '98 but was sent to the Pirates after the season. Reacquired in 2000, he had to wear #35 for one series—ironically enough, against the White Sox on the road—until he could swap numbers with pitcher **Scott Downs.**

Since Downs's trade to Montreal a few weeks after his number swap with Brown, more middle (and middling) relievers have worn #37: **Mike Remlinger** (2003–05) wasn't quite the All-Star reliever they paid for, but the lefty did pitch 156 times in less than three years as a Cub; **Jermaine Van Buren** (2005), no relation to the eighth President, could throw hard but couldn't throw strikes; and its latest occupant, **Angel Guzman** (2006–08), had talent but couldn't stay healthy, spending most of his Cubs career on and off disabled lists.

MOST OBSCURE CUB TO WEAR #37: **Manny Seoane** (1978). Acquired on October 25, 1977 in trade from the Phillies for one of the most popular Cubs of the 1970s, Jose Cardenal, Cubs fans had high hopes for the twenty-three-year-old right-hander. Instead, they got one start, in the second game of a doubleheader, on September 3, 1978; Seoane went only an inning and a third, allowing three walks and three hits in a game the Cubs eventually won, 4-2. Six relief appearances later, he was sent back to the minors, never returning to the Cubs.

GUY YOU NEVER THOUGHT OF AS A CUB WHO WORE #37: **Ed Lynch** (1986-87). This may seem a strange choice, as Lynch was a Cubs pitcher for a season and a half and also served as the team's general manager from 1994–2000. But to most Cubs fans, the enduring memory of Lynch was as the Mets pitcher who threw at Keith Moreland during a memorable August doubleheader in 1984, sparking a bench-clearing brawl. He wasn't very good as GM, either, trading then-minor leaguer and future solid starter Jon Garland for what remained of Matt Karchner's talent (not much), and on August 23, 1999, forcing the Cubs and Giants to sit with the tarp on the field for two hours *while it wasn't raining.* They easily could have gotten an official game in, but when the skies finally did open up the postponement cost the Cubs the revenue from a sellout crowd. He was fired in the middle of the following season.

Loss Leaders

Since #31 leads all numbers in Cubs history in terms of pitching wins, games, strikeouts, and walks, it only makes sense that it also holds the lead in losses. Fergie Jenkins (132) and Greg Maddux (112) combined for 244 losses for #31, more than half of the "Ls" absorbed by the number. Still, those two #31 aces' winning percentage for the Cubs is a combined .551. Given the ups and downs of the Cubs during the forty-year window that began with Jenkins throwing his first pitch as a Cub in 1966 and Maddux tossing his last in the blue pinstripes in 2006, that's quite a percentage. But you can't win 'em all.

Uniform #	Losses	Uniform #	Losses
31	447	40	203
32	344	38	178
30	310	39	165
36	289	44	149
34	264	18	146
46	245	47	146
33	242	45	137
37	241	13	133
49	231	22	122
48	218	53	119

#38: Z!

Well he went down to dinner in his Sunday best
Excitable boy, they all said
And he rubbed the pot roast all over his chest
Excitable boy, they all said
Well he's just an excitable boy...
—Warren Zevon, "Excitable Boy"

Rubbing pot roast on his chest is about the *only* thing the very excitable **Carlos Zambrano** (2001–08) hasn't done on the pitcher's mound.

We're exaggerating here, of course. Z's exuberant nature—and we're talking about Zambrano, not the late Mr. Zevon—his histrionics on the mound, his clear passion for playing baseball, are all things that make him the exciting player we all love to watch, the pitcher who's already, at age twenty-seven, a dominant force in the major leagues. But he's also the guy who infuriates us when he breaks bats over his leg after striking out, or stomps off the pitcher's mound like a petulant child when being removed. Z's talent is monumental, as shown by the no-hitter he threw on September 14, 2008, one of the most dominant pitching performances ever by a Cubs pitcher.

Z first came to the majors on August 20, 2001, debuting just two months past his twentieth birthday to become the first player born in the 1980s to reach the

CARLOS ZAMBRANO

major leagues. Struggling at first as a reliever, he didn't pitch consistently until manager Don Baylor put him in the starting rotation, ironically, only a few days before Baylor was fired in July 2002. (That's the only legacy of Baylor for which Cubs fans can thank him.) Z immediately took to starting. Though posting only a 4–8 record in 16 starts in 2002, he had a 3.68 ERA and struck out ten Astros on July 20.

Z went 13–11, 3.11 in 2003, and had a memorable confrontation with Barry Bonds at Wrigley Field on July 31 after fanning Bonds. Z went off the field pumping his fists and pounding his chest and threw the ball into the stands. Afterwards Zambrano was quoted as saying: "Well, I just try to be myself. I don't try to embarrass anybody. He's a big man in baseball. It was a situation that was a big deal in the game. I was happy."

Bonds's response? "I don't get upset about things like that, brother. He will learn respect eventually. I promise you. He'll learn respect, I guarantee that."

Major league hitters learned to respect Z over the next several seasons, but not before he had a meltdown in Game 5 of the 2003 NLCS. He had to be yanked with the Cubs down 2-0 after five innings, because he had walked four and thrown 113 pitches (a pattern that would repeat itself, disturbingly, far too often in the next few years). To be fair, no one was going to hit Josh Beckett that day—he threw a two-hit shutout—but Z had a chance to clinch the pennant for the Cubs and failed.

He hasn't failed too many other times, though, posting ninety-six career wins in his first eight seasons, making three All-Star teams and being considered the ace of the Cubs staff, culminating with the no-hitter. Cubs fans only wish he'd harness his tremendous energy and talent into his pitching, instead of the histrionics.

Before Z's time, #38 was the forgotten stepchild of Cubs numbers. Only one other player—**Willie Hernandez** (1977–83)—wore it for more than two seasons. Guillermo "Willie" Hernandez, a hard-throwing lefty, was infuriating: he'd be dominant for a while, then totally hittable. In his rookie year, 1977, he had a 3.03 ERA, but he also gave up 11 homers in 110 innings, all in relief save for one start Herman Franks gave him against the Cardinals on September 6. He threw well in that start, but Hernandez got scant hitting support and the Cubs lost, 3-1. After several more up-and-down years, Dallas Green finally soured on Hernandez and sent him to the Phillies in another one of his "Philly Shuttle" deals, acquiring one of his personal favorites, Dick Ruthven. The Phillies should have hung on to him; instead, just before the 1984 season, they sent him to the Tigers for John Wockenfuss and Glenn Wilson, both useful players—but Hernandez helped the Tigers to the world championship and won both the AL Cy Young and MVP awards. Come to think of it, the '84 Cubs could have used him, too.

The rest of the #38s can be separated into three different groups. There's the short-timers in the World War II era: **Dick Barrett** (1943), **Mickey Livingston** (1943), **Garth Mann** (1944), **Mack Stewart** (1944–45), **Johnny Moore** (1945, a return wartime engagement at age forty-three, Moore had been one of the first Cubs to wear a number, donning #5 in 1932), and **Ray Starr** (1945), several of whom also wore other numbers. Then there's the collection of guys who were better for other teams, either long before or long after they were Cubs: **John Buzhardt** (1959), **Jim Brewer** (1962–63), **Bobby Tiefenauer** (1968), **Don Nottebart** (1969), **Jack Aker** (1972–73), **Geoff Zahn** (1975–76), **Jeff Robinson** (1992), and **Jaime Navarro** (1995–96), who actually had two good years for the Cubs but had seen his better days for the Brewers. And there were prospects and suspects who never made it: **Bob Zick** (1954), **Seth Morehead** (1960), **Jack Warner** (1962), **Dick Scott** and **John Flavin** (both in 1964 and both with an ERA north of ten), **Rick James** (1967), **Ron Tompkins** (1971), **Tom Grant** (1983), **Ron Meridith** (1984–85), **Mike Capel** (1988), whose main claim to fame was that he was a college teammate of Roger Clemens's at Texas, **Dean "No Relation To Rick" Wilkins** (1989–90), **Randy "Not The *Seinfeld* Character" Kramer** (1990), **Dave Swartzbaugh** (1997), and **Manny Aybar** (2001).

There are three other stories worth telling among the #38 slugs. **Roe Skidmore** (1970), a native of downstate Decatur, is one of the few major leaguers to retire with a perfect 1.000 batting average. Acquired from the Giants in the 1968 minor league draft, Skidmore was sent up to pinch-hit for pitcher Joe Decker in the seventh inning on September 17, 1970, with the Cubs trailing, 8-1. He singled, and was forced at second to end the inning. Despite being sent to the White Sox, Reds, Cardinals, Astros and Red Sox in various deals over the next four years, that was his only major league plate appearance.

Jose Bautista (1993–94) was born in the Dominican Republic and had four so-so years for the Orioles before the Cubs signed him as a free agent at the end of the 1992 season. He had one good year ('93) and one not-quite-so-good ('94), but his background is the most interesting part of his story. He is the son of a Dominican father and an Israeli mother, and he and his family are apparently quite observant Jews. When asked about his faith, Bautista told the *Village Voice*: "My family and I go to synagogue when we can and we pray every Friday. We fast on Yom Kippur and not only do I not pitch, I don't even go to the ballgame."

Finally, **Darcy Fast** (1968) had a name that seemed destined for fame; it's a great baseball name, especially for a pitcher, although his full name (Darcy Rae Fast) seemed as if his parents expected a girl rather than a boy. Fast, a left-hander, was selected in the sixth round of the 1967 draft and a year later was in the major leagues; he pitched in eight games, starting one, and posted a 5.40 ERA at age twenty-one. Hopes were high for him to be in the 1969 rotation or bullpen—except for one thing. Uncle Sam called him up first. He was drafted into the Army, and though the Cubs tried to get him an exemption by sending him back to college to finagle a student deferment or getting him into the National Guard, there was some sensitivity to that sort of thing—athletes getting preferential treatment—and so he spent 1969 in a military uniform rather than a Cubs uniform. He tried to come back in 1970 but hurt his arm and was traded to the Padres. When he submitted his voluntary retirement papers from baseball at age twenty-four, commissioner Bowie Kuhn sent him a letter telling him he was one of the youngest, if not the youngest, to ever do so. Eventually he went into the ministry; Cubs fans are left to wonder what might have been had Darcy Rae Fast been in Leo Durocher's bullpen on the fateful day of September 7, 1969, when Willie Stargell stepped to the plate in Wrigley Field with two out and a victory on the line.

MOST OBSCURE CUB TO WEAR #38: **Garth Mann** (1944). Though a pitcher by trade, Mann's only major league appearance came as a pinch runner in the second game of a doubleheader at Wrigley Field on May 14, 1944. The Cubs had lost the first game to the Dodgers 4-2 to drop to a 2–16 record, already twelve games out of first place only eighteen games into the season. Mann ran for Lou Novikoff, who had led off the eighth inning with a single. After Bill Nicholson doubled him to third, Mann scored on an Andy Pafko single. The Cubs won the game, 8-7. Six days later, Mann was sent back to the minors. He was recalled later in the season and issued #45, but never again appeared in a major league game.

GUY YOU NEVER THOUGHT OF AS A CUB WHO WORE #38: **Rick Aguilera** (1999-2000). When Rod Beck went down with an injury in early 1999, the Cubs, then considering themselves contenders (and they were, peaking at 32–23, only a game out of first place on June 8, 1999), felt they needed an "established" closer. So they sent two minor leaguers to the Twins for Aguilera, who had posted 281 saves for the Twins, Red Sox, and Mets and who had played for two World Series winners. Aguilera was awful. He blew a save to the Marlins in spectacular fashion in his second Cubs appearance, capped by a three-run homer hit by Kevin Millar, and "Aggie" (could that nickname be short for "Aggravating"?) was routinely booed after that. Though he posted 37 saves in a Cubs uniform—including the 300th of his career—he also had 13 blown saves and a 4.31 ERA. The guy the Twins were after in the deal was Jason Ryan, at the time the Cubs' top pitching prospect. But they asked for another pitcher as a "throw-in"—and that was Kyle Lohse. Ryan pitched in only 16 major league games with a 1–5, 5.94 mark, but Lohse became a solid rotation starter and is still active, winning 15 games for the Cardinals in 2008.

No-No Numbers

The Cubs have thrown fifteen no-hitters in franchise history. Eight of those came before the Cubs wore numbers, including three by Larry Corcoran in the early 1880s. That doesn't count the nine-plus hitless innings by Bob Wicker (1904) and Hippo Vaughn (1917) because they did not finish those games with no-hitters. It's not fair, but them's the rules.

Seven Cubs no-hitters have come since the numbers first went on the uniforms in 1932, from the Toothpick (Sam Jones) to El Toro (Carlos Zambrano). The only number worn for more than one Cubs no-no is #30 because Kenny Holtzman tossed both. All were thrown at Wrigley Field except for Holtzman's second—in Cincinnati—and Zambrano's 2008 no-hitter, the first indoor Cubs no-no. The game took place at Milwaukee's Miller Park after the Astros were forced to host two games there because of Hurricane Ike.

#	Pitcher	Opponent	Score	Date
#22	Sam Jones	Pirates	4-0	May 12, 1955
#43	Don Cardwell	Cardinals	4-0	May 15, 1960
#30	Kenny Holtzman	Braves	3-0	August 19,1969
#30	Kenny Holtzman	Reds	1-0	June 3, 1971
#44	Burt Hooton	Phillies	4-0	April 16, 1972
#32	Milt Pappas	Padres	8-0	September 2, 1972
#38	Carlos Zambrano	Astros	5-0	September 14, 2008

#39: ABBY, KRUKE, AND SOUP

Ted Abernathy's signature submarine pitching motion has been implemented over the years by several successful relief pitchers, notably Dan Quisenberry, and today Chad Bradford, whose knuckles occasionally scrape the ground. For Abernathy, the underhanded motion was adopted out of necessity, not choice. He had shoulder surgery and after a few attempts to make the Washington Senators in the late 1950s, he spent two years in the minors reinventing himself as a reliever.

For one spectacular season—1965, after the Cubs purchased his contract from the Indians—Abernathy was virtually unhittable. Posting a 2.57 ERA, he threw what today would be an unheard-of 136.1 innings in relief. His record total of 31 saves is modest by the standards of today, where his long-surpassed mark was doubled by Francisco Rodriguez of the Angels in 2008. "Abby" was the first pitcher to save 30 games in a season; the record of 29 had been set in 1961, but as recently as 1949, Firpo Marberry's retroactive (because the save wasn't made an official stat until 1969) record of 22 had stood since the 1920s.

Abernathy was a pioneer—he wasn't used as modern closers are, pitching only in the ninth inning with a lead—but he was

Ted Abernathy | PITCHER

among the first pitchers to be used exclusively to close out or "save" games. His 84 appearances set a major league record, and he was only the second pitcher since 1900 to pitch in more than the nineteenth century record of 76—back when 76 games meant *76 games started* (or, technically, 75 starts and one relief appearance, by Will White in 1879 and matched by Pud Galvin in 1883, but you get the idea). Abernathy's 84 games broke Bill Hutchinson's franchise record of 75 appearances (70 starts) set in 1892; Abernathy's mark is still the team record (it's been tied twice, by Dick Tidrow in 1980 and Bob Howry in 2006). It was a spectacular year by Abernathy—for a ninety-loss Cubs team.

But when Abby got off to a bad start in 1966, the Cubs figured he was done at age thirty-three, and dumped him to the Braves, who in turn shipped him to Cincinnati—where he had two fine years in 1967 and 1968. That prompted the Cubs to reacquire him for what we'd now consider a set-up role to Phil Regan, this go-around wearing #37.

Most of the other players to wear #39—virtually all pitchers—were short-timers with the club. One notable exception was **Mike Krukow,** who came up through the Cubs farm system and first made the rotation at age twenty-five in 1977. Solid but unspectacular, he was basically a .500 pitcher for the North Siders and was sent to the Phillies by Dallas Green before the 1982 season in one of several deals with his old club. Later traded to the Giants, he has made his home in the Bay Area and become one of the better broadcasters in the game, for Giants TV.

The Krukow deal made room for #39 to be worn by **Bill "Soup" Campbell,** he of one of the more contrived nicknames in recent baseball history (really—they couldn't do better than "Campbell Soup"?). Several years removed from some big winning and saving years for the Twins and Red Sox (17 wins, 20 saves in 1976; 13 wins, 31 saves in 1977), Campbell was supposed to be the Cubs' closer . . . but Green hadn't counted on Lee Smith grabbing that job by the horns. Relegated to a set-up role, Campbell's sour countenance mirrored his play.

A 4.49 ERA in 1983 got him traded to—where else?—Philadelphia, as part of the deal that brought Gary Matthews and Bob Dernier to the Cubs, two key parts of the '84 NL East champions.

Another pitcher, **Ray Prim,** would be a forgotten footnote in Cubs history had he not had one of those seasons that historians would say was made possible by a "war-weakened" league. Prim went 13–8, 2.40 for the 1945 NL champions, leading the NL in ERA. He was thirty-eight years old and hadn't pitched in the majors in eight years before the war, and didn't pitch in the '45 World Series. His ERA ballooned to 5.79 in '46 and he retired.

The only significant non-pitcher to wear #39 was **Roy Smalley**, whose son, Roy Jr., had a thirteen-year career mostly in the AL, hitting 163 homers. Roy Sr. had power, too. His 21 homers in 1950 helped the Cubs to total of 161, good for second in the league. Roy Sr. also made 51 errors in '50, which led the league, and made Cubs fans with a wicked sense of humor say that the seventh-place club's double play combination was "Miksis to Smalley to Addison Street."

The usual lists of prospects/suspects include **Chuck Tanner** (1957), later better known as a major league manager; **Paul "Four Games of the" Jaeckel** (1964); **Archie Reynolds** (1968, 1970), the only Cub ever named "Archie"; **Jose Nunez** (1990), who had a 2.57 ERA in eleven relief appearances but a 7.71 ERA when then placed in the rotation; **Laddie Renfroe** (1991), the only Cub ever named "Laddie"; **Scott May** (1991), not the former NBA player—and not much of a pitcher, either, with an 18.00 ERA in two games; **Eddie Zambrano** (1993), the second banana Zambrano; and **Robin Jennings** (1996), the only major leaguer born in Singapore. Three players playing out the string were **Monte Irvin** (1956), **Curt Simmons** (1966–67), and **Ellie Hendricks** (1972), each of whom prompt the question, "*He* played for the Cubs?" Yes, they did: Irvin and Simmons spent their final major league seasons at Wrigley while Hendricks played briefly in 1972 (batting .116) before making a U-turn and being traded back to Baltimore, from whence he came, two months after he arrived. **Willie Greene** (2000), who never played in the majors again after hitting .201 in 299 at bats for that 97-loss team, rounds out the list of 39ers.

Pitcher **Dick Selma** (1969) deserves special mention because, despite spending less than one season on the North Side, he will be remembered in Wrigley Field lore forever for his antics with the Bleacher Bums. The Bums, in those days a quasi-organized yellow-helmeted group in left field, befriended Selma, who used to lead them in cheers. From his acquisition in late April 1969 through August 17, Selma went 10–2 with a 2.96 ERA and it looked like the twenty-five-year-old would be a Cub for years to come. But Selma got himself into Leo Durocher's doghouse permanently when he made an attempted pickoff throw toward Ron Santo on September 11, 1969 in Philadelphia—only Santo wasn't covering the base. The Phillies tied the game and eventually won it, giving the Cubs their eighth loss in a row. Selma was sent, ironically, to the Phillies along with Oscar Gamble for Johnny Callison before the 1970 season in one of the Cubs' worst deals of the time.

MOST OBSCURE CUB TO WEAR #39: **Tony Balsamo** (1962). Sounding more like a character from *The Sopranos*, Balsamo was one of the revolving-door pitchers who pitched for the revolving College of Coaches in the horrid 1962 season. Balsamo, who played college ball at Fordham, never pitched in a winning major league game. Pitching entirely in April, May, and June, he was the very definition of mop-up man, earning only one decision (a loss in a thirteen-inning game to the horrid Mets on May 15). The Cubs were outscored 165-77 in his eighteen appearances.

GUY YOU NEVER THOUGHT OF AS A CUB WHO WORE #39: **Hoyt Wilhelm** (1970). You can win trivia contests with this one. Hall of Famer Wilhelm, who is the only player to hit a homer in his first major league at bat and never hit another one, pitched in three games for the 1970 Cubs, who picked him up off waivers with ten games left in the season. Several years removed from his successful years as a White Sox reliever, the forty-seven-year-old Wilhelm threw mop-up duty in three losses and then was sent to Atlanta; he had two more major league years left with the Braves and Dodgers.

How 'Bout Them Colts?

One thing you need to know about the Cubs is that they are old. That's not a dig on the advancing age of Jon Lieber or Jim Edmonds, the two most senior Cubs in 2008. We're talking about the franchise.

The Cubs, along with the Braves, are the oldest existing franchises in baseball, dating to 1871 (the National League was founded in 1876). In the early years, the Braves—then in Boston—were referred to as the Red Stockings and the Cubs were the White Stockings. By 1901 the Cubs had abandoned "White Stockings," and so the upstart American League franchise granted to Chicago that year took it as its own, to trade off the popularity of the Chicago National League Ball Club; the name had a decent enough ring to still be in use today (albeit shortened to "Sox") in that nouveau 108-year-old AL.

Sports nicknames weren't as much a part of the culture in the nineteenth century as they are in the twenty-first. The team was often called the Chicagos on the road and by a range of names when at home, including Remnants, Babes, Rainmakers, Recruits, Orphans, Cowboys, and Broncos. Colts was perhaps the most popular and Orphans the most memorable; they were called the latter after legendary first baseman and manager Cap Anson was discharged following the 1897 season.

The team's home shifted almost as often as its nickname: Union Street Grounds (1871), 23rd Street Grounds (1874–77), two versions of Lakefront Park (1878–84), West Side Park (1885–1891), South Side Park—gasp! (1891–1893), and West Side Grounds, where the franchise had its greatest years from 1893 until they moved into Weeghman Park in 1916. The park changed monikers to Wrigley Field a decade later, but the Cubs name stayed.

Keep in mind that all these names came to pass before a Cub ever donned a uniform number. The number they were predominantly known as were the Chicago nine. And Chicagoans, whether in suits and bowler caps or floppy hats without any shirt, have always loved 'em.

#40: 16-1!

When **Rick Sutcliffe** (1984–91) was acquired by the Cubs from the Indians just before the then-trading deadline of June 15, 1984, most Cubs fans scratched their heads. Sutcliffe? The guy who had overturned Tommy Lasorda's desk at Dodger Stadium when removed from the rotation for pitching badly? The guy who had started the '84 season 4–5, 5.15 for the then-moribund franchise in Cleveland?

Sutcliffe immediately proved Cubs fans (and Indians management, though they got many productive years out of Joe Carter) wrong. He threw eight innings against the Pirates and won 4-3 in his first Cubs start, and then, five days later—the day after the famous "Sandberg Game"— on June 24, he threw a five-hit shutout against  the Cardinals, striking out fourteen, and had Cubs fans standing and cheering, thinking perhaps it was to be something special.

It was. Sutcliffe kept winning . . . and winning . . . and winning. The only game he lost in a Cubs uniform in '84 was the start following that 14-K gem; it was against Lasorda and the Dodgers, and Rick admitted that he was overthrowing, trying far too hard to beat his old team. He threw six more complete games and two more shutouts and on

September 3, he struck out fifteen Phillies, tying the then-club record set by Dick Drott in 1957 and tied by Burt Hooton in 1971. His 20–6 record made him only the second pitcher at that time to win twenty games combined (16–1 in the NL, 4–5 in the AL) between both leagues—and the other, Hank Borowy in 1945, had led the Cubs to a pennant. Hopes were high entering the NLCS against the Padres, and Rick didn't disappoint, throwing seven shutout innings in Game 1 and also hitting a home run.

And then the wheels fell off. Cubs fans debate to this day whether Jim Frey should have brought Sutcliffe back on short rest to start Game 4. Instead, Rick was held to Game 5, and despite a valiant effort . . . well, you don't need us to remind you what happened.

Hopes were high again in 1985, but one by one, the starting rotation went down to injury until all five of them were, at one time, on the DL. Sutcliffe, who'd won the '84 Cy Young Award, was first, tweaking a hamstring on April 28 while trying to beat out an infield hit in Philadelphia. He kept pitching, but finally succumbed to this and other related injuries in late July. He wound up 8–8, and the Cubs wound up with a losing record.

Sutcliffe came back to win eighteen games in 1987—many thought he should have won a second Cy, rather than the eventual winner, Steve Bedrosian—and sixteen games for the 1989 NL East champions. But the next year he went down again to injury and finished his career with the Orioles and Cardinals. Since retirement Sutcliffe has been a respected broadcaster, mainly with ESPN.

Cubs fans, though, will never forget 16–1. And Sutcliffe would not have had #40 to wear had **Dennis Eckersley** not desired the #43 he had worn with Cleveland and Boston. Eckersley was assigned #40 when he was acquired on May 25, 1984, but wore it for only one start—a 4-3 loss to the Reds on May 27—before switching back to #43, leaving #40 available for Sutcliffe, who joined the Cubs only three weeks later. Perhaps it was the bench-clearing brawl triggered by a reversed home run call on an apparent three-run dinger hit by Ron Cey that prompted Eck to switch shirts—one wonders what he must have been thinking, seeing opposing pitcher Mario Soto charge and bump an umpire, his manger, Jim Frey, ejected, and the game played under protest. (The fan who caught the ball said it was clearly foul.)

Another Sutcliffe, or another Kerry Wood, might have been **Glen Hobbie** (1959–64). Hobbie, who wore #28 during a couple of briefer stints with the Cubs in 1957 and 1958, made his mark in the rotation full-time in '59, going 16–13 with a respectable 3.69 ERA and finishing 10th in the NL in strikeouts with 138. At age twenty-three he seemed to have a bright future, and despite losing twenty games the next year, he also won sixteen—for a horrid club that lost ninety games—and it was hoped he'd be a mainstay for a decade. Alas, he got hurt in 1961, and his workload decreased. After a poor start in 1964, he was sent to the Cardinals—who wasn't, in those days?—for Lew Burdette. Burdette wasn't very good for the Cubs, and Hobbie's career ended after '64.

Dee Fondy (1951–57), whose given name actually was "Dee," was originally signed by the Dodgers, but was shipped to the Cubs along with Chuck Connors (more about Connors later in this chapter) after the 1950 season. Fondy was a first baseman with speed, a commodity lacking in Chicago. In 1954, he became the first Cub to steal twenty bases since 1940. He also twice led the team in hits and his .309 average in '53 was the highest by a Cubs first baseman until '78. A solid fielder, he made his major league debut as Opening Day first baseman for the Cubs in 1951. In one of the few 1950s deals that actually worked out better for the Cubs than their trading partner, the Cubs sent him to Pittsburgh on May 1, 1957, along with Gene Baker for Lee Walls and Fondy's replacement, Dale Long.

The rest of the #40s are the typical collection of hopefuls, never-wases, and ne'er-do-wells, going all the way back to the 1940s. **Tot Pressnell** (1941–42) had a couple of decent years for the Dodgers, but Tot had little impact in a Cubs uniform, going 6–4, 3.95 in two seasons. Even manager **Jimmie Wilson** (1943–44) wasn't a difference-maker; he had managed four poor years in Philadelphia before coming to Chicago, and he had a season and a half of bad managing for the Cubs before being replaced by franchise icon **Charlie Grimm** (1944–49), who led the Cubs to the 1945 pennant. Substandard pitchers wearing #40 included **Ed Mayer** (1957) and **Jack Warner** (1964–65), 0–2, 5.10

in four different stints with the Cubs over four seasons, during which he also tried on #33, #34, and #38. In the "let's try to resurrect his career" category came **Bill Hoeft** (1965–66); **Don Larsen** (1967); **Pete Mikkelsen** (1967–68); **Jack Lamabe** (1968); **Eddie "Buddy" Solomon** (1975), whose last name caused many to ask—before people met the African-American Solomon—if he was Jewish; **Pete Broberg** (1977), a former first overall pick of the Washington Senators—out of an Ivy League school, Dartmouth, no less—who went 1–2, 4.75 in 22 Cubs relief appearances; and **Lynn McGlothen** (1978–81), who did win 31 games over his four seasons as a Cub, but who carried a high ERA for the day, 4.25, and whose name was often misspelled "McGlothlin" because there was a better known pitcher in the seventies with that last name (Jim McGlothlin of the Reds).

The procession of pedestrian-level pitching was briefly interrupted for the 3-for-25 performance of **Fernando Ramsey** (1992), the only position player to wear #40 between Dee Fondy in 1957 and Henry Rodriguez in 1998 (and one of only three Cubs born in Panama; the others are Adolfo Phillips and Julio Zuleta).

After Ramsey, the #40 Parade of Pitching Mediocrity continued through the nineties: **Dave Stevens** (1997), a Cubs draftee later dealt to the Twins, returned via waivers and posted a 5.70 ERA in 41 games before being released; **Manny Aybar** (2001) and **Todd Wellemeyer** (2003–05) also threw poorly in Cubs uniforms (and Aybar threw poorly in both #38 *and* #40 in 2001), though, surprisingly, Wellemeyer resurrected his career as a Cardinal starter in 2007.

The only interruption to the 1990s' pitching-poor pageant at #40 came off the strong left-handed bat of **Henry Rodriguez** (1998–2000), who, after his acquisition from Montreal before the '98 season, posted a fine 31 homer season and had many "O! Henry!" candy bars thrown onto the left field turf at Wrigley Field, helping the Cubs to the 1998 wild card. He hit 26 homers in 1999, but even though Henry hit 18 homers in half a season in 2000, he was traded to Florida as the Cubs tried to retool. Perhaps brokenhearted at leaving the left field bleacher fans who showered him with affection, he hit only two homers for the

Marlins and none after, finishing his career with a weak 1-for-20 for his original team, the Expos, in 2002.

Cubs fans, at last, have hope that #40 will be worn for many years by a star who helped lead them to the postseason. **Rich Harden** (2008) was acquired from Oakland midseason, much as Rick Sutcliffe had been in 1984. If Harden can avoid the injury bug that hit Sutcliffe, he can, having just turned twenty-seven, be an ace for the Cubs for years to come.

MOST OBSCURE CUB TO WEAR #40: **Oswaldo Mairena** (2000). Even the name sounds obscure. One of nine major leaguers in history born in Nicaragua, Mairena was one of two minor leaguers acquired from the Yankees on July 21, 2000, for Glenallen Hill. Less than two months later, Mairena was in the majors, even though he had a 4.80 ERA in eleven relief appearances at Triple-A Iowa. He was the mop-up man in two blowouts (the Cubs lost them by a combined score of 24-6) and the following March was traded to the Marlins.

GUY YOU NEVER THOUGHT OF AS A CUB WHO WORE #40: **Chuck Connors** (1951). Maybe this one should be titled "Guy You Never Thought of as a Baseball Player." Connors was a tough guy. For kids who watched too much TV as children, black-and-white reruns of *The Rifleman* were pretty cool when your options for quality viewing/time wasting were limited. When it was discovered that the show's star played major league baseball—and was a Boston Celtic, too—that transformed *The Rifleman* into a low-grade sporting event. He fought for justice away from the tube. As an aging prospect on a Brooklyn Dodgers team loaded with talent, Connors complained bitterly about management's parsimony. So it was no surprise when Branch Rickey traded Connors and Dee Fondy to the Cubs for Hank Edwards and, of course, cash. Connors hit and fielded poorly as the Cubs' semi-regular first baseman in 1951. He returned to the Pacific Coast League, which he actually preferred to the big leagues because of the money, weather, and proximity to his next career. Connors earned his first bit part in a movie while he was with the PCL's Hollywood Stars. He then went into television when the Western was king. He may have used his memories of baseball executives as inspiration for his last major role: as a vindictive slave owner in the 1977 miniseries *Roots.*

The "System" by Yosh

When teams began numbering players in the 1920s and 1930s, most started simply: they gave the lowest numbers, the single digits, to the players who regularly had that spot in the batting order: the leadoff man got #1, the second-place hitter #2, and so on. That's why Yankees legends Babe Ruth and Lou Gehrig wore #3 and #4 respectively, for example.

The Cubs began that way, too; but, eventually, Yosh Kawano, who had become clubhouse manager in 1953, designed a system for numbering players and coaches. This system was first put into full practice in the first College of Coaches year, 1961. That year, the eleven coaches were all issued numbers 50 or higher. Pitchers got numbers in the thirties and forties; outfielders numbers in the twenties; infielders numbers in the tens, and catchers single digits, primarily #6 through #9. There were only two exceptions: outfielder Richie Ashburn wore his old Phillies #1 in 1960 and 1961, and Jimmie Schaffer, a backup catcher, wore #5 in 1963 and 1964. Apart from those two, #1 through #5 didn't get issued at all from 1961-65.

When Leo Durocher became manager in 1966, coaches shifted from the highest numbers to the lowest: Durocher had worn #2 as manager of the Giants and Dodgers and took that number with the Cubs. Coaches followed suit. Only three coaches in the Durocher era did not wear a number between 3 and 7. They were Ernie Banks, who coached in Leo's last two years and wore his familiar #14; Mel Wright, pitching coach in 1971, who wore #1, and Al Spangler, who wore #20 after returning to the team from the minors in 1970 as a player-coach (the #21 Spangler had worn from 1967-69 had been taken by Jack Hiatt.) Folllowing Leo's departure, the coach/manager numbering system broke down and managers and coaches were allowed to choose numbers as they pleased.

Yosh's system began to crumble big-time (he had granted a few exceptions and had to give a few out-of-system numbers in the 1960s when certain categories filled up) in 1970, when Johnny Callison arrived in an offseason deal from the Phillies. He requested #6, which he had worn in Philly; no non-catcher had worn #6 since Jim McKnight in 1960 (and McKnight, an infielder, was switched to #15 in 1962). Yosh granted Callison's request and also that of Jack Hiatt, a catcher acquired from the Giants on May 12. Hiatt thus became only the second Cubs catcher to wear #21, after Clyde McCullough, and the first to wear more than a single digit since Sammy Taylor (#15) and Moe Thacker (#20) did so in 1960. Blow-drying rebel Joe Pepitone continued the breakthrough when he asked for—and got—#8 when he arrived by trade on July 29, 1970. Ken Rudolph, a catcher who had worn #8, switched to #15—the lowest available number, because Yosh was averse to assigning #1 (no player wore it between

1961 and 1972). All the other single digits were taken, #13 was shunned by most players in that era, and #12 had been taken by yet another "crack in the system," J. C. Martin, who had gotten his old White Sox number after being acquired from the Mets just before Opening Day in 1970 (J. C.'s Mets number, 9, was already taken by Randy Hundley).

Yosh continued to grant similar requests and make exceptions until he officially "retired" as Cubs clubhouse manager in 2000 (Yosh continued as a visiting clubhouse assistant until his full retirement from the team at age eighty-six in 2008, after having worked for the Cubs in various capacities for sixty-five years).

In the spirit of this system, a kid infielder was told, on first reporting to the Cubs for spring training in 1982, that he should choose a number in the teens. Ryne Sandberg, knowing nothing of Cubs history, asked for #14—the number he'd worn as a high school quarterback in Spokane, Washington. Yosh explained to Ryno who Ernie Banks was and issued Sandberg a number that wasn't part of his infielder system: #23. Perhaps he sensed Sandberg's greatness to come and wanted him to stand out.

And Mark Grace, who had worn #56 in 1988 spring training, was issued #28 when first called up, during a series at San Diego. When the Cubs came home, Grace was given #17 and told by Yosh, "That's a first baseman's number." Grace, who idolized Keith Hernandez, was happy to be issued his hero's number, which still graces a popular replica jersey sold by the team.

#41: WEATHERS, RAIN, AND DIRT

After only two seasons, perhaps the most famous wearer of uniform #41 in Cubs history is manager **Lou Piniella.** He wore #14 as a player but, for the second time in his managing career, Lou had to reverse this number because he managed a team for which #14 was unavailable (Reds: Pete Rose, and Cubs: Ernie Banks). Lou is the third Cubs skipper to don #41. He's certainly cut a far more colorful and successful path than **Jim Essian** or **Tom Trebelhorn**.

But we're here to get down and dirty with three pitchers who wore #41: **Dick "Dirt" Tidrow, Steve Rain,** and **David Weathers**.

And the order in which they appeared in Cubs uniforms seems appropriate, too. First, "The Dirt Man," Dick Tidrow, a sidewinding right-hander with a classic seventies walrus stache and a uniform that he managed to get filthy *before* he even got into the game. In the typical style of the later years of the Wrigley ownership of the team, Tidrow was acquired after he had success elsewhere (two World Series rings with the Yankees in 1977 and 1978), hoping he could replicate that success on the North Side.

While Tidrow did have several decent seasons as a middle reliever—including going 11–5, 2.72 in 63 games for the 1979 Cubs after his acquisition for Ray Burris on May 23—the Cubs never had a winning record in his nearly four seasons. Dirt was durable. Counting his outings with the Yankees, he pitched 77 times in '79 and led the Cubs in appearances for three consecutive years. Dirt's 84 appearances for the woeful 1980 Cubs tied Ted Abernathy's 1965 record. That mark still stands, having been tied again by Bob Howry for yet another horrid Cubs team in 2006.

The Dirt was washed away, so to speak, by the "Rain Man." Steve Rain was considered a top Cubs relief prospect in the late 1990s. Despite a decent performance for yet another execrable Cubs team in 2000 (54 strikeouts in 49.2 innings over 37 appearances), Rain became a free agent and never again pitched in the major leagues.

The number was next worn by David Weathers, maintaining our meteorological bent, but not without some confusion. He was initially issued #49 in his first games after his acquisition by the Cubs on July 30, 2001, games all played on the road. When the Cubs returned home to Chicago he was going to switch to #48—and the printed Wrigley Field scorecards had him listed that way—but Joe Borowski, who appeared in only one 2001 Cubs game, was still on the forty-man roster and had claim to #48, so Weathers took #41 instead. The 2001 Cubs, contenders up to that time, hoped he would help them make the postseason. They didn't weather the rest of the season, though, finishing third. Weathers left the Cubs as a free agent after appearing in only 28 games.

Number 41, famously retired by the New York Mets for Tom Seaver, has a more checkered history for the Cubs. Before World War II, #41 was worn by the forgettable **Don Hurst** (1934), **Ken O'Dea** (1935–36), **John Bottarini** (1937), and **Bob Logan** (1938). In the prewar era, only **Dolph Camilli** (1933–34), who was traded to the Phillies on June 11, 1934 for Hurst in perhaps the worst trade the Cubs made in the thirties (Camilli went on to have eight straight twenty-plus homer seasons for the Phillies and Dodgers, while Hurst hit .199 in 51 games and left the majors after '34), is a recognizable name on the #41 roster. **Vance Page** (1938–41) did start nine games, winning five, for the 1938 NL champions, but when called on to keep a 4-3 game close in Game 4 of the '38 World Series, he gave up two runs and the Yankees wound up winning that clinching game, 8-3. The equally forgettable **Carmen Mauro** (1948–51), **Seth Morehead** (1959), and **Taylor Phillips** (1959) wore it through most of the rest of the forties and fifties. **Art Ceccarelli** (1959–60) went 5–5, 4.85 in 28 games before he was sent to the Yankees on May 19, 1960, leaving #41 for Hall of Famer **Billy Williams** to wear during his second September call up (he wore #4 in 1959). Williams was assigned his now-retired #26 for his Rookie of the Year campaign in 1961.

From the 1960s on #41 has been almost exclusively reserved for pitchers, and mostly forgettable ones (**Tom Baker, Sterling Slaughter, Rob Gardner, Mike Mason, Roberto Rivera, Bryan Hickerson,** and **Jesus Sanchez** are perhaps the least memorable of the forgettable; none of them were Cubs for more than a season). **Jeff Pico** (1988–90) threatened to rescue #41 from obscurity when he shut out the Reds on four hits in his major league debut on May 31, 1988, but Pico's three-year Cubs (and major league) career ended with a 13–12 record and 4.24 ERA, and he wore #41 for all but one game— that first one; he threw that four-hit shutout in #51 (maybe he should have kept that number). And #41 was worn briefly by **Adolfo Phillips** before he switched to #20, and by catcher **Mike Martin** (1-for-13 in 1986), the last position player to wear #41.

Roberto Pena was a non-roster playing during the spring of 1965; in camp, he wore #1, which wasn't worn by a player during the regular season between 1961 (Richie Ashburn) and 1972 (Jose Cardenal). Ron Campbell, who had worn #7 in 1964, was sent to the minors at the end of spring training and Pena made the club, taking over Campbell's #7. On May 29, the Cubs acquired Harvey Kuenn from the Giants, and Kuenn was given #7, the number he'd worn in San Francisco. Pena switched to #41—but only for a couple of weeks, as on June 10, he was sent to the minors. In September, he was recalled and given #28, which he wore through the rest of 1965 (though he played in only one September game) and six games in April 1966. By Yosh's System, as described in chapter 40, Pena, an infielder, should have worn a number in the teens, but they were all taken (save #16, which was still being set aside in memory of Ken Hubbs). Pena, Wimpy Quinn (#4, #16, #19: 1941) and Ryan Theriot (#55, #7, #3: 2006) are the only Cubs to wear three different numbers in a single season. What did all this numerical maneuvering do for Pena? It's hard to say, but the numbers that linger for the rookie shortstop—.218, two homers, 12 RBI, 17 errors in 51 games—weren't good. He played for four other teams and was better at the plate and in the field, though only once did he wear the same uniform number in successive seasons.

MOST OBSCURE CUB TO WEAR #41: **Bud Hardin** (1952) wore #41 and played in three games between April 15 and May 1, having seven at bats and one hit, a single. We put him in this book because otherwise no one outside his family would remember him. And if you do remember William Edgar Hardin: This Bud's for you.

GUY YOU NEVER THOUGHT OF AS A CUB WHO WORE #41: **Lou Johnson** (1968) actually came up as a Cub in 1960, was sent packing after hitting .206 in 68 at bats, had several good seasons as a Dodgers outfielder (hitting .296 in the 1965 World Series), and was reacquired for Paul Popovich and Jim Williams in the 1967-68 offseason. After hitting .244 in half a season, he was sent to Cleveland for Willie Smith in one of the better transactions of the John Holland era.

Making Music in '41

Of all the singers of "Take Me Out to the Ballgame" over the years, Harry Caray is the best remembered today. He started singing the song over the PA at Comiskey Park when White Sox owner Bill Veeck tricked him into doing it in the 1970s, but it was serendipity that in 1982 teamed him with the place that had the first organ in the big leagues: Wrigley Field. By then, Veeck was sitting in the bleachers on the North Side as well. Veeck had helped plant the Wrigley ivy in 1937 while working for his dad, club president Bill Veeck Sr. Bill Veeck the Younger had also been around when the Cubs brought organ music to the big leagues.

No stadium had a ballpark organ until Wrigley Field installed one on April 26, 1941. According to Craig Wright at baseballpast.com, the Cubs hooked up the organ to the public address system as a one-time gimmick. The fans loved it and it became permanent. It would be almost another half-century before Wrigley would light up the nights, but the organ would brighten the days at the Friendly Confines for generations.

#42: GAME OVER

+ Worn only on April 15 in honor of Jackie Robinson.

Bruce Sutter was a pioneer. He was the first to throw the now-common split-finger pitch with any accuracy or success. And he came about it almost by accident—trying it out only because his fastball topped out at 88 MPH and the Cubs were going to release him. Instead, minor league pitching coach Fred Martin taught him—and all the pitchers at the Cubs' Class A affiliate at Key West—the pitch. Sutter's minor league numbers improved from 3–3, 4.13 in 1973 to a 1.35 ERA in 40 innings in 1974, when he allowed only 26 hits and struck out 50. The Key West team, which also included future Cubs Dennis Lamp, Donnie Moore, and Mike Krukow, finished 34–97, but Sutter was dominant.

Two years later he was in the major leagues, serving as a set-up man—apparently, manager Jim Marshall didn't recognize his talent at first—picking up ten saves and posting a 2.70 ERA. But it was the next year, 1977, when Sutter and his split-finger fastball broke through. Hitters would stand and stare at what they thought was a fastball, only to see it drop down at the last possible moment, either called a strike, or swung on and missed badly. Sutter struck out 123 and walked only 29 in 107.1 innings, posting a 1.35 ERA and saving 31 games. They weren't the quickie one-inning saves we know from closers today, either; Sutter pitched at least two innings in fifteen of his saves and three innings in five of them.

Unlike previous relievers of that type, who would often post gaudy victory totals when they'd come in trailing and their team would come back and win, manager Herman Franks would only put Sutter in the game if the Cubs were tied or leading, a precursor to today's closers who only throw the ninth inning when their teams are ahead.

The heavy workload—99 or more innings each of his four full seasons with the Cubs from 1977–80—began to wear on Sutter, as throwing the splitter put stress on his arm. He spent some time on the DL in '77, one of many reasons that team fell out of the race, and had to be rested from time to time the following years. But it wasn't the injuries that sent him out of Chicago, it was money. The Cubs were creaking to the end of the P. K. Wrigley ownership era, and Sutter, the best reliever in baseball and coming off the NL Cy Young Award, submitted an arbitration request before the 1980 season. He was awarded $700,000, which may not seem like a lot of money in 2009, but it was at that time the largest arbitration award yet given. Wrigley said the Cubs couldn't afford him and sent him to the Cardinals for Leon Durham and Ken Reitz after the 1980 season. The trade, at least, brought a productive player, but Cubs fans were crushed to see Sutter help lead the Cardinals to the 1982 World Series title.

The Cubs got some measure of revenge in the aforementioned 1984 "Sandberg Game," and also later that year when, on September 30, the last day of the season, Sutter needed to save the game to top Dan Quisenberry's then-record 45 saves. The Cubs came back and won in the last of the ninth, denying Sutter the record. When Sutter went into the Hall of Fame in 2006, however, it was with a Cardinals cap on his plaque.

Other 42ers, mostly pitchers, have been an up-and-down lot. **Jim Brosnan** (1956–57), who also wore #27 and another retired number, #23, had two good years as a reliever and spot starter for the Cubs in '56 and '57 but he is better remembered for his two diary-style books, *The Long Season* and *Pennant Race*, after he was traded from Chicago.

Chuck "Twiggy" Hartenstein (1965–68), so nicknamed for his skinny build (5-foot-11, 165), was also an effective relief pitcher, saving ten games in 1967 (that may not seem like many today, but that ranked seventh in the NL that year) and backing up Phil Regan as a set-up man in '68. Then, in one of the least popular and most inexplicable trades of the era, the Cubs shipped him to the Pirates, along with Joe Campbell, for thirty-year-old outfielder Manny Jimenez, who had six Cubs at bats with one hit. Twiggy saved ten games for the '69 Pirates. The '69 Cubs could have used him. **Dave Smith** (1991–92) had been an effective closer for the Astros for a decade, but when the Cubs signed him as a free agent, he was awful, posting a 6.00 ERA in '91 and then pitching in mop-up duty the next year before retiring. The Cubs failed to learn their lesson, signing washed-up closers Doug Jones and Mel Rojas before ceasing this practice.

Others weren't even that good: **Walter Stephenson** (1935–36) had only 38 at bats for the Cubs before being shipped to the Phillies; **Hy Cohen** (1955) pitched in seven games with a 7.94 ERA; **Elmer Singleton** (1958–59) won more than 100 games in the Pacific Coast League in the 1950s, but he was thirty-eight before he donned a Cubs uniform (originally wearing #20), going 3–2 in 28 games (three starts); **Lou Jackson** (1959), who also wore #22 in 1958 and part of 1959, went 1-for-4 wearing #42 in 1959; and **Freddie Burdette** (1962–64), who was not Lew Burdette's brother nor in his league, but they were on the same staff in 1964. Freddie, a decade younger, got his lone major league decision that year—a win!—in a sixteen-inning game in which the soon-to-be-loathed Ernie Broglio got his first career save.

In the 1980s, more pitchers wore #42, but none had any lasting impact: **Rich Bordi** (1983–84) had a good year in '84, posting a 3.46 ERA with a 5–2 record and four saves; he was left off the playoff roster in favor of Dallas Green's former Phillies favorite Dick Ruthven. Shout if you've heard this before: The Cubs could have used him. Bordi was traded to the Yankees the following offseason along with Porfi Altimirano, Henry Cotto, and Ron Hassey for Ray Fontenot and Brian Dayett. **Lary Sorensen** (1985), the man with the seemingly misspelled first name (where's the other "r"?), took over #42. A former eighteen-game winner with the Brewers, Sorensen's North Side tenure was short a few "W"s as well as the "r"—a 3–7, 4.26 mark earned his release. **Bob Tewksbury** (1987–88) was next. The Cubs never really gave him a chance, as his Chicago tenure happened when he was rehabbing from an arm injury. Let go after only eight appearances and an 0–4 record, he was signed by the Cardinals, where he had his best year: a 16–5 mark in 1992, walking just 20 batters in 233 innings and finishing third in the Cy Young balloting. He won exactly 100 games over ten seasons after his release by the Cubs.

Number 42 went out the way came in, on a coach's back. **Charley O'Leary** wore #42 in '32 when the uniforms were handed out and coaches **Moe Drabowsky** (1994) and **Dan Radison** (1995–97) finished the shift. It was officially retired by MLB to honor Jackie Robinson on April 15, 1997, the fiftieth anniversary of Robinson's debut with the Dodgers, at which time Radison moved over to #3. Since then, four Cubs players—**Cliff Floyd** (2007), **Jacque Jones** (2007), **Derrek Lee** (2007–08), and **Daryle Ward** (2007–08), and coaches **Gerald Perry** (2007–08) and **Lester Strode** (2007–08)—have donned #42 for one day in honor of Robinson.

MOST OBSCURE CUB TO WEAR #42: **Jim Qualls** (1969). The last guy off the bench on the 1969 club, Qualls hit a respectable .250 in 43 games. After Don Young was benched at the beginning of July, Qualls started most of the games that month in center field, and on July 9 (the day after Young had missed two catchable fly balls that cost the Cubs a game at Shea Stadium), he singled with one out in the ninth to break up a perfect game being thrown by Tom Seaver. Now, forty years later, with Shea extinct, still no Met has pitched a no-hitter (though Seaver, among others, tossed them for other clubs). As for Qualls, this bit of history didn't get him any more play for the Cubs; he was traded to the Expos the next April and eventually had a handful of at bats for the 1972 White Sox.

GUY YOU NEVER THOUGHT OF AS A CUB WHO WORE #42: **Tony LaRussa** (1973). At the time, no one would have thought anything about a guy whose name wasn't even printed on the Opening Day scorecard. But LaRussa, who had been acquired from the Braves the previous offseason in exchange for reliever Tom Phoebus, was sent in to pinch-run for Ron Santo after Santo had reached on an error in the bottom of the ninth. The Cubs were trailing 2-1 and had a runner already on first. Three walks later, LaRussa scored the winning run. Shortly afterward, he was sent to Triple-A and never again played in the major leagues. An infielder with 176 career at bats—none as a Cub—he's gone on to manage more than 4,600 games in the big leagues and capture a World Series in each league.

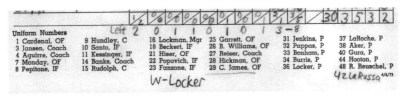

Uniform Numbers					
1 Cardenal, OF	9 Hundley, C	16 Lockman, Mgr	25 Garrett, OF	31 Jenkins, P	37 LaRoche, P
3 Jansen, Coach	10 Santo, IF	18 Beckert, IF	26 B. Williams, OF	32 Pappas, P	38 Aker, P
4 Aguirre, Coach	11 Kessinger, IF	21 Hiser, OF	27 Reiser, Coach	33 Bonham, P	40 Gura, P
7 Monday, OF	14 Banks, Coach	22 Popovich, IF	28 Hickman, OF	34 Burris, P	44 Hooton, P
8 Pepitone, IF	15 Rudolph, C	23 Fanzone, IF	29 C. James, OF	36 Locker, P	48 R. Reuschel, P

Hall of Fame Cubs

When you're dealing with a franchise that was formed during the Ulysses S. Grant administration, there's a lot of ground to cover. With their long lineage, the Cubs are well-represented in the National Baseball Hall of Fame, with forty-five past Cubs having plaques in Cooperstown. That number includes everyone who's played for the team or managed it at some point, from Grover Cleveland Alexander (elected in 1938) to Rich Gossage (elected in 2008). Alex the Great wore no number; Goose wore #54, though only for one year as a Cub. They all count, whether they played in Chicago for a year or a lifetime.

Here's a list of the Cubs in the Hall of Fame who played before there were uniform numbers:

Cub	Year of Induction:
Grover Cleveland Alexander	1938
Cap Anson	1939
A. G. Spalding	1939
Hugh Duffy	1945
Roger Bresnahan	1945
King Kelly	1945
Frank Chance+	1946
Johnny Evers	1946
Joe Tinker	1946
Clark Griffith	1946
Rube Waddell	1946
Mordecai "Three-Finger" Brown	1949
Rabbit Maranville	1954
Joe McCarthy*	1957
John Clarkson	1963
George Kelly	1973
Hack Wilson+	1979
William Hulbert	1995
Frank Selee*	1999

Below are the Hall of Famers who served the Cubs in uniform after numbers were added in 1932 (the order of the uniform numbers is the order in which each player wore them).

Cub	Year of Induction	Uni#
Rogers Hornsby	1945	9
Frankie Frisch*	1947	3
Jimmie Foxx	1951	16, 26
Dizzy Dean	1953	22
Gabby Hartnett+	1955	7, 9, 2
Burleigh Grimes	1963	16, 21
Kiki Cuyler+	1968	3
Lou Boudreau*	1970	40, 5
Monte Irvin	1973	39
Ralph Kiner	1975	4
Billy Herman+	1975	2, 4
Robin Roberts	1976	36
Fred Lindstrom	1976	7
Ernie Banks+	1977	14
Chuck Klein	1980	6, 4
Lou Brock	1985	24
Hoyt Wilhelm	1985	39
Billy Williams+	1987	4, 41, 26
Ferguson Jenkins+	1991	31
Tony Lazzeri	1991	15
Leo Durocher	1994	2
Richie Ashburn	1995	1
Dennis Eckersley	2004	40, 43
Ryne Sandberg+	2005	23
Bruce Sutter	2006	42
Rich Gossage	2008	54

* Denotes manager only.
+ Signifies the player wears a Cubs hat on his plaque.
Numbers are not included if players wore different numbers as nonplaying coaches.
William Hulbert was owner of the club and helped found the National League in 1876.

#43: WHAT THE ECK?

On May 15, 1960, not even a month into the season, the campaign had already turned dismal for the Cubs. After losing the first game of a doubleheader that Sunday to the Cardinals they stood at 8–14, sixth in an eight-team league, already eight games out of first place. Taking the mound for the Cubs in game two, as the shadows crept over the infield, was **Don Cardwell** (1960–62), who had been acquired from the Phillies two days earlier along with Ed Bouchee, in exchange for Tony Taylor and Cal Neeman.

Cardwell had the most auspicious debut with a new team of any player in baseball history—he threw a no-hitter, nearly a perfect game; the only baserunner was Alex Grammas, who drew a first-inning walk. The footage of the ninth inning, one of the earliest surviving pieces of WGN-TV videotape, lets the viewer feel the excitement as George Altman catches the last out, a fly ball to the rightfield wall, and as Moose Moryn snags the final out, as Jack Brickhouse would say, "off the top of a tall blade of grass out there!"

DON CARDWELL
Pitcher

Chicago Cubs

It was a hard act to follow. Cardwell seemed to have a bright future; he was only twenty-four years old. He had a fine 15–14, 3.82 season for another woeful, ninety-loss Cub team in 1961, but slumped to 7–16, 4.92 the following season and was sent to the Cardinals in one of the few trades that helped both teams: St. Louis got Cardwell, George Altman, and Moe Thacker, and the Cubs got a solid starting pitcher in Larry Jackson, a backup catcher to replace Thacker in Jimmie Schaffer, and **Lindy McDaniel,** who inherited Cardwell's #43.

McDaniel immediately paid dividends; he went 13–7 and had 22 saves (leading the NL in that still-unofficial category) in 1963. In a memorable game on June 6 at Wrigley Field, Lindy came into a tie game in the top of the tenth with the bases loaded. He picked off Willie Mays and struck out Ed Bailey to end the inning and then hit a walkoff homer leading off the bottom of the inning against Billy Pierce. The win put the Cubs into a first-place tie, a heady position for a team that had lost 103 games the previous season.

Lindy's workload increased and his saves decreased (to fifteen and then two) in the next two years and then he continued the profitable trade chain—one of the few for the Cubs in that era—when he was traded, along with outfielder Don Landrum, to the Giants for Bill Hands and Randy Hundley, two key cogs for the good Cub teams of the late sixties.

Before Lindy and Don, #43 could have been dubbed the "All-Nickname" team: **Dutch Meyer** (1937), **Rabbit Warstler** (1940), **Peanuts Lowrey** (1942), **Moose Moryn** (1956–57)—he'd swap down to #7 in time to save Cardwell's no-no—and **Riverboat Smith** (1959). But the best of all the nicknames was **Bill Nicholson** (1943–48), simply known as "Swish." You be the judge of whether that was for his large strikeout totals, or his prodigious home runs. Swish, a Maryland native, had worn #8 for his first four years as a Cub, but upon switching to #43 in '43, he had his best two years in the majors. In the war era, when the composition of the baseballs was different because of material shortages, Nicholson's 29 homers in '43 led the league by 11, and when he hit 33 for a fourth-place team in '44, he was the only thirty-homer man in the majors. His power dipped in '45, when he hit only 13 dingers, but he still drove in 88 runs for the NL champs. One of the most popular players of his era, fans started staying away in droves after Swish, still productive with a 19-homer season at age thirty-three, was traded to the Phillies after the 1948 season. (Well, that and the last-place finish.)

Another old-timer who contributed to a Cubs pennant season was **Carl Reynolds** (1937–39). Reynolds, who had taken advantage of the "rabbit ball" of 1930 to have a 22 homer, .359 season for the White Sox, had been sold by the Senators to the minors in 1937. The Cubs rescued him and he contributed a .302 average to the 1938 NL champions, also playing a solid center field. Unfortunately, Reynolds's offense vanished in the '38 World Series; he went 0-for-12 as the Cubs were swept by the Yankees.

Returning to the 1960s, the number was worn by several "temporary" Cubs: **Don Lee** (16 games in 1966); **Wes Covington** (11 at bats in 1966 after Lee was let go); **Dick Radatz** (20 games in 1967, long after his "Monster" status was gone); **Roberto Rodriguez** (23 games in 1970); and **Chris Cannizzaro** (.213 in 71 games in 1971).

Paul Reuschel, brother to Rick, just as large a man but not as large a pitcher, wore #43 (and very thick horn rim glasses) for four seasons. His 4.40 ERA in 163 relief appearances for the Cubs was nothing special, but on August 21, 1975, he and Rick became the first brothers in major league history to combine on a shutout. Rick threw 6.2 innings and Paul finished a six-hit, 7-0 win over the Dodgers.

In the eighties, most of the #43s are the usual never-weres, although two of them, **Herman Segelke** (1982) and **Don Schulze** (1983–84), were former first-round picks. Between them they appeared in eight games and neither recorded a victory in a Cubs uniform. Also appearing, briefly and unmemorably, were **Randy Stein** (1982) and **Joe Kraemer** (1989–90). The resident #43 as of the end of the 2008 season, **Michael Wuertz** (2004–08), has held the number for as many years as any player since Swish Nicholson, but Wuertz's hold on it hasn't always been firm. Though he twice surpassed seventy appearances in a season, enjoyed a solid 2007, and pitched twice in that year's NLDS, he

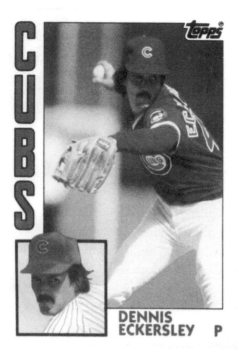

DENNIS
ECKERSLEY   P

spent much of the summer of '08 in Des Moines and was left off the October roster.

If only Dallas Green had known that **Dennis Eckersley** (1984–86), who had declined from his 10-8, 3.03 start in 1984 that helped the Cubs to the NL East, spent the 1986–87 offseason getting help for a serious alcohol problem, perhaps he might have had a little more patience and wouldn't have traded the future Hall of Famer. Eckersley came to spring training in 1987 in shape, but he had a poor spring and the Cubs had a kid named Maddux they wanted to try in the rotation. No one with the Cubs thought of using Eckersley in the bullpen; he was considered superfluous and so was dealt to Oakland for three minor leaguers, none of whom played a single major league game. Eckersley got off to a poor start for the A's, who rotated him between the bullpen and two underwhelming starts. But on June 6, 1987, he replaced Moose Haas with the A's down 4-0 in the fourth inning; he threw six perfect innings in relief with five strikeouts, as the A's came back to win 6-4; Eck never started again. The rest of the Eckersley story is a well-known ride to the World Series with the A's (three times) and a trip to Cooperstown . . . a ride that could have been made wearing blue pinstripes.

MOST OBSCURE CUB TO WEAR #43: **John Hairston** (1969). Call John "The Forgotten Hairston" in a three-generation baseball family. Sam Hairston, his father, played in four games for the 1951 White Sox after a stellar career in the Negro Leagues; brother Jerry had a long career, mostly on the South Side; and John's nephews Jerry Jr. and Scott are still active in the major leagues today. But John, a September call up to the star-crossed '69 team, played in only three games behind the plate, starting the last game of the season and never again returning to the majors.

GUY YOU NEVER THOUGHT OF AS A CUB WHO WORE #43: **Rico Carty** (1973). Carty, who had won the NL batting title in 1970 with a .366 average—plus a .454 OBP—had suffered some severe knee injuries that made it nearly impossible for him to play the field by '73. That didn't stop the DH-less Cubs from acquiring him on August 13, 1973, from the Rangers. He fared poorly in 22 games for the Cubs, hitting .214 in 70 at bats, so they sold him to the A's. Two years later he embarked on a nice run in the AL as a first generation DH, hitting 89 homers in a four-year period for Cleveland, Oakland, and Toronto.

Tales from the Crypt: Ones that Almost Got Away

You've read, earlier in this volume (see chapter 13), about the "Gassaway Conundrum," our inability to locate any source for two-game 1944 Cub Charlie Gassaway to indicate what number he wore. But there were others nearly as difficult to locate—although eventually we got everyone but good ol' Charlie—dating from the 1960s to the 2000s.

In 1994, Kasey Ignarski got a list of numbers from the Cubs which helped a great deal in sorting out discrepancies. But that list showed Bob Humphreys, who played only one season for the Cubs (1965), wearing both #36 and #39 that year. Ted Abernathy, who set a major league record with 31 saves in '65, wore #39 all year and Humphreys wore #36. So where did the information that Humphreys had worn two numbers come from? After checking various sources, including 1965 scorecards, we learned that Abernathy had been acquired the day before Opening Day—April 11—by which time the Opening Day scorecards had already been printed with Humphreys shown wearing #39. Abernathy, who was older and who had been around longer than Humphreys, claimed #39, so Humphreys took #36—but anyone seeing that scorecard years later would have been led astray.

Jophery Brown, who pitched in only one game in 1968, had been listed in various sources as wearing #34 and #47. Players do often change shirts during a game, but never put on a different number, so unofficial Cubs historian Ed Hartig was consulted. He confirmed #47 was the number worn by Brown and believes #34 may have been a number from a spring-training list.

We had Archie Reynolds, who pitched a handful of games from 1968–70, listed as #39 in 1968 and 1970, but #46 *and* #39 in 1969. Dick Selma, who had worn #39 with other clubs, claimed it when he was acquired by the Cubs in April 1969. So when Reynolds was recalled to start two games in June, #39 wasn't available, and Yosh Kawano issued him #46. Later that year, Ken Johnson was acquired and issued the then-vacant #46—Reynolds had been sent back to the minors. Both Johnson and Selma were gone in 1970, so when Reynolds returned to the majors for another brief (seven-game) stint that year, he was again given his original #39.

Both Kasey and Al Yellon were in attendance on August 7, 2001 and bought scorecards with #48 listed for newly acquired David Weathers, who had worn #49 on the just-ended road trip. Yet Weathers entered the game—and earned a hold—wearing #41. Why? Ed Hartig again helped sort it out. Joe Borowski, the previous year's #48 held on to that number though he had been on the disabled list all year. Borowski came off that week, donned #48, and got hurt again. By the time Borowski came back in '02, he still had #48 and Weathers was a Met.

#44: CAVVY

Phil Cavarretta was a leader on the Cubs' pennant-winning teams of the 1930s and 1940s, and one of the greatest all-time Cubs, still ranking tenth on the team's all-time lists for both runs and hits. He was NL MVP in 1945, helped the Cubs win three pennants while twice batting .400 in the World Series, and managed the club for the better part of three seasons. He got some Hall of Fame consideration, receiving a number of votes in the 1960s and 1970s including 35 percent of the necessary vote in 1975. To compare him to a modern-day Cub, his numbers—good average, little power—were similar to Mark Grace's. Numbers-wise, he was the first Cub to wear #43 and #44. He did everything the club ever asked of him, except lie.

The Lane Tech High School star hit for the cycle in his first professional game in Peoria in 1934. Soon after, Cavarretta was promoted to the majors at age eighteen, and he was Chicago's first baseman as a teenager in the 1935 World Series loss to the Tigers. The Cubs won the pennant again three years later, with Cavarretta moving to right field to make room for Ripper Collins. An ear problem exempted him from military service during World War II and he provided stability to a lineup in constant flux. In 1945 he won the NL batting title and MVP while helping the Cubs reach the World Series for the third time in a decade. He made the All-Star team four straight times and in his later years took a seat on the Cubs bench to let younger players get a chance. Even

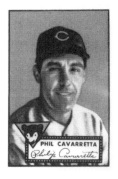

PHIL CAVARRETTA
Phil Cavarretta

as a reserve he was still a crack hitter and a preacher of patience—he had more walks than strikeouts in fifteen of his final sixteen seasons.

The Cubs fired Frankie Frisch midway through the 1951 season and made Cavarretta player-manager. In 1952 the team finished at .500—no small feat for those Cubs, and the only time between 1946 and 1963 that they didn't have a losing record—and the '53 club, although seventh at 65–89, still did better than expected given the team's scoring (for and against). The following spring, Cavarretta was asked by owner P. K. Wrigley how he felt the team would do, and, being honest, said, "They're a second-division club." (In 1950s baseball speak, that meant he thought the team wouldn't be any good.) Wrigley promptly fired the Chicago legend, saying he had a "defeatist attitude," making Cavvy the first post-1900 manager to be dismissed during spring training. Cavarretta was asked about this for a July 2008 article that appeared in the *Chicago Sun-Times,* and said:

> *Like a dumb dago, I told the truth in a meeting with my owner. I was raised that way. My dad would always say: 'Tell the people the truth. Tell them what's on your mind.' I told the truth to Mr. Wrigley and got fired.*

Cavvy was telling the people the truth—the 1954 Cubs lost ninety games and finished seventh under Cavarretta's former teammate, Stan Hack.

Finally, according to a *Chicago Tribune* article published April 2, 1954, the Cubs "officially" retired Cavarretta's #44 the previous day. No ceremony was held for the just-fired manager, and on May 24, 1954 Cavvy signed with the rival crosstown White Sox, with whom he finished his career as a bench player. The number wasn't reissued until 1971, when University of Texas star **Burt Hooton,** who had worn the number in college, asked to wear it (it had been worn in spring training, but not in the regular season, between 1954 and 1970). Cubs clubhouse manager Yosh Kawano, who issued numbers for players from the 1940s through the 1980s, actually called Cavarretta to ask his permission to reissue the number.

Fifteen other Cubs have worn Cavarretta's #44, which probably should have stayed retired in honor of one of the franchise's greatest players. In fact, #44 is a retired number for many greats in baseball and other sports, from Henry Aaron to Willie McCovey to Reggie Jackson to the NFL's Floyd Little and the NBA's Jerry West. But for the Cubs, it's been donned mostly by a succession of journeymen, all but one (**Ken Reitz,** 1981) a pitcher.

Burt Hooton started his Cubs career as if he, not Cavarretta, would be the one they'd be retiring #44 for someday. Following a brief appearance right after he was taken with the second overall pick in the June 1971 draft, Hooton spent the rest of the year in the minors until a late-season call up. In his first major league start on September 15, he tied the Cubs' then club record of 15 strikeouts against the Mets. Six days later, facing those same Mets, he threw a two-hit shutout. Though he threw a no-hitter at Wrigley in the second game of the 1972 season, Hooton received little run support from his teammates and poor instruction from coaches who tried to get him to throw pitches other than his pioneering knuckle-curve. Stardom eluded Hooton with the Cubs, and after going 34–44 in three-plus years and starting out poorly in 1975, he was traded to the Dodgers for Eddie ("Buddy") Solomon, who pitched six times as a Cub, and Geoff Zahn, who won 105 games *after* the Cubs released him. Hooton, meanwhile stayed in L.A. for nearly a decade and was a key contributor to three Dodgers pennant winners.

After Hooton was dealt #44, once worn with such pride by Cavarretta, the number was sported by journeyman pitchers such as **Mike Garman** (1976), whose main claim to fame is that he pitched one year for the Cubs and then helped bring Bill Buckner to the North Side when traded to the Dodgers; **Dick Ruthven** (1983–86), one of the Phillies Connection guys brought over by Dallas Green when he took over as GM after Tribune Co. bought the team; **Drew Hall** (1986–88), yet another in a long line of failed Cubs top choices; **Bill Brennan** (1993), whose stork-like pitching delivery didn't help him post better numbers; and

Amaury Telemaco (1994), whose name sounds like a South American telephone company. In recent years, #44 has been sported by **Chris Haney** (1998), **Tony Fossas** (1998), **Roberto Novoa** (2005–06), and **Chad Fox** (2008). All of the aforementioned pitchers should be happy we mention nothing more than their names in this chapter.

And that leaves the best—well, weirdest, anyway—story for last. **Kyle Farnsworth** (1999–2004), heartthrob of female Cubs fans and known (sort of) affectionately as "Dr. Tightpants" for, well, the way he wore his uniform trousers. Farnsworth was a forty-seventh-round draft pick in 1994 who came up through the system throwing a fastball at speeds up to 100 MPH, although not always knowing where it would end up. He arrived in the bigs as a twenty-three-year-old starter in 1999. On August 29, he threw the only complete game of his career, a two-hit shutout at Dodger Stadium. The Cubs needed heat in the pen and felt that the Georgia native was durable enough to take the daily usage. Starting in 2001, he had a strong alternating-year pattern— good one year, bad the next. One of the NL's top set-up men in 2001, Farnsworth broke his foot the following April. The official story was that it was while warming up in the bullpen, but rumor had it that Farnsworth had been fooling around before a game kicking footballs in the outfield. He missed two months, and was ineffective thereafter. After a good season in 2003 his fastball started to lose its punch and with his velocity down and work ethic in question, he was dealt to the Tigers after the 2004 season for Roberto Novoa (who took over Kyle's #44), Scott Moore, and Bo Flowers.

MOST OBSCURE CUB TO WEAR #44: **Jeff Hartsock** (1992), who had been highly touted when acquired in 1991 from the Dodgers for fellow #44er **Steve Wilson** (1989-91), went 5-12, 4.37 for the Cubs' Triple-A team at Iowa in '92, and for some reason got a September recall anyway. Hartsock pitched in relief four times, was bad in all of them (posting a 6.75 ERA in 9.1 innings) and the Cubs lost each game he appeared in, by a combined score of 46–13.

GUY YOU NEVER THOUGHT OF AS A CUB WHO WORE #44: We could have given this to **Ken Reitz**, the only non-pitcher to wear the number since Cavarretta; he had been the Cardinals' third baseman

---

for most of the 1970s (save a one-year detour to San Francisco), and was acquired along with Leon Durham in the Bruce Sutter trade after the 1980 season. The slick-fielding Reitz couldn't hit a lick (.215 in 82 games) and was released just before the 1982 season. But the guy who *really* didn't seem as if he belonged in a Cubs uniform was palmballist **Dave Giusti** (1977), a former closer for the Pirates who seemed to take delight in tormenting the Cubs during Pittsburgh's heyday in the early 1970s. Also pitching for Houston and St. Louis, Giusti had put up a 23–9, 2.98, 15-save record against the Cubs, his best record against any team he faced for more than 100 career innings. As was typical of the Cubs in that era, they went out of their way to acquire a washed-up guy (age thirty-seven) who had dominated them years earlier (fortunately, they only gave money, not prospects, to get him), and he was awful, recording a 6.04 ERA in twenty games before being released at the end of the season.

Native Sons by the Numbers

Native Son is the 1940 novel by Richard Wright about a young man from Chicago named Bigger Thomas who . . . well, we'll hope your high school English teacher helped you sort that out. This sidebar is about young men born in the city of Chicago who grew up to be Cubs and the numbers that they wore. It does not include people born outside the city limits or players who moved to the Windy City as youths; nor does it include Cubs from before they started wearing numbers in 1932, though we're all very proud of those native sons, too. Coaches who wore numbers, including "head coach" Bob Kennedy of the College of Coaches fiasco, are included (in italics) because a lot of kids grow up hoping they'll one day find a great job near home.

Chicago Kid	Position	Years as Cubs	Numbers as Cubs
Aberson, Cliff	OF	1947-49	11
Bartell, Dick	SS	1939	2,5
Carpenter, Bob	P	1947	32
Cavarretta, Phil	1B-OF	1934-53	43,23,3,44
Church, Len	P	1966	45
Coomer, Ron	3B-1B	2001	6
Fanning, Jim	C	1954-57	48,1
Felske, John	C	1968	24

Chicago Kid	Position	Years as Cubs	Numbers as Cubs
Floyd, Cliff	OF	2007	15,42*
Hargesheimer, Alan	P	1983	50
Holm, Billy	C	1943-44	12,10
Johnson, Don	2B	1943-48	20
Kennedy, Bob	*Coach*	*1963-65*	*61*
King, Ray	P	1999	56
Kush, Emil	P	1941-42, 1946-49	20,22,29
Lindstrom, Freddie	3B	1935	7
Miklos, Hank	P	1944	39
O'Leary, Charley	*Coach*	*1932-33*	*42*
Ostrowski, Johnny	3B-OF	1943-46	47,50,27
Otto, Dave	P	1994	53
Pappas, Erik	C	1991	37
Pall, Donn	P	1994	47
Rothschild, Larry	*Coach*	*2002-08*	*47,41,40,50*
Stelmaszek, Rick	C	1974	8
Stock, Milt	*Coach*	*1944-48*	*41*
Walker, Mike	P	1995	39
Wiedemayer, Charlie	P	1934	11
Winceniak, Ed	3B-SS	1956-57	12

* wore #42 for one day as a tribute to Jackie Robinson on April 15, 2007.

#45: JUG, FLASH, AND NIPPER

In Cubs lore, #45 is like a bad UHF channel that has poor reception and never has anything good on. Take **Billy Jurges,** the regular shortstop for three Cubs pennant winners while wearing other numbers. Returning to the North Side in 1946 as a player-coach, he took #45 and retired after two years of part-time play, remaining one more year as a full-time coach. He's the star in this cast.

Many of the other #45s were one-shot pitchers who either never made it or made it elsewhere. **Dave "Jug" Gerard** (1962) toiled for seven years in Chicago's farm system, only to have his sole major league year be with the horrible 1962 Cubs, who lost a franchise-record 103 games. As bad as that team was, Gerard was used almost always in mop-up time: the Cubs were 7–32 in games in which he appeared. The origins of his nickname are lost to the mists of time, as was the reason he also wore #31.

Fred Norman (1964), was like a guest star on a TV show of the day—for the hell-like quality of the College of Coaches regime, let's call it the gritty black-and-white World War II drama, *Combat!* Norman makes a cameo and based on his 0–4, 6.54 performance, maybe his only lines are in German, but he later becomes a familiar face in the colorful, prime-time 1970s hit "The Big Red Machine." **Billy Connors** (1966) had no such future stardom in his arm—he never won a game in three seasons in the bigs (and posted a stratospheric 7.31 ERA for the '66 Cubs)—though he became a fine pitching coach.

Also starring, in order of appearance: **Dick Calmus** (1967); **John Upham** (1967); **Bobby Tiefenauer** (1968), who had a 6.08 ERA in nine Cubs appearances after several good years as a Milwaukee Brave; **Alec Distaso** (1969); **Bob Miller** (1970–71), whose main claim to fame came as a 1962 Met, when he was continually confused with another guy named Bob Miller who played for the same team (the Bob Miller here went 1–12 as an original Met and had, by comparison, a perfect 0–0 mark as a not-so-original Cub); and featuring **Ray Newman** (1971) as Mop-up Guy out of the Pen #45.

Quickly cancelled were **Karl Pagel** (1978–79), older brother of NFL quarterback Mike Pagel—he hit 39 homers in Triple-A in '78, but only three Cubs at bats (all strikeouts) and at last report was driving a UPS truck in Phoenix; **Trenidad Hubbard** (2003), who had almost 4,000 minor league at bats, but over ten major league seasons averaged only 76 trips to the plate a year; and 1998 AL Rookie of the Year **Ben Grieve** (2005), who never lived up to the hype of being the second player chosen in the draft. His 20 Cubs at bats in #45 in '05 resulted in a .250 batting average.

There were other failed pilots, too. **Ed Sauer** (1945) was the wrong Sauer—Ed hit 283 fewer homers than his better-known sibling Hank, who came to Chicago four years later. **Ben "Not the Sprinter" Johnson,** whose full name was Benjamin Franklin Johnson, spent a decade in the minor leagues before the Cubs gave him 21 appearances in 1959 and 1960. He made his last appearance on June 12, 1960, and only weeks later the #45 shirt was given to the almost-identically sized **Jim Brewer** (both were 6-foot-2; Johnson was listed at 190 and Brewer 195 pounds). Brewer, who also wore #38 and #48, was wearing #45 when, on August 4, 1960, he threw a pitch high and tight to Billy Martin, then playing for the Reds. Martin charged the mound and punched Brewer in the face, breaking his cheekbone and putting him out for the season. The Cubs and Brewer sued Martin for $1 million for "loss of services" in regard to Brewer's injury. The suit dragged on for nine years before being settled for $10,000, and it was said that the bad blood between Martin and the Cubs made them reject the idea of signing him as manager after one of his many firings by George Steinbrenner. **Oscar Zamora** (1974–76) debuted well, posting a 3.12 ERA in '74, but the five-plus ERAs he put up in '75 and '76 had Cubs fans sadly singing, "If the pitch is so fat, that the ball hits the bat, that's Zamora" (to the tune of "That's Amore"). **Jay Howell** (1981) posted 155 major league saves; unfortunately, none of those came as a Cub. He had been acquired in a steal of a deal from the Reds (for backup catcher Mike O'Berry) but was sent to the Yankees a year later; he didn't round into closer form until New York traded him to Oakland. **Al Nipper** (1988) was acquired along with Calvin Schiraldi in the lamentable Lee Smith deal. Nipper had won ten games for the 1986 AL champion Red Sox, but his Cubs career was nipped in the bud—2–4 in 22 games (12 starts), after which he was released. **Tim Worrell** (2000) was the wrong Worrell; brother Todd was the star of the family. Tim did have a 38-save season for the Giants in 2003 after the Cubs sent him there for Bill Mueller.

A couple of relief pitchers wore #45 with some positive impact. **Paul Assenmacher** was a solid middle reliever after his acquisition in late 1989 (for a couple of minor leaguers who never made it); he helped the club to the '89 NL East title and then saved 33 games over the next three seasons. The Cubs wouldn't have won the 1998 wild card without **Terry Mulholland,** who made 70 appearances, including six spot starts, had three saves, and a 2.89 ERA and was known for having the best move to first base of any pitcher of his era.

Tom "Flash" Gordon could have been a longtime Cub, and was the best Cubs pitcher ever to don #45. He had gone back and forth between starting and closing in his career with the Royals and Red Sox (12–9 as a starter in 1996; 46 saves in 1998). He had an injury-plagued 1999 season with Boston and didn't pitch at all in 2000, after which the Cubs signed him as a free agent. He was still hurt when 2001 began and Jeff Fassero filled in admirably in April. Flash did a fine job until September came; he saved 27 of 29 chances until a disastrous outing in Florida on September 5—Preston Wilson crushed a three-run, walkoff homer—revealed further arm problems. Shut down until July 2002, he returned but by then had been supplanted as closer by Antonio Alfonseca. He sulked until the Cubs traded him to the Astros in August.

A couple of final names before we switch off #45, with intriguing plots for different reasons. **Kent Bottenfield** (1996–97) threw competent middle relief for the Cubs for two years and then signed with the Cardinals as a free agent. His 18-win season in 1999, by far the best year of his career, got him traded to the Angels for future Cub Jim Edmonds, one of the worst deals in

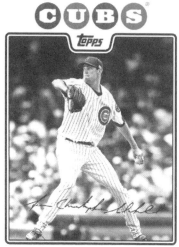

SEAN MARSHALL

Angels history. Bottenfield went 7–8, 5.71 in half a year in Anaheim before being shipped to Philadelphia, and since his departure from baseball he has become a well-known Christian music singer. The current occupant of the number, **Sean Marshall,** has a chance to be the best #45 of them all. Brought to the majors way too soon (with only 10 appearances above A-ball) in 2006, he struggled; but in 2008 he was an excellent swingman, starting and relieving, showing promise for the future and a live left arm.

MOST OBSCURE CUB TO WEAR #45: **Len Church** (1966). Lane Tech High School, located less than two miles from Wrigley Field, had produced Phil Cavarretta, a star right out of school at age eighteen and for many years after. The Cubs tried this again in 1957 when they signed Jim Woods and put him on the field at Wrigley a few months after graduation. Woods, though, was no Cavarretta; he played in only two games as a Cub, both as a pinch runner, wearing #48, and was out of baseball by age twenty-one. So when the Cubs signed Len Church out of Lane (along with his classmate John Felske), it wasn't until after college and seasoning in the minors for a couple of years before Church made his major league debut on August 27, 1966. The Lane magic had apparently run out—Church got pounded in his four relief appearances, posting a 7.50 ERA. He did face five Hall of Famers in those four games: Joe Morgan, Phil Niekro, Hank Aaron, Roberto Clemente, and Bill Mazeroski. He gave up a single to Morgan, a double to Mazeroski, and retired the other three. Sent back to the minors, he retired after 1969 to become a golf pro in Texas, where he died, far too young, of a heart attack in 1988, only forty-six years old.

GUY YOU NEVER THOUGHT OF AS A CUB WHO WORE #45: **Bobby Shantz** (1964). Everyone remembers the Brock-for-Broglio deal. But what you may not remember is that there were four other players involved in that trade: pitchers Jack Spring and Paul Toth went to St. Louis, and outfielder Doug Clemens and Shantz, a right-handed pitcher, came to the Cubs. None of the four had any impact on their teams, and the Cubs, typical for those days, were trying to recapture the long-gone glory years of a former All-Star. Shantz, one of the smallest players in modern baseball history at 5-foot-6, 142 pounds, had won 24 games in 1952 and been named AL MVP, leading the Philadelphia Athletics to their last winning season. (He was, in fact, the last Philadelphia Athletic active in the majors.) Shantz was an effective middle reliever for the Yankees, pitching in the World Series in 1957 and 1960. But by 1964 he was playing out the string at age thirty-eight, and posted a 5.56 ERA in 20 Cubs appearances. Two months after the disastrous Brock deal, he was sold back to Philadelphia—this time, to the Phillies, where he finished his career with Philly's fabled fall from first.

Quantity, Not Quality

One category in which #31 does not lead all other Cubs uniform numbers is in the actual number of Cubs pitchers who have worn it. It's close, but #45 has taken the top spot for most pitchers in the last four seasons. Thank you, Will Ohman and Sean Marshall. With the possibility of retiring #31 for Hall of Famer Fergie Jenkins and Cooperstown shoo-in Greg Maddux, it would be a surprise if any other pitchers joined that list, and #38 may be on hold for a while with Carlos Zambrano; #33—a more itinerant number—might yet make reach for the sky.

Uniform #	Number of Pitchers
45	32
33	31
38	31
32	30
37	30
31	27
34	25
39	25
41	23
30	22
36	22
40	22
35	19
43	19
47	19
49	18
48	17
22	14
42	14
44	14
46	14
50	14

#46: WHAT MIGHT HAVE BEEN, PART DEUX

The story of #46 is a twofold tale of "too late" and "too soon." Of the seventeen players who have worn the number, all but three (**Marv Rickert, Dom Dallessandro,** and **Ed Mickelson**) have been pitchers, and no position player has worn it since Mickelson did so briefly in 1957.

But of the others—oh, how a change here or there might have made this number famous. Or retired. **Al Lary** wore it for the awful 1962 Cubs (eight years after wearing #31, in 1954). He went 0-1, 7.15 in 15 appearances. If only instead of Al, the Cubs had his brother Frank, a four-time 15-game winner for the Tigers.

Larry Jackson won 24 games for the Cubs in 1964, the most any Cubs pitcher has won in a season (tied by Fergie Jenkins in 1971) since Grover Cleveland Alexander's 27 in 1920. But what if Jackson had been averaging 15 wins a year from 1957–62 for the Cubs instead of the Cardinals? Maybe they'd have had a chance to contend, particularly in 1959 when Ernie Banks had one of his two MVP seasons and the team finished only thirteen games out of first place. At least Jackson helped bring Fergie to the Cubs in the 1966 deal with Philly.

Dave Dowling was hyped as a pitching prospect after being acquired from St. Louis, and perhaps he could have joined Fergie, Bill Hands, and Kenny Holtzman in 1969 and beyond. But he only started one game for the Cubs, on September 22, 1966, a complete-game, 7-2 win, before leaving baseball to go to dental school. He now practices as an orthodontist in the Phoenix area.

Ken Johnson? Too late; five years after he threw the only nine-inning, complete-game, no-hit loss in major league history, he made nine decent relief appearances for the Cubs, then got released. **Juan Pizarro?** Too late; after pitching in the 1957 and 1958 World Series for the Milwaukee Braves at just barely drinking age and winning 61 games for the White Sox from 1961–64, the Cubs tried to catch lightning in a bottle by acquiring him from the Angels for Archie Reynolds. Pizarro was decent—going 7–6, 3.46 with three shutouts in 1971—but the Cubs still didn't win.

And that brings us to the #46 who could have had the number retired in his honor: **Lee Smith** (1980–87). Big Lee, a Louisiana native, stood 6-foot-5, threw hard, and wound up holding the major league saves record from 1993–2006. But at first the Cubs couldn't figure out what to do with him. In 1982 he actually started five games. He eventually settled in as closer and he saved 33 games for the 1984 NL East champs; Smith repeated that number the next year. But by 1987, even though he tied what was then the club record with 37 saves, he blew 12 save chances and was being booed regularly. Jim Frey, who was out of his league after being promoted from dugout boss to general manager, supposedly rejected offers to trade Smith to the Dodgers for Bob Welch, and to the Braves for John Smoltz and Jeff Blauser (while the shortstop still had his best years ahead of him, rather than the ghost-Blauser the Cubs got in 1998). Instead, Frey shipped Smith to the Red Sox for Al Nipper and Calvin Schiraldi, neither of whom will ever make any top-ten Cubs list (unless it's a negative list). Smith, meanwhile, went on to have 298 more saves, including 18 against the Cubs (or 13 more saves than Schiraldi had in a Cubs uniform), and Big Lee may eventually make the Hall of Fame.

RYAN DEMPSTER

Steve Trachsel (1993–99) won't make the Hall of Fame, but the Stall of Fame is a possibility for the deliberate—who are we kidding?—downright slow right-hander. He had one fine year in Chicago—1998—going 15–8 and winning the wild-card tiebreaker game against the Giants on September 28. Nationally, though, he'll always be remembered for the pitch that year that Mark McGwire served over the fence in St. Louis for his 62nd home run. Trachsel later had several solid seasons for the Mets after the Cubs let him leave via free agency. When he returned to the Cubs in 2007 for a not-so-great encore (1–3, 8.31), he wore #52, as #46 had been taken for several years by **Ryan Dempster** (2004–08).

Dempster may at last take the "too late" tag off #46, because he had two fine years as a closer, 2005 and 2007 (the 2006 season, he'd likely want to forget). His 4.73 ERA in 2007 was inflated by two disastrous four-run outings in September, one of which came after the Cubs clinched the NL Central. During the 2007–08 offseason, Dempster let it be known that he wanted to try starting again, as he had enjoyed some success in that role with the Marlins (he made the All-Star team as a Florida starter in 2000). He began a tough workout routine, including running up and down Camelback Mountain in Arizona, one of the toughest trails in that state, and it paid off—he once again made the All-Star team in 2008 and had the best record of his career, going 17–6 with a 2.96 ERA.

MOST OBSCURE CUB TO WEAR #46: **Ed Mickelson** (1957). Mickelson had a couple cups o'coffee with the two St. Louis teams, going 1-for-10 for the Cardinals in 1950 and 2-for-15 with the Browns in 1953. Those poor performances didn't stop the Cubs from taking him north with the club in 1957, in the days when rosters could be larger than twenty-five for the first weeks of the season. Mickelson was an afterthought; he started two games and subbed in four others, going 0-for-12 and getting his only Cub RBI on a foul pop-up on which Ernie Banks scored.

GUY YOU NEVER THOUGHT OF AS A CUB WHO WORE #46: **Steve Barber** (1970). A hard- and wild-throwing lefty (130 walks and 150 strikeouts in 1961), Barber won 101 games for the Orioles from 1960 through 1966, though he didn't pitch in the O's World Series sweep of the Dodgers. Like fellow #46 Ken Johnson, Barber threw a no-hitter and lost (though Stu Miller got the last out); and like a lot of hard throwers of that era, Barber got hurt. Without modern surgical techniques available, he drifted from team to team, trying to get back his old form. The Cubs signed him on April 23, 1970, and after five appearances and a 9.53 ERA, they released him on June 30. He managed to resurrect his career and have a couple of fine years as a middle reliever with the Angels in 1972 and 1973.

Save It

The save, an important modern statistic, is a Chicago invention. Chicago sportswriter Jerome Holtzman came up with the system that first quantified the late-inning reliever's role and eventually led to many becoming wealthy men. The Cubs have been keeping track of saves since 1960 and Holtzman's creation has been an official stat since 1969.

The Cubs have racked up a ton of saves in the last half century. Some numbers seem better equipped than others, or more accurately, have better pitchers who wind up wearing those numbers. Not surprisingly the three most successful Cubs closers of 1960–2008 correspond with the top three numbers on the chart:

1. Lee Smith #46 (180 career saves)
2. Bruce Sutter #42 (133)
3. Randy Myers #28 (112)

Uni #	Number of pitchers	Total saves for uniform number	Uni #	Number of pitchers	Total saves for uniform number
46	5	273	50	3	24
42	5	167	30	3	22
28	2	164	35	4	21
38	10	110	37	8	21
45	16	106	57	1	19
32	8	80	40	6	14
36	10	70	62	1	14
47	6	67	13	2	13
39	9	65	31	4	13
27	3	64	54	1	13
43	7	64	44	6	12
48	5	59	52	1	11
41	6	55	17	1	9
34	6	49	21	1	3
51	5	45	16	1	2
33	6	40	29	1	1
49	8	35	55	1	1

#47: SHOOTER, PEANUTS, AND SPUD

DENNIS LAMP
PITCHER

Rod "Shooter" Beck was one of the most genuine individuals ever to wear a Cubs uniform. Signed as a free agent before the 1998 season, his droopy mustache and arms-flailing delivery became fan favorites as he saved 51 games for the NL wild card winners, including the wild card tiebreaker on September 28. But he got hurt the next season—later, he admitted he was injured at the end of 1998 and could have had offseason surgery—and, blowing saves left and right, he finally went to the DL. He was traded to the Red Sox at the 1999 waiver trading deadline on August 31. He re-signed with the Cubs as a free agent before the 2003 season, and they assigned him to Iowa, where he lived in his trailer behind the scoreboard at the ballpark, holding cookouts for anyone to attend. He had had an agreement with the Cubs that if he received another major league offer, they'd let him go—so when the Padres called, he went, saving 20 games that year for San Diego. Too bad, as the Cubs could have used him in the postseason. (Same song, different verse.) The popular Beck passed away suddenly, far too young at thirty-eight, in June 2007.

Jack Brickhouse once made a groaner of a pun of **Dennis Lamp**'s name on a dark, gloomy day by saying, "It's really dark here at the ballpark even though there's a Lamp on the mound!" Lamp was another example of a player whose Cubs performance, decent though it was (28 wins in three-plus seasons), simply got him a ticket out of town. Or, in Lamp's case, to the other side of town: he was traded to the White Sox for Ken Kravec, who won two games as a Cub while Lamp's solid pitching helped lead the Sox to the 1983 playoffs. Later, he went 11–0 in 53 games (one start) for the Blue Jays in their 1985 AL East title year. His lone Cubs highlight was a one-hit shutout of the Padres on June 9, 1978.

Harry "Peanuts" Lowrey, who got his nickname from his 5-foot-8, 170-pound stature, was the regular center fielder for the 1945 NL champion Cubs. He had to cover a lot of ground, as right fielder Bill Nicholson was mostly immobile. Lowrey had good speed, stealing 13, 11, and 10 bases in 1943, 1945 (he missed the 1944 season due to military service), and 1946, and while those don't seem like huge numbers today, consider the era: the 13 steals in 1943 ranked second in the National League. He was traded in one of the better deals the Cubs made in that fallow period: Lowrey and Harry Walker were sent to Cincinnati on June 15, 1949, for two mainstays of the Cubs lineup in the 1950s, **Hank Sauer** and **Frankie Baumholtz,** both of whom wore #47 for part of '49. Lowrey later returned to Chicago as a coach, wearing #7 in 1970 and 1971 and #2 in 1977, 1978, 1979, and 1981.

Most of the other #47ers were single-season guys: **Dale Alderson** (1944); **Solly Drake** (1956); **Don Prince** (1962), who, having thrown only one inning, would have won the "Most Obscure" nod for this chapter if not for someone far more interesting whom you'll read about later; **Arnie Earley** (1966), acquired too late in his career (age thirty-three) to be of any real use to the Cubs; **Chuck Estrada** (1966); **Gary Krug** (1981); **Derek Botelho** (1985), another refugee from the Phillies organization brought over by Dallas Green, as was **Dickie Noles** (1987; Noles also wore #48 in an earlier Cubs stint); **Bill Landrum** (1988), who pitched in seven games for the Cubs, departed and had three decent years as a closer for the Pirates; and Chicago native **Donn Pall** (1994), known as "the Pope" for the way his name rhymed with the pontiff's. Pall had several good years for the White Sox, but pitched only four innings (with two runs allowed) on the North Side.

Four other pitchers wore #47 for brief flings with the Cubs with a few good days followed by more bad ones. **Ken Frailing** (1974–76)—you can hear him telling the payroll secretary on his first day, "You spell it 'failing,' only you throw in an 'r' "—was one of four players acquired from the White Sox for Ron Santo after the 1973 season. He was installed immediately into the starting rotation, and flopped immediately; he had to be demoted to the bullpen after going 5–7, 4.83 as a starter. He was better in relief—a 2.08 ERA in 40 relief appearances—but lasted only two more seasons before leaving baseball for good. **Doug Bird** (1981–82), who was acquired in the Rick Reuschel trade from the Yankees, posted a decent 4–5 mark with a 3.58 ERA in '81, but regressed to 9–14, 5.14 the next year and was sent to the Red Sox. **Shawn Boskie** (1990–94) could have been Ryne Sandberg's stunt double (a very strong facial resemblance). Boskie, a first-round pick by the Cubs in 1986, had a promising 5–6, 3.69 season for a poor 1990 Cubs team at age twenty-three, but the next three years brought a 14–23 mark with a combined 4.68 ERA and a trade to the Phillies. Boskie landed on his feet after baseball, becoming one of the managing partners in a Phoenix-area venture capital firm. **Todd Van Poppel** (2000–01) was a highly-ballyhooed first-round draft pick of the A's. (He had let the then-woebegotten Braves know, in 1990, that he wouldn't sign with them if picked first overall; he fell to Oakland with the fourteenth selection. Ironically, of course, had he let the Braves choose him, he'd have been with the singular powerhouse NL franchise of the 1990s, but maybe Atlanta wouldn't have been so good if they'd picked Van Poppel instead of some kid named Chipper.) By 2000 Van Poppel was a mediocre middle reliever who put up two good years as a set-up man for the Cubs, which got him one of the first big free-agent deals offered to such a pitcher (two years, $4.5 million from the Rangers), but he never again threw as well as he had in his two years in Cubs blue.

Virgil "Spud" Davis (1950–53), the other title subject of this chapter, was a catcher for the original Gas House Gang in St. Louis in 1934, and played sixteen seasons in the National League, none of them for the Cubs. When Frank Frisch, one of the key players in that Cardinals era, was named Cub manager, he brought his bud Spud over as a coach. Frisch was fired in 1951, but Davis (who had coached under, and then replaced, Frisch for the final three games of the 1946 season as manager of the Pirates when Frisch was fired there) stayed on for two more years as a coach under Frisch's successor, Phil Cavarretta. All of Cavarretta's coaches—Charlie Root, Roy Johnson, Ray Blades, and Davis—were either fired or reassigned after the '53 season and Davis left baseball and returned to his hometown of Birmingham, Alabama, where he worked in various businesses until his death in 1984.

MOST OBSCURE CUB TO WEAR #47: **Jophery Brown** (1968). Brown not only wins the "most obscure #47" award—he pitched in only one game, throwing two innings and allowing a run in a 5-1 loss to the Pirates on September 21, 1968—but also gets the prize for "Most Interesting Post-Baseball Career." He became a renowned Hollywood stuntman, doing stunts in over 100 films, even as recently as 2007's *Feast of Love* at age 62, and having bit parts as an actor in about a third of them. Remember the worker who gets eaten by the raptor in the first *Jurassic Park*? That was Jophery Brown. He also had small roles in *Rocky III*, *Sudden Impact*, *The Presidio*, and the first *Spider-Man*.

GUY YOU NEVER THOUGHT OF AS A CUB WHO WORE #47: **Miguel Batista** (1997). Batista could also be called "the guy you never thought of as an Expo, Pirate, or Marlin," because he bounced around those organizations before being acquired by the Cubs on waivers on December 17, 1996. He was 0–5, 5.70 in 11 appearances (five starts) for the 94-loss '97 Cubs, but he produced for the organization anyway: after the 1997 season he was traded back to his original club, the Expos, for Henry Rodriguez, who had a couple of productive years in Chicago. Meanwhile, Batista became a competent starter for several teams, pitching in the 2001 World Series for Arizona and also having a 31-save season for Toronto. The versatile and sensitive Batista also published a book of poetry in Spanish and a thriller in English.

Oh, Those Bases on Balls

You have to take the good with the bad. If #31 is going to lead in all the favorable pitching categories—plus losses—it's got to take it on the chin with the walks. The funny thing is, though, that Fergie Jenkins, whose dominance helped push #31 to top in the other stats categories, didn't even make the top ten in issuing walks. He's number eleven with 620—#31 Greg Maddux is fourteenth with 547. Carlos Zambrano already has more free passes than either of them, but he's barely nudged #38 into the top ten. Still, the individual record for walks is pretty safe. Bill Hutchinson, born during the Civil War and whose last pitch for the franchise was thrown in 1895, is the only pitcher in Cubs history to have a career four-digit walk total. His 1,109 bases on balls—long before uniform numbers, needless to say—were almost as many walks as Maddux and Jenkins combined.

Uniform #	Walks by Pitchers	Uniform #	Walks by Pitchers
31	2,477	49	1,307
36	1,937	17	1,288
34	1,895	48	1,174
30	1,871	39	1,096
32	1,848	35	980
33	1,617	22	955
37	1,420	18	931
38	1,416	41	876
46	1,380	44	850
40	1,359	45	827

#48: BIG DADDY AND HANDY ANDY

Rick Reuschel was a giant of a man (listed at 6-foot-3, 235, he may have been even heavier than that); in spite of that, he

RICK
REUSCHEL
CHICAGO CUBS   PITCHER

was an excellent athlete who was a good hitter (35 career doubles) and was occasionally used as a pinch runner. This, despite being teased by his teammate Steve Stone, who once was asked how the clubhouse food spreads were when he played for the Cubs. His response: "I have no idea. I never had any, because there was always 500 pounds of Reuschels between me and the spread."

Younger brother of big-boned Cubs reliever Paul Reuschel, who debuted later and retired earlier than his sibling, Rick Reuschel reached the majors only two years after he was drafted in 1970. Reuschel went a respectable 10–8 with a fine 2.93 ERA in his rookie season, puzzlingly not getting a single vote in the 1972 NL Rookie of the Year balloting. (Jon Matlack won it for the Mets.)

The following year he began to define the term "workhorse." From 1973 through 1980, Reuschel never pitched fewer than 234 innings, starting between 35 and 39 games each year. Even so, he was really no better than a .500 pitcher until 1977, when he and the rest of the Cubs roared out to a 48–33 start and an 8½-game lead in late June. On July 28, he was sent into the game against the Reds in relief in the thirteenth inning, and his base hit began a rally in the bottom of the inning; the pure-joy grin on his face as he scored the winning run on Davey Rosello's single in a 16-15 victory is a singular memory for any Cubs fan from the 1970s.

After that win, Reuschel was 15–3 with a 2.14 ERA and was the odds-on favorite for the NL Cy Young Award. Needless to say, it didn't happen—the team collapsed and despite pitching reasonably well the rest of the year, Rick wound up 20–10 and finished third in the Cy Young balloting behind Steve Carlton. It was the only 20-win season for a Cubs pitcher between Fergie Jenkins's 24-win season in 1971 and Greg Maddux's 20-win season in 1992.

By 1981, the Cubs had fallen to the depths of the NL, and Rick was off to a 4–7 start (though with a team that was 15–37 at the time, maybe that wasn't so bad). Given the pressure to "do something," GM Bob Kennedy traded him to the Yankees the day that year's strike started. When the strike was settled, the Cubs received Doug Bird and a prospect named Mike Griffin, who never panned out. Bird was a marginally useful starting pitcher, and Reuschel went 4–4 for the Yankees in 11 starts, pitching for them in both the split-season 1981 division series, and the 1981 World Series. A torn rotator cuff ruined most of the next two years for Rick, but the Cubs re-signed him (he looked odd wearing #47 in 1983, but he reclaimed his familiar #48 the next season) and he contributed to the 1984 NL East champions, though he was disappointed to not be named to the playoff roster. They could have used him as the rest of the bullpen collapsed in the NLCS. Never a favorite of the Dallas Green regime, he was allowed to depart as a free agent after the 1984 season—and, fully recovered from arm surgery, he won

14 games for the Pirates in 1985, and later had a 19-win season for the Giants in 1988 and a 17-victory season in '89, when he started—and won—the decisive Game 5 of the NLCS against his former team.

Andy Pafko (1944–51) patrolled the outfield at Wrigley Field for more than eight seasons. The Wisconsin native, purchased in 1941 from Green Bay in the Wisconsin State League, was in the major leagues less than two years later (wearing #33 at the end of the 1943 season) and batted .379 as a call up. He was installed in center field the following year and had a nice rookie season. Pafko helped lead the Cubs to the pennant in 1945 with 12 HR (that may not sound like many today, but league-leader Tommy Holmes had only 28), 110 RBI (good for third in the league), and a .298 average; he finished fourth in the NL MVP voting. He continued to put up solid seasons for the Cubs as the team free-fell to the bottom of the NL standings. Pafko was named to the All-Star team five times in six years, including 1948, his only year in the major as a regular third baseman. He hit a career-high 36 homers in 1950 as the Cubs finished seventh.

The next year, inexplicably, management, perhaps wanting to shake up a moribund franchise, traded the still-in-his-prime Pafko to the Dodgers in an eight-player deal. None of the players acquired matched the performance or popularity of Pafko. Meanwhile, Handy Andy settled right in to left field with the Dodgers, where he achieved photographic immortality for the wrong reason. He was the outfielder looking dejectedly at Bobby Thomson's "Shot Heard 'Round The World" at the Polo Grounds on October 3, 1951.

Pafko played in three more World Series—with the Dodgers in 1952 and his home-state Milwaukee Braves in 1957 and 1958, but, in his own words quoted in *The Sporting News* of June 27, 1951, his biggest thrill in baseball came much closer to home:

> *It was 1945 and the Cubs were battling for the pennant. It was the next-to-the-last week of the season and the Pirates were at Wrigley Field. It was a Saturday and the fans were giving me a day. My mother and father had come down from Wisconsin to see me play. My mother had never seen me play before. I never*

wanted to hit one so much in my life. Preacher Roe was pitching for the Pirates. My first time up I found the bases loaded. I guess I was trying too hard, because Preach struck me out. But I was lucky. I got another chance. The next time up the situation was exactly the same. The bases were loaded again.

This time I didn't miss. I hit one into the stands and I don't think I'll ever have another thrill like that one. Looking back now, it's even bigger. Because that was the only time my mother ever saw me play. She'd never seen me play before and she was never to see me again. She died a couple of years ago without ever getting another chance.

Many times, ballplayers get the details wrong but this one, Pafko got right, except for the day of the week (it was Sunday, not Saturday). He hit what the *Tribune* termed "a four-run homer" and the Cubs beat the Pirates, 7-3.

The 1950s produced a bunch of lackluster hitters at #48: **Gene Hermanski** (1951), who came over from Brooklyn in the eight-player deal, took over Pafko's number but didn't hit like him; **Jim Fanning** (1954) had a better career as an executive; **Luis Marquez** (1954); **Jim King** (1955–56), who later hit 89 homers in six and a half seasons with the expansion Senators in the 1960s; and Lane Tech grad **Jim Woods** (1957).

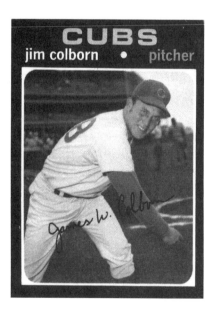

After Woods's brief appearance in #48, it became exclusively a pitcher's number, specializing in has-beens: **Frank Baumann** (1965) and **Dennis Rasmussen** (1992), who won 91 major league games in 12 seasons—all of them for other teams (0–0, 10.80 in three Cubs appearances); never-weres: **Dickie Noles** (1982–84), **Jay Baller** (1985–

87), who had a great fastball but no idea where or how to throw it, **Dave Stevens** (1998), and **Ruben Quevedo** (2000), who had a good repertoire but ate his way out of baseball; and guys who had better careers elsewhere: **Jim Brewer** (1961; Brewer also wore #38 and #45); **Jim Colborn** (1969–71), who went 4-2, 3.78 in three brief Cubs call ups, yet became the first 20-game winner in Milwaukee Brewers history in 1972; and **Mark Clark** (1997; Clark switched to #54 in 1998). **Ryan O'Malley** (2006) pitched in only two major league games, but his first, on August 16, 2006, was memorable. Called up from Triple-A on only a few hours' notice after the Cubs had played an eighteen-inning night game in Houston, he was driven by limousine from the Iowa Cubs' road trip in Round Rock, Texas early the next morning; he threw eight five-hit, shutout innings against the Astros in a 1-0 victory, one of the few highlights of the misbegotten 2006 season. Six days later at Wrigley Field, he took the field to a standing ovation against the Phillies, and after allowing three runs in 4 $^2/_3$ innings, he left the major league field, never to return.

One other #48 who deserves mention is **Joe Borowski** (2001–05). "Lunch Bucket Joe," signed almost as an afterthought by the Cubs out of the Mexican League in 2000, was brought to the majors for one start in 2001, replacing Kerry Wood, who had to skip a start. Borowski wound up giving up Barry Bonds's 50th homer of the season and took the loss while giving up six runs in less than two innings. It was his only major league start. Working hard, he came back the next year as a reliever and in 2003 saved 33 games for the NL Central champions. In 2004, his performance declined and it took two months before he admitted to a shoulder problem. He had surgery and came back a year later, but, inexplicably, the Cubs let him go. He wound up having solid years for the Marlins in 2006 (36 saves) and for the 2007 AL Central champion Indians, leading the AL with 45 saves despite a 5.07 ERA. It's Joe's bulldog attitude and work ethic that will always make him a fond memory for Cubs fans.

MOST OBSCURE CUB TO WEAR #48: **Dave Lemonds** (1969). Lemonds, drafted out of the University of North Carolina in the first round of what was then termed the "secondary phase" of the 1968 draft, was deemed "ready" in June 1969 and so, at age twenty-one, he was recalled to start a game in Montreal against the Expos. Lemonds gave up four hits, three walks, and two runs in 2.2 innings and was the losing pitcher in a 5-2 Cubs loss, but that wasn't the story of the game, which was delayed two hours by a torrential rainstorm. In the second inning Ernie Banks hit what appeared to be a home run. Expos outfielder Rusty Staub, taking advantage of the poor field conditions and visibility (the game probably shouldn't have been played at all, as there was an afternoon game scheduled the next day), told umpire Tony Venzon that the ball had gone *under* the fence at Parc Jarry. Venzon believed Staub and despite an angry tirade from Leo Durocher, the play stood as a ground-rule double; Banks advanced to third base on a flyout, but wound up stranded. Durocher played the game under protest, but as in most of those situations, the protest was denied. As for Lemonds, he threw two scoreless innings of relief against the Cardinals five days later, and eventually he was traded to the White Sox in a five-player deal. And Banks is still out that 513th home run.

GUY YOU NEVER THOUGHT OF AS A CUB WHO WORE #48: **Joe Niekro** (1967-69). Phil's younger brother had a twenty-two-year major league career in which he won 221 games (combined with Phil, they had a brother-record 539 wins). Unfortunately for Cubs fans, only 24 of those wins were in the blue pinstripes. Joe, off to a slow start in 1969 after good years in '67 and '68, was shipped to the Padres for Dick Selma, who became popular for leading the Bleacher Bums in cheers but who spent only one year in a Cubs uniform. Niekro, meanwhile, put together two decades of pitching, winning 197 games in other uniforms and appearing in the postseason three times, including two scoreless innings in the World Series for the champion 1987 Twins.

Boy, the Way Hank Sauer Played

This "All in the Family" segment features Cubs father-son and brother combinations and the numbers they wore. It's a pretty nondescript bunch, with the Sauer, Matthews, Hundley, and Reuschel clans the only ones on anyone's Christmas card list. Out of respect, we'll mention here the Cubs family pairs that played before there were numbers: father and son Jimmy Cooney, plus Herm and Jack Doscher (the former appeared as a Cub in 1879). Larry and Mike Corcoran were the first fraternal teammates in Cubs history in 1884. They were followed by Jiggs and Tom Parrott in 1893 and Kid and Lew Camp in 1894.

Of the number-wearing families, Todd Hundley was the only son to wear his father's number (and he had to wear another number until that became available). Four of the five fathers in the list below went on to coach for the Cubs (Marty Keough being the lone exception) and an asterisk is placed next to the number they wore as coaches. Bobby Adams wore #51 as a coach in 1961–65 and #2 while coaching in 1973. Randy Hundley was a player-coach wearing #4 in 1977. Gary Matthews was a coach wearing familiar #36 (2003-06). Chris Speier wore #35 as a coach (2005-06). None of these four got to coach their sons in Chicago.

The Breedens and Reuschels are the only number-wearing brother combos to be Cubs teammates.

Cubs father	Year(s) Playing	Uni #
Bobby Adams	1957–60	#7, #16, #51*, #2*
Marty Keough	1966	#28
Randy Hundley	1966–73, 1976–77	#9, #5, #4*
Gary Matthews	1984–87	#36*
Chris Speier	1985–86	#28, #35*
Cubs son	Year	Uni #
Mike Adams	1976–77	#21, #30
Matt Keough	1986	#33
Todd Hundley	2001–02	#99, #9
Gary Matthews, Jr.	2000–01	#51, #19
Justin Speier	1998	#56

Cubs brother	Year	Uni #
Ed Sauer	1943–45	#29, #49, #45
Hank Sauer	1949–55	#43, #47, #9
Mort Cooper	1949	#34
Walker Cooper	1954–55	#25
Solly Drake	1956	#47
Sammy Drake	1960–61	#19
Danny Breeden	1971	#19
Hal Breeden	1971	#25
Rick Reuschel	1972–81, 1983–84	#48, #47
Paul Reuschel	1975–78	#43

#49: BILL HANDS ON DECK

Bill Hands (1966-72) wasn't the first pitcher you thought of when the Cubs came to town in the late 1960s or early 1970s. On a roster that included future Hall of Famer Fergie Jenkins and hard-throwing lefty Kenny Holtzman, Hands was sometimes an afterthought, but he helped complete a formidable staff. Hands came to the Cubs with Randy Hundley in a heist from San Francisco on December 2, 1965. (Lindy McDaniel and Don Landrum went west in exchange.) In 1968 Hands won 16 games and walked the fewest batters in the league per nine innings, although he also led the NL in homers allowed. He won 20 games and threw 300 innings in '69, and Jenkins still led the club in both categories. Hands's 2.49 ERA, however, led the team. He won 41 games over the next three seasons, but his ERA was 3.00 or higher each season. In 1972 the Cubs traded Hands and two youngsters to Minnesota for lefty Dave LaRoche. While his pitching skills slipped in the AL, Hands benefited from the advent of the designated hitter in '73 as his putrid batting average could go no lower than .078. His lack of batting prowess was legendary among his Cubs teammates, and at one time Ron Santo had a standing bet that Hands would never hit a home run. On September 4, 1970, when Hands hit a long fly ball to center field at Wrigley Field against the Mets, Santo found himself rooting for the ball *not* to go out of the park, even though the game was tied at the time. It didn't—Hands settled for a double, one of only six in his career. The Cubs did win the game, 7-4.

Vince Barton (1932) was the first #49, starting in right field the first day the numbers were handed out. His batting numbers—.224/.273/.351—quickly put that uni number into circulation. **Carroll Yerkes** later that year became the first pitcher to wear it, followed by young third baseman **Stan Hack** (1933), who went through eight numbers in a career that kept him in a Cubs uniform, as a player, coach and manager, into the mid-1960s.

Kirby Higbe (1937) wore #49 on his first recall to the Cubs at age twenty-two. As was customary for young, unproven players, he was assigned different numbers in his other two years with the Cubs: #25 in 1938 and #29 in 1939, the only full season he spent in a Cubs uniform (not a very good one: 12–15 in 43 games, 28 starts, with a 4.67 ERA). Higbe went on to a solid career, mostly with the Dodgers, and pitched for them in the 1941 World Series. He left the Cubs in one of the better deals they made in that era: traded to the Phillies on May 29, 1939, along with Joe Marty and Ray Harrell, in exchange for Claude Passeau, who would become a mainstay in the Cubs rotation for most of the 1940s.

Frank Secory (1944-46) had 156 at bats as a part-time outfielder for the Cubs between 1944 and 1946, hitting .237, and went 2-for-5 in the 1945 World Series. Even at that, he wouldn't really be worth a mention here except that in 1952 he became a National League umpire, calling games for nineteen seasons and umpiring in four World Series.

The lot of the 49er, for the most part, has been to pitch. Of the twenty-six Cubs to don the number, two were coaches, eighteen were pitchers, and six position players, but no non-moundsman has worn it since **Steve Bilko** (1954), a huge man (6-foot-1, 230 pounds) for his time who would hit monstrous home runs and also strike out monstrously. (He'd have made a perfect DH had they had them in those days.) The Cubs bought him from the Cardinals early in the 1954 season and didn't quite seem to know what to do with him. For several seasons he bounced up and down between the Cubs and their then-top farm team in the Pacific Coast League, the pre-major league L.A. Angels. He dominated the PCL, hitting 148 homers from 1955-57 and winning the league Triple Crown in 1956 when he hit .360 with 55 HR and 164 RBI. But he played only 47 games for the North Siders, hitting .239 in 92 at bats with four homers. He'd have been a natural hitting in Wrigley Field in the 1950s. Eventually Bilko went to the major league Angels in the expansion draft, and, ironically, hit the last home run in Wrigley Field—but not in Chicago; that blast was hit in Wrigley Field in Los Angeles, the Angels' first major league home, in 1961.

No non-pitcher has worn #49 since Bilko; it lay fallow for eleven years until Hands wore it; **Frank Castillo** (1991-97) shares the record with Hands for the longest tenure in the #49 shirt. Castillo had a promising 10–11, 3.46 season at age twenty-three in 1992, but was then beset by injuries and never really made it. His shining Cubs moment was a near no-hitter thrown against St. Louis on September 25, 1995; it was broken up with two outs in the ninth by a Bernard Gilkey triple. Castillo also struck out 13 that night.

Jamie Moyer (1986-88), a sinkerballing, Tommy John–style lefty, looked good but was traded away in the Mitch Williams deal, a trade that helped the Cubs to the 1989 NL East title. No one could have guessed that Moyer would still be

FRANK CASTILLO
CUBS

JAMIE MOYER

pitching twenty years later, finally reaching his first World Series in his twenty-second major league season in 2008, including the Rangers and Cardinals, who released him, and the Cubs, who signed him back before the 1992 season and then released him at the end of spring training—but not before offering him a minor league coaching job. Moyer thanked the Cubs but told them he thought he could still pitch. Guess he was right.

So through most of the 1980s and 1990s, #49, which longtime Cubs fans had remembered fondly from Hands's days, went to guys who were World Series heroes with other teams (**Rawly Eastwick**, 1981, a hero for the 1975-76 Reds); guys who had been on NCAA college basketball championship teams (**Tim Stoddard**, 1984, a member of the 1974 North Carolina State Wolfpack), or never-wases-and-never-will-bes (**Steve Engel**, 1985; **Will Cunnane**, 2002; **Jimmy Anderson**, 2004, **and John Koronka**, 2005).

But after the detritus of the early 2000s, #49 lay waiting for the man who may, over time, become its most famous occupant: **Carlos Marmol** (2006-08), the man with the electric slider.

MOST OBSCURE CUB TO WEAR #49: **Kennie Steenstra** (1998) was one of the Cubs' better pitching prospects in the 1990s, but he never got a real opportunity to prove himself in Chicago. He toiled for seven seasons in the farm system, winning 66 games before getting a token opportunity in four games early in the 1998 season. (We're wondering about the spelling of "Kennie," too. What's up with that?)

GUY YOU NEVER THOUGHT OF AS A CUB WHO WORE #49: **Donnie Moore** (1975-79) had four decent years as a middle reliever, starting one game each year, but the Cubs in those years had plenty of good relief pitchers. They dealt him to the Cardinals for Mike "Not the Chicken Guy" Tyson and later, of course, Moore gave up a devastating home run in the 1986 ALCS, said to have unhinged him and led to his eventual suicide.

Clown College

The College of Coaches was the poster child for bad ideas from the mind of owner P. K. Wrigley. In the first ninety years of the franchise's existence, dating back to the National Association in 1871, the franchise had never lost more than 94 games in a season. Two years into the College—and the 162-game schedule—the Cubs got an F, or the baseball equivalent of that grade: their first 100+ loss season, a 59–103 mark.

Wrigley had announced the system to a skeptical press by saying, "The dictionary tells you a manager is the one who bosses and a coach is the one who works. We want workers." They may have had workers, but the system never worked. First of all, few coaches with managerial options or aspirations would go anywhere near the Cubs. (Though Harry Craft did go from the 1961 College of Coaches to manager of the first-year Houston Colt .45s, who would finish ahead of the '62 Cubs.) Second, Wrigley could replace head coaches even quicker than he did managers—and only seven years earlier he had fired popular and honest Phil Cavarretta while the team was still in spring training. Third, not all coaches got chances to be head coach; most lamentably Buck O'Neil, who was baseball's first African-American coach and could have been the first manager of color. (It took thirteen more years for that barrier to be broken, by Frank Robinson in Cleveland.) O'Neil, a championship manager in the Negro Leagues, getting a chance to lead the Cubs? Now that would have been innovative.

The experiment continued, though Bob Kennedy ran the team on the field for the next two-plus seasons. The Cubs showed an improvement of twenty-three games and had a winning season in '63. Kennedy was eventually replaced in June 1965 by Lou Klein, who had twice previously served as head coach. Leo Durocher was brought in the next year to clean up the mess, stating, memorably, at his introductory press conference: "If no announcement has been made about what my title is, I'm making it here and now. I'm the manager. I'm not a head coach. I'm the manager." Starting from scratch, the Cubs again lost 103 games. They followed with a winning record each of the next six seasons. No Cubs team has put together that many consecutive winning seasons since Leo—but no other Cubs team has hit 100 losses, either.

Here's the rundown by the numbers of College of Coaches in order of P. K.'s whim.

Head Coach	Year	Record	Uni#
Vedie Himsl	1961	5–6	#4
Harry Craft	1961	4–8	#53

Head Coach	Year	Record	Uni#
Vedie Himsl	1961	5–12	#4
El Tappe	1961	2–0	#52
Harry Craft	1961	3–1	#53
Vedie Himsl	1961	0–3	#4
El Tappe	1961	35–43	#52
Lou Klein	1961	5–6	#60
El Tappe	1961	5–11	#53
*El Tappe	1962	4–16	#53
Lou Klein	1962	12–18	#60
Charlie Metro	1962	43–69	#63
Bob Kennedy	1963–65	182–198	#61
Lou Klein	1965	48–58	#60

*The only "Player–Head Coach" in baseball history.

#50–#59: THE NOT-SO-FABULOUS 50s

Player	years
50	
Walter Signer	1943
Joe Stephenson	1944
John Ostrowski	1944–46
George Piktuzis	1956
Charlie Grimm (manager)	1960
(coach)	1961–63
Whitey Lockman (coach)	1965
Steve Renko	1976–77
Mike Griffin	1981
Tom Filer	1982
Alan Hargesheimer	1983
Dave Beard	1985
Guy Hoffman	1986
Les Lancaster	1987–91
Alex Arias	1992
Jason Maxwell	1998
Phil Norton	2000, 2003
Julian Tavarez	2001
Kent Mercker	2004
Will Ohman	2005–06
Matt Lawton	2005
Clay Rapada	2007
Larry Rothschild (coach)	2008
51	
Frank Demaree	1932
Red Corriden (coach)	1933–34
Augie Galan	1935–36
Ival Goodman	1943–44
Reggie Otero	(1945)
Bobby Adams (coach)	1961–65
Fred Koenig (coach)	1983
Jeff Pico	1988
Kevin Blankenship	1988–90
Heathcliff Slocumb	1991–93
Blaise Ilsley	1994
Terry Adams	1995–99
Mel Rojas	1997
Brian Williams	2000
Gary Matthews, Jr.	2000
Juan Cruz	2001–03
Jon Leicester	2004–05
Juan Mateo	2006

One hundred players have taken the field in a Cubs uniform with a number in the 50s. And as sure as you're holding this book in your hands, there'll be more 50s coming right along. One thing that isn't a stretch is to assume that they won't be getting their numbers retired anytime soon. The 50s are generally the domain of marginal players and of coaches, lots of coaches. There are thirty instances of numbers in the 50s being handed to coaches, or coaches who at one point wore that same number as Cubs manager. As a bonus, there's **Frank Lucchesi** (#53), who wasn't a Cubs coach, but who was appointed to finish out the last 25 games of 1987 as manager after Gene Michael resigned at 68–68. Everyone knew they'd be looking for a new manager—it would eventually be Don Zimmer—so it was a low pressure situation; the Cubs played accordingly, finishing 8–17. It still ended better than Lucchesi's last managing job a decade earlier in Texas, when he was punched out by a disgruntled Lenny Randle and subsequently fired.

Two members of this elite over-50 crowd have multiple representation in this section: coach **Red Corriden** (who wore #51 in 1933 and 1934 and #56 in 1935 and 1936) and **El Tappe** (who wore #55 as a player in 1954–56 and #52 as a player/coach/head coach from 1962–65).

Player	Years
52	
Pete Elko	1944
Red Smith (coach)	1945–48
Spud Davis (coach)	1950
Don Robertson	1954
George Myatt (coach)	1957
El Tappe (player, coach, and head coach)	1961–65
Reggie Patterson	1983–85
Jim Bullinger	1992–96
Ramon Tatis	1997
Matt Karchner	1998–2000
Joey Nation	2000
Pat Mahomes	2002
Sergio Mitre	2003–05
Wade Miller	2006–07
Steve Trachsel	2007
53	
Cy Block	1945
Johnny Schmitz	1946–51
Joe Hatten	1951–52
Cal Howe	1952
Dave Hillman	1955–57
Harry Craft (coach and head coach)	1961
Buck O'Neil (coach)	1962–65
Frank Lucchesi (manager)	1987
Jorge Pedre	1992
Doug Jennings	1993
Dave Otto	1994
Chris Nabholz	1995
Kurt Miller	1998–99
Micah Bowie	1999
Francis Beltran	2002–04
Rich Hill	2005–08
54	
Clarence Maddern	1946
Vedie Himsl (coach and head coach)	1961–64
Stan Hack (coach)	1965
Rich Gossage	1988
Jeremi Gonzalez	1997
Mark Clark	1998
Ron Mahay	2001–02
David Aardsma	2006

Before the 1950s, only Corriden, **Johnny Schulte** (#56, 1933), **Mike Kelly** (#56, 1934), **Red Smith** (#52, 1945–48), and **Spud Davis** (#52, 1950) had been coaches wearing 50-pluses. The rest were part-timers or short-timers or guys like **Frank Demaree,** who wore #51 when first called up in 1932, before he switched to #6 and #8 for the rest of his Cubs career. Journeyman outfielder **Lance Richbourg** (#56, 1932) was the other Cub to go into the 50s that first year the club wore numbers. He hit .257 and wasn't on the World Series roster in the sweep by the Yankees, yet Richbourg—who as a rookie had been traded for an outfielder named Casey Stengel—was still appealing enough as a veteran (though he would never again play in the majors) to be part of the retinue the Cubs shipped to Cincinnati for Babe Herman.

Only two players—**John Ostrowski** (1944–46) and **Johnny Schmitz** (1946–51)—wore a 50-plus for more than one year before 1950, and both also modeled other numbers during their tenure with the Cubs; #27 and #47 for Ostrowski and #7 and #31 for Schmitz.

With the advent of the 1960s and the College of Coaches, numbers 50 and higher became the exclusive jurisdiction of non-players. As noted in chapter 40, clubhouse manager Yosh Kawano devised a "system" for assigning numbers in that era: #6 through #9 for catchers, teens for

Player	Years
55	
El Tappe	1954–56
Ripper Collins (coach)	1961–63
Alex Grammas (coach)	1964
Al Dark (coach)	1965
Larry Casian	1995–97
Jeff Pentland (coach)	1997
Andrew Lorraine	1999–2000
Augie Ojeda	2000
Jamie Arnold	2000
Courtney Duncan	2001–02
Shawn Estes	2003
Ryan Theriot	2005–06
Les Walrond	2006
Koyie Hill	2007–08
Kevin Hart	2007
56	
Lance Richbourg	1932
Johnny Schulte (coach)	1933
Mike Kelly (coach)	1934
Red Corriden (coach)	1935–36
Al Epperly	1938
Verlon Walker (coach)	1961–65
Brian McRae	1995–97
Justin Speier	1998
Ray King	1999
Jason Smith	2001
Cliff Bartosh	2005
Billy Petrick	2007
57	
Vito Valentinetti	1956–57
Goldie Holt (coach)	1961–65
Rich Garces	1995
Augie Ojeda	2000
Antonio Alfonseca	2002–03
Jerome Williams	2006
Rocky Cherry	2007
Sam Fuld	2007
Chad Gaudin	2008

infielders, 20s for outfielders, 30s and 40s for pitchers, and 50-plus for coaches and managers. During the 1960s alone, sixteen different men coached (or "head coached," in the tortured vernacular invented by Col. Robert Whitlow, the "athletic director" of the Cubs) wearing numbers in the 50s. Even former great player **Stan Hack,** who returned briefly as a 1965 coach, could not don any of the numbers—seven to choose from!—he wore as a player. Instead of his most familiar #6, or #20, #25, #31, #34, #39, or even #49 (just a number away from sacred #50), Hack sat in the dugout sporting #54.

Something similar happened to **Charlie Grimm.** During Jolly Cholly's previous two stints as manager of the Cubs—during which time they won three pennants and captured a fourth after he was dismissed in midseason—he wore an array of numbers: #1, #6, #7, #8, and #40—plus #38 as a coach. When P. K. Wrigley fired Bob Scheffing after consecutive 70-win seasons in 1958 and 1959—the first time the franchise had managed even that modest achievement since 1945–46—Grimm took over again at age sixty-one and was given #50. But after starting out 6–11 in 1960, P. K. made the bizarre Grimm-for–Lou Boudreau, manager-for-broadcaster swap discussed in chapter 5. Boudreau wore #42 and then #5; no wonder he didn't last past the season. Why #42? Because Lou was forty-two years old in 1960 and claimed he was "more mature" as a manager than he was in his Cleveland managing days.

Player	Years
58	
Fred Martin (coach)	1961-65
Ben Van Ryn	1998
Richard Barker	1999
Mike Mahoney	2000, 2002
Geovany Soto	2005-07
Jose Ascanio	2008
59	
Dick Cole (coach)	1961
Mel Wright (coach)	1963-64
Mel Harder (coach)	1965
Rodney Myers	1996-99
Ismael Valdez	2000
Juan Lopez (coach)	2003-06
Ivan DeJesus (coach)	2007

Mature or not, the swap didn't work either way—Boudreau went 54–83 in the dugout and Grimm was, well, grim in the booth, so in '61 Grimm returned as a coach wearing #50, but the owner was too far gone. Mr. Wrigley was preparing to send coaches one and all—Grimm included—back to College.

The great **Buck O'Neil,** who had been responsible for signing so many of the first African-American players for the Cubs, including Ernie Banks, Billy Williams, George Altman, and Lou Brock, was made a coach in 1962. One of his lifelong disappointments was not being part of the College of Coaches rotation for head coach; O'Neil was never used in more than an instructional role. Unfortunately, there was still some racism in the Cubs organization (some say orchestrated by Grimm) in those days and that may have prevented O'Neil from being on the field, even on a temporary basis. One day when head coach Charlie Metro and third base coach El Tappe were both ejected, O'Neil would have been the next logical choice to coach third, but instead Fred Martin, the pitching coach, was waved in from the bullpen to take over.

CUBS STEVE RENKO PITCHER

No player wore a number in the 50s between the trade of **Vito Valentinetti** (#57, 1956–57) to the Brooklyn Dodgers on May 23, 1957 and the acquisition of **Steve Renko** from the Montreal Expos one day short of nineteen years later; Renko made his first Cubs appearance on May 22, 1976. Renko had worn #50 for the Expos and requested it from Yosh; it was the first "crack" in his system for pitchers.

And so the occasional player would take a flyer on the high numbers. The list is filled with September call ups: **Jorge Pedre** (#53, 1992), **Jason Maxwell** (#50, 1998), **Richard Barker** (#58, 1999), **Phil Norton** (#50, 2000, 2003), **Joey Nation** (#52, 2000), **Mike Mahoney** (#58, 2000,2002), **Les "I Am The Eggman, (Whoo!) I Am The" Walrond** (#55, 2006), and **Sam Fuld** (#57, 2007); guys who, like Steve Renko, wore higher numbers for other teams and kept them when they came to Chicago, such as **Rich Gossage** (#54, 1988), **Brian McRae** (#56, 1995–97), **Mark Clark** (#54, 1998), **Ismael Valdez** (#59, 2000), **Julian Tavarez** (#50, 2001), **Antonio Alfonseca** (#57, 2002–03), **Shawn Estes** (#55, 2003), **Kent Mercker** (#50, 2004), and **Wade Miller** (#52, 2006–07); plus a handful who eventually made it, though only one in his original 50-plus: **Rich Hill** (2005–08), who kept his spring training #53 when having his breakout season in 2007. Others such as **Justin Speier** (#56, 1998), **Micah Bowie** (#53, 1999), **Ray King** (#56, 1999), **Gary "Little Sarge" Matthews Jr.** (#51, 2000), **Juan Cruz** (#51, 2001–03), and **David Aardsma** (#54, 2006) never had success until they moved on to other teams. **Ryan Theriot** (#55, 2005–06) and **Geovany Soto** (#58, 2005–07), key parts of the 2008 NL Central champion Cubs, became better known wearing other numbers (#2 for Theriot, #18 for Soto).

Ivan DeJesus took #59 in his first coaching year, 2007, because the #11 he wore as a player was taken by Jacque Jones. When Jones left after 2007, DeJesus reclaimed his old #11. On the other end, pitching coach **Larry Rothschild** was twice bumped: from #41 to #40 when Lou Piniella became his boss, and from #40 to #50 when Rich Harden arrived in 2008 to become a prized pupil.

MOST OBSCURE CUB TO WEAR A NUMBER IN THE 50s: **Jason Smith** (#56, 2001). There are so many examples to choose from, but Smith is the most interesting because his only Cubs appearances came against AL teams and he has actually put together a decent, though itinerant (six post-Cubs teams) career as a backup infielder. In 548 career at bats, just about a full season's worth, he's hit 17 homers. Only one of those at bats came in a Cubs uniform; he pinch-hit (and struck out) in the sixth inning of a 5-4 win over the Twins on June 17, 2001. Later, he played the ninth inning at shortstop in a 15-9 win over the Tigers on July 6; a month after that he was sent to Tampa Bay as the player to be named later in the Fred McGriff trade.

GUY YOU NEVER THOUGHT OF AS A CUB WHO WORE A NUMBER IN THE 50s: **Matt Lawton** (#50, 2005). In one of the most useless trading-deadline deals in recent years, the Cubs acquired Lawton from the Pirates for Jody Gerut (who had been a Cub for only two weeks) on July 31, 2005. Marginally in contention at four games out of the wild-card lead on that date, the Cubs went 7–12 in games Lawton played for them and 8–16 overall before they dumped him to the Yankees on August 27. The collapse wasn't necessarily Lawton's fault, but neither did he help matters, hitting .244 with only one homer in 78 at bats.

Put Me In, Coach

The Cubs and their coaches have a bond that seems to transcend other franchises. They've handed out uniforms to some of their greatest players and kept them around in the dugout, even after they could no longer play. They've borrowed some of the greats from other teams and added them to their brain trust and sometimes kept them on as active players to get a few more swings. And most famously, or infamously, the Cubs even sent their coaches to school. The College of Coaches may be one of the most questionable methods of running a dugout in major league history, but the Cubs wouldn't have done it if they didn't have a lot of faith in their coaches.

The coaches in the list are chronologically separated by number, with a running count of how many coaches served wearing each number. Head coaches from the 1960s College of Coaches are included.

Last Name	First name	Uniform Number	Years served
Wright	Mel	1	1971
Rojas	Cookie	1	1978–1981
		#coaches	2
Hartnett	Gabby	2	1938
Tappe	Elvin	2	1960
Adams	Bobby	2	1973
Marshall	Jim	2	1974
Saul	Jim	2	1975–1976
Lowery	Peanuts	2	1977–1979, 1981
Vukovich	John	2	1982–1987
Oliveras	Mako	2	1996–97
Pentland	Jeff	2	1998–99
Alomar	Sandy	2	2000–2002
Clines	Gene	2	2003–2006
		# coaches	11
Craft	Harry	3	1960
Klein	Lou	3	1960
Fitzsimmons	Freddie	3	1966
Becker	Joe	3	1967–1970
Spangler	Al	3	1971, 1974
Jansen	Larry	3	1972–1973
Bloomfield	Jack	3	1975–1976
Clines	Gene	3	1980–1981
Connors	Billy	3	1982–1986
Starrette	Herm	3	1987
Martinez	Jose	3	1988–1994
Oliveras	Mako	3	1995
Radison	Dan	3	1997–99
Glynn	Gene	3	2000–2002
Kim	Wendell	3	2003–2004
Trammell	Alan	3	2008

Last Name	First name	Uniform Number	Years served
		# coaches	16
Himsl	Vedie	4	1960
Root	Charlie	4	1960
Walker	Verlon	4	1966–70
Aguirre	Hank	4	1972–1973
Dunlop	Harry	4	1976
Hundley	Randy	4	1977
Roarke	Mike	4	1978–1980
Hiatt	Jack	4	1981
Zimmer	Don	4	1984–1986
Connors	Billy	4	1992–1993
Pentland	Jeff	4	2000–2002
		# coaches	11
Lockman	Whitey	5	1966
Amalfitano	Joe	5	1967–1971, 1978–1980
Lowe	Q.V.	5	1972
Noren	Irv	5	1975
Dark	Alvin	5	1977
MacKenzie	Gordy	5	1982
Amaro	Ruben	5	1983–1986
Snyder	Jim	5	1987
Cottier	Chuck	5	1988–1991, 1994
Lachemann	Rene	5	2000–2002
		# coaches	10
Reiser	Pete	6	1972
Martin	J.C.	6	1974
Schultz	Barney	6	1977
Moss	Les	6	1981
Altobelli	Joe	6	1988–1991
Jackson	Sonny	6	2005–2006

Last Name	First name	Uniform Number	Years served
Trammell	Alan	6	2007
		# coaches	7
Reiser	Pete	7	1966–1969
Lowrey	Peanuts	7	1970–1971
		# coaches	2
Harmon	Tom	8	1982
Dyer	Duffy	8	1983
Acosta	Oscar	8	2001
Quade	Mike	8	2007–2008
		# coaches	4
Hornsby	Rogers	9	1958–1959
Koenig	Fred	9	1983
Oates	Johnny	9	1984–1987
		# coaches	3
Tappe	Elvin	10	1959
		# coaches	1
Shea	Merv	11	1948
DeJesus	Ivan	11	2008
		# coaches	1
Banks	Ernie	14	1967–1973
		# coaches	1
Lazzeri	Tony	15	1938
Cottier	Chuck	15	1992–1993
Jackson	Sonny	15	2003–2004
		# coaches	3
Jackson	Sonny	16	2003
		# coaches	1
Clines	Gene	18	1979
Quade	Mike	18	2007
		# coaches	2
Corriden	Red	19	1937–1940

Last Name	First name	Uniform Number	Years served
Martin	Pepper	19	1956
		# coaches	2
Johnson	Roy	20	1937–1939
Uhl	George	20	1940
Leonard	Dutch	20	1954–1956
Hatton	Grady	20	1960
Spangler	Al	20	1970
		# coaches	5
Dean	Dizzy	22	1941
Mueller	Ray	22	1957
		# coaches	2
Foxx	Jimmie	26	1944
Williams	Billy	26	1980–1982,1986–1987,1992–2001
		# coaches	2
Reiser	Pete	27	1973
Regan	Phil	27	1997–1998
		# coaches	2
Perry	Gerald	28	2007–2008
		# coaches	1
Blades	Ray	29	1953
		# coaches	1
Jenkins	Fergie	31	1995–1996
		# coaches	1
Fitzsimmons	Freddie	33	1957–1959
		# coaches	1
Pole	Dick	34	1988–1991
		# coaches	1
Cox	Larry	35	1988–1989
Speier	Chris	35	2005–2006
Strode	Lester	35	2007–2008
		# coaches	3

Last Name	First name	Uniform Number	Years served
Kranitz	Rick	36	2002
Matthews	Gary	36	2003–06
		# coaches	2
Spalding	Dick	37	1941–1942
Franks	Herman	37	1970
Aguirre	Hank	37	1974
		# coaches	3
Grimm	Charlie	38	1941
Cuyler	Kiki	38	1941–1942
Connors	Billy	38	1991
		# coaches	3
Gamboa	Tom	39	1998–1999
Pole	Dick	39	2004–2006
Sinatro	Matt	39	2007–2008
		# coaches	3
Muser	Tony	40	1993–1997
Rothschild	Larry	40	2007–2008
		# coaches	2
Corriden	Red	41	1932
Stock	Milt	41	1944–1948
Blades	Ray	41	1954–56
Trebelhorn	Tom	41	1992–1993
Rothschild	Larry	41	2003–2006
		# coaches	5
O'Leary	Charley	42	1932–1933
Cuyler	Kiki	42	1943
Johnson	Roy	42	1944–1953
Drabowsky	Moe	42	1994
Radison	Dan	42	1995–1997
Perry	Gerald	42*	2007, 2008
Strode	Lester	42*	2007, 2008
		# coaches(legit)	5

Last Name	First name	Uniform Number	Years served
		# coaches wearing 42 for 1 day	2
Spalding	Dick	43	1943
Foley	Marv	43	1994
Bialas	Dave	43	1995–1999,2002
		# coaches	3
Jurges	Billy	45	1947–1948
Shea	Merv	45	1949
Bloomfield	Jack	45	1977–1978
		# coaches	3
Scheffing	Bob	46	1954–1955
Hayworth	Ray	46	1955
Reiser	Pete	46	1974
Grissom	Marv	46	1975–1976
Ellis	Sammy	46	1992
Acosta	Oscar	46	2000
Pole	Dick	46	2003
		# coaches	7
Davis	Spud	47	1950–53
Rothschild	Larry	47	2002
		# coaches	2
Roof	Phil	48	1990–1991
DeMerritt	Marty	48	1999
		# coaches	2
Baker	William	49	1950
Root	Charlie	49	1951–1953
		# coaches	2
Grimm	Charlie	50	1961–63
Lockman	Whitey	50	1965
Rothschild	Larry	50	2008
		# coaches	2

Last Name	First name	Uniform Number	Years served
Corriden	Red	51	1933–1934
Adams	Bobby	51	1961–1965,
Koenig	Fred	51	1983
		# coaches	3
Smith	Red	52	1945–1948
Davis	Spud	52	1950
Myatt	George	52	1957
Tappe	Elvin	52	1961–1965
		# coaches	4
Craft	Harry	53	1961
O'Neil	Buck	53	1962–1965
		# coaches	2
Himsl	Vedie	54	1961–1964
Hack	Stan	54	1965
		# coaches	2
Collins	Rip	55	1961–1963
Grammas	Alex	55	1964
Dark	Alvin	55	1965
Pentland	Jeff	55	1997
		# coaches	4
Schulte	Johnny	56	1933
Kelly	Mike	56	1934
Corriden	Red	56	1935–1936
Walker	Verlon	56	1961–1965
		# coaches	4
Myatt	George	57	1958–59
Holt	Goldie	57	1961–1965
		# coaches	2
Martin	Fred	58	1961–1965
		# coaches	2
Cole	Dick	59	1961

Last Name	First name	Uniform Number	Years served
DeJesus	Ivan	59	2007
Wright	Mel	59	1963–1964
Harder	Mel	59	1965
Lopez	Juan	59	2003–06
		# coaches	4
Klein	Lou	60	1961–1965
		# coaches	1
Johnson	Roy	61	1935–1936
Kennedy	Bob	61	1963–1965
		# coaches	2
Dixon	Walt	62	1964–1965
		# coaches	1
Metro	Charlie	63	1962
Freese	George	63	1964–1965
		# coaches	2
Macko	Joe	64	1964
Peden	Les	64	1965
		# coaches	2
Quade	Mike	81	2006
		# coaches	1

#60–#99: SIXTY AND BEYOND

Player	Year
60	
Lou Klein (coach, head coach)	1961–65
61	
Babe Phelps	1933–34
Roy Johnson (coach)	1935–36
Bob Kennedy (coach, head coach)	1963–65
Jose Reyes	2006
62	
Walt Dixon (coach)	1964–65
Felix Sanchez	2003
Bob Howry	2006–08
63	
Charlie Metro (coach, head coach)	1962
George Freese (coach)	1964–65
Jon Leicester	2003
Carmen Pignatiello	2007–08
64	
Joe Macko (coach)	1964
Les Peden (coach)	1965
72	
Robert Machado	2001–02
76	
Daniel Garibay	2000
81	
Mike Quade (coach)	2006
94	
Felix Heredia	2001
96	
Bill Voiselle	1950
99	
Todd Hundley	2001

Twenty men have dared to wear a Cubs uniform bearing a number 60 or higher. Those who have tempted mojo with this numeric audacity have often paid the price by having performance numbers that did not approach the uniqueness of their uniform numbers.

Babe Phelps, a backup catcher who hit .286 in 77 at bats in 1933 and 1934, was the first to reach for such heights. The reasons he chose #61 are lost to the mists of time; Phelps went to the Dodgers on waivers in early 1935 and made three All-Star teams in Brooklyn. On Phelps's departure, #61 was claimed by coach **Roy Johnson,** who wore it for two years and later also appeared in #20 and #42.

After that, though, only one man wore a number higher than 60 for the Cubs until . . . well, the sixties. That was **Bill Voiselle,** acquired by the Cubs for Gene Mauch on December 14, 1949, from the Boston Braves, for whom he had lost the last game of the 1948 World Series. Voiselle hailed from Ninety-Six, South Carolina, a town so named because early settlers thought (incorrectly) that it was 96 miles from there to a Cherokee Indian village. So he insisted on wearing #96. Voiselle, an All-Star in 1944 with the Giants, posted an 0-4, 5.79 mark in 19 games (seven starts) with the Cubs in 1950 and then retired back to Ninety-Six.

High numbers then took a hiatus until the College of Coaches got men back into the big digits. Coaches **Lou Klein** and **Bob Kennedy,** both of whom eventually served as "head coach," wore #60 and #61, respectively. **Charlie Metro,** #63 in '62, also served as head coach. Klein has the distinction of being the final "head coach" of the College of Coaches system; after the Cubs slipped from their winning 82–80 record in '63 to 76–86 in '64 and a 24–32 start under Bob Kennedy in '65, Kennedy was moved to the front office, Klein finished the '65 season, "guiding" the team to a 48–58 record before being replaced by the man who said, "I'm the manager"—Leo Durocher.

Three other coaches: **Walt Dixon** (#62, 1964–65), **Joe Macko** (father of future Cub Steve, the only one of these coaches to wear the number of the year he served, #64 in '64), and **Les Peden** (#64 in '65), also wore the higher numbers reserved for coaches in the late and unlamented College of Coaches era.

The 60-pluses were not seen again until more than thirty years later, at the very end of the twentieth century. When pitcher **Daniel Garibay** broke camp with the Cubs for the 2000 season, his #76 was the highest uniform number worn by anyone other than Bill Voiselle. Garibay pitched in 30 games (eight starts) with little distinction; a 2–8 record and 6.03 ERA sent him back to the Mexican League from whence he came.

While there wasn't much rhyme or reason for the 60s preferences of **Jon Leicester** (#63, 2003), **Bob Howry** (#62, 2006–08), and **Carmen Pignatiello** (#63, 2007–08), a few of the higher-numbered Cubs have used numerological reasons for their choices. Pitcher **Felix Heredia,** who wore #35 and then #49 from 1998–2001, gave up #49 to the more-senior David Weathers when he was acquired in 2001. Heredia then reversed the #49 to make #94. Too bad his poor pitching that year—a 6.17 ERA—couldn't have also been reversed. Similarly, coach **Mike Quade,** who wore #18 in 2007, gave it up to Jason Kendall when the catcher was acquired from Oakland, and reversed the digits to make #81.

Todd Hundley couldn't get his dad's old #9 when he was signed as a free agent in 2002; his former Mets teammate Damon Buford already had it. So Hundley doubled the digit and made #99. Unfortunately, his performance was about half as good as his previous years with the Mets, and it didn't get any better when Buford left and Todd took over #9. Another catcher, **Robert Machado** (2001–02), took #72 to honor Hall of Famer Carlton Fisk, who was the catcher when Machado was coming up in the White Sox organization. (Fisk had famously reversed the #27 he'd worn with Boston when he came to Comiskey.) Machado couldn't bring any Pudginess to the North Side in his season and a half as a Cub. Hard as it is to admit, numbers can only do so much.

MOST OBSCURE CUB TO WEAR #60 OR ABOVE: **Felix Sanchez** (#62, 2003). Sanchez, a southpaw signed out of the Dominican Republic as a teenager, debuted on September 3, 2003 at Wrigley against the Cardinals at age twenty-three, pitching to lefty-swinging Fernando Vina. He walked him. J. D. Drew, another lefty, followed with a three-run homer. The Cubs were down, 6-0, but they rallied to win, 8-7, and Sanchez got another chance in two losses in Pittsburgh as the Cubs were trying to take the NL Central crown. He got Matt Stairs to bounce into a double play; the next night Sanchez sandwiched a double and a walk in between two strikeouts. The problem was that the walk was to the pitcher and Sanchez never appeared again in the bigs after that.

GUY YOU NEVER THOUGHT OF AS A CUB WHO WORE #60 OR ABOVE: **Jose Reyes** (#61, 2006). Gotcha! The speedy Mets shortstop has never been a Cub, or you might have heard about it before now. The Cubs did have a slow-footed catcher of the same name born in the same country (Dominican Republic) a few months before the others Reyes (1983). Jose Ariel Reyes spent the last few weeks of 2006 as a Cub, with his lone major league hit a two-run single to cap off a 14-6 rout of the Brewers at Wrigley on September 26. After that he joined the Mets' minor league system and started confusing people over there.

Zero Zeroes

The Cubs have never had a player wear zero or double zero. So 0 and 00 are a subset of a minority of single and double-digit numbers that haven't been worn by any Cubs players, managers, or coaches. The missing numbers read like a Who's Who of linemen and wide receivers: 65, 66, 67, 68, 69, 70, 71, 73, 74, 75, 77, 78, 79, 80, 82, 83, 84, 85, 86, 87, 88, 89, 90, 91, 92, 93, 95, 97, and 98.

CUBS ALPHABETICAL ROSTER (1932–2008)

Players, managers, and coaches

A	
Aardsma, David (2006)	54
Abernathy, Ted (1965–66,1969–70)	39,37
Aberson, Cliff (1947–49)	11
Abrego, Johnny (1985)	32
Acosta, Oscar (2000–01)	46,8
Adams, Bobby (1957–59, 1961–65,1973)	7,16,51,2
Adams, Mike (1976–77)	21,30
Adams, Red (1946)	18
Adams, Terry (1995–99)	51,33
Addis, Bob (1952–53)	16
Adkins, Dewey (1949)	37
Aguilera, Rick (1999–00)	38
Aguirre, Hank (1969–70, 1972–74)	34,4,37
Aker, Jack (1972–73)	38
Alderson, Dale (1943–44)	31,47
Alexander, Manny (1997–99)	24
Alexander, Matt (1973–74)	42
Alfonseca, Antonio (2002–03)	57
Allen, Ethan (1936)	4
Alomar Sr, Sandy (2000–02)	2
Alou, Moises (2002–04)	18
Altamirano, Porfi (1984)	33
Altman, George (1959–62, 1965–67)	21,29
Altobelli, Joe (1988–91)	6
Amalfitano, Joey (1964–71, 1978–81)	17,5
Amaro, Ruben (1983–86)	5
Amor, Vicente (1955)	35

Anderson, Bob (1957–62)	32
Anderson, Jimmy (2004)	49
Andre, John (1955)	29
Andrews, Shane (1999–00)	7,24
Arcia, Jose (1968)	17
Arias, Alex (1992)	24,50
Arnold, Jamie (2000)	55
Asbell, Jim (1938)	30
Ascanio, Jose (2008)	58
Ashburn, Richie (1960–61)	1
Aspromonte, Ken (1963)	15
Assenmacher, Paul (1989–93)	45
Atwell, Toby (1952–53)	11
Averill, Earl (1959–60)	6
Ayala, Bobby (1999)	31
Aybar, Manny (2001)	38,40

B	
Baczewski, Fred (1953)	31
Baecht, Ed (1932)	16
Bailey, Ed (1965)	6
Baker, Bill (1950)	49
Baker, Dusty (2003–06)	12
Baker, Gene (1953–57)	37
Baker, Tom (1963)	41
Bako, Paul (2003–04)	9
Baller, Jay (1985–87)	48
Balsamo, Tony (1962)	39
Banks, Ernie (1953–73)	14
Banks, Willie (1994–95)	35,27
Barber, Steve (1970)	46
Barberie, Bret (1996)	20
Barker, Rich (1999)	58
Barragan, Cuno (1961–63)	9

Barrett, Dick (1943)	38
Barrett, Michael (2004–07)	5,8
Bartell, Dick (1939)	2,5
Barton, Vince (1932)	49
Bartosh, Cliff (2005)	56
Batista, Miguel (1997)	47
Bauers, Russ (1946)	18
Baumann, Frank (1965)	48
Baumholtz, Frank (1949, 1951–55)	47,7
Bautista, Jose (1993–94)	38
Baylor, Don (2000–02)	25
Beard, Dave (1985)	50
Beck, Rod (1998–99)	47
Becker, Heinz (1943–46)	24,7
Becker, Joe (1967–70)	3
Beckert, Glenn (1965–73)	18
Bell, George (1991)	11
Bellhorn, Mark (2002–03)	28
Beltran, Francis (2002–04)	53
Benes, Alan (2002–03)	35
Benton, Butch (1982)	9
Bere, Jason (2001–02)	46
Berry, Joe (1942)	31
Berryhill, Damon (1987–91)	34,9
Bertel, Dick (1960–65, 1967)	6
Bialas, Dave (1995–99, 2002)	43
Bielecki, Mike (1988–91)	36
Biittner, Larry (1976–80)	26,33
Bilko, Steve (1954)	39,49
Bird, Doug (1981–82)	47
Bithorn, Hi (1942–43,1946)	17,35,25
Blackwell, Tim (1978–81)	9
Blades, Ray (1953–56)	3,29,41
Bladt, Rick (1969)	20
Blanco, Henry (2005–08)	9,24
Blankenship, Kevin (1988–90)	51
Blauser, Jeff (1998–99)	4

Block, Cy (1942,1945–46)	32,53,34
Bloomfield, Jack (1975–78)	3,45
Bobb, Randy (1968–69)	6
Boccabella, John (1963–68)	22,12
Bolger, Jim (1955,1957–58)	30,3
Bonds, Bobby (1981)	25
Bonetti, Julio (1940)	43
Bonham, Bill (1971–77)	33
Bonura, Zeke (1940)	18
Bordi, Rich (1983–84)	42
Borkowski, Bob (1950–51)	22
Boros, Steve (1963)	17
Borowski, Joe (2001–05)	48
Borowy. Hank (1945–48)	26
Boskie, Shawn (1990–94)	47
Bosley, Thad (1983–86)	20,27
Botelho, Derek (1985)	47
Bottarini, John (1937)	41
Bottenfield, Kent (1996–97)	45,34
Bouchee, Ed (1960–61)	11
Boudreau, Lou (1960)	5,42
Bourque, Pat (1971–73)	19
Bowa, Larry (1982–85)	1
Bowen, Rob (2007)	4
Bowie, Micah (1999)	53
Bowman, Bob (1942)	21
Breeden, Danny (1971)	19
Breeden, Hal (1971)	25
Brennan, William (1993)	44
Brewer, Jim (1960–63)	45,48,38
Brewster, Charlie (1944)	26
Briggs, Dan (1982)	11
Briggs, John (1956–58)	15,30
Bright, Harry (1965)	29
Brinkopf, Leon (1952)	43
Broberg, Pete (1977)	40
Brock, Lou (1961–64)	24
Brock, Tarrik (2000)	22

Broglio, Ernie (1964–66)	32
Brosnan, Jim (1954,1956–58)	27,42,23
Brown, Brant (1996–98,2000)	37,35
Brown, Jophery (1968)	47
Brown, Roosevelt (1999–02)	28,24
Brown, Tommy (1952–53)	12
Browne, Byron (1965–67)	29
Brumley, Mike (1987)	17
Brusstar, Warren (1983–85)	41
Bryant, Clay (1935–40)	18,26
Bryant, Don (1966)	25
Buckner, Bill (1977–84)	22
Buechele, Steve (1992–95)	24
Buford, Damon (2000–01)	9
Buhl, Bob (1962–66)	31
Bullett, Scott (1995–96)	10
Bullinger, Jim (1992–96)	52
Burdette, Freddie (1962–64)	42
Burdette, Lew (1964–65)	33
Burgess, Smoky (1949,1951)	4,8,11
Burke, Leo (1963–65)	15
Burnitz, Jeromy (2005)	3
Burris, Ray (1973–79)	34
Burrows, John (1943–44)	36
Burton, Ellis (1963–65)	21,24
Burwell, Dick (1960–61)	34
Bush, Guy (1932–34)	14,17
Buzhardt, John (1958–59)	23,38
Bynum, Freddie (2006)	4

C

Cairo, Miguel (1997,2001)	20,40
Callison, Johnny (1970–71)	6
Calmus, Dick (1967)	45
Camilli, Dolph (1933–34)	41
Campbell, Bill (1982–83)	39
Campbell, Gilly (1933)	15
Campbell, Joe (1967)	25
Campbell, Mike (1996)	33

Campbell, Ron (1964–66)	7,15,23
Cannizzaro, Chris (1971)	43
Capel, Mike (1988)	38
Capilla, Doug (1979–81)	35
Cardenal, Jose (1972–77)	1
Cardwell, Don (1960–62)	43
Carleton, Tex (1935–38)	16
Carlsen, Don (1948)	16
Carpenter, Bob (1947)	32
Carter, Joe (1983)	33
Carty, Rico (1973)	43
Casey, Hugh (1935)	21
Casian, Larry (1995–97)	55
Castillo, Frank (1991–97)	49
Caudill, Bill (1979–81)	36
Cavarretta, Phil (1934–53)	43,23,3,44
Ceccarelli, Art (1959–60)	41
Cedeno, Ronny (2005–08)	11,5
Cey, Ron (1983–86)	11
Chambers, Cliff (1948)	32
Cherry, Rocky (2007)	57
Chiasson, Scott (2001–02)	37
Chipman, Bob (1944–49)	31
Chiti, Harry (1950–52, 1955–56)	16,32
Choi, Hee Sop (2002–03)	19
Christmas, Steve (1986)	18
Christopher, Loyd (1945)	32
Church, Bubba (1953–55)	33,23
Church, Len (1966)	45
Clark, Dave (1990,1997)	30,22
Clark, Mark (1997–98)	48,54
Clemens, Doug (1964–65)	27
Clement, Matt (2002–04)	30
Cline, Ty (1966)	20
Clines, Gene (1977–81, 2003–06)	18,3,2
Coats, Buck (2006)	30

Coffman, Kevin (1990)	42
Coggins, Frank (1972)	17
Cohen, Hy (1955)	42
Colborn, Jim (1969–71)	48
Cole, Dave (1954)	23,39
Cole, Dick (1961)	59
Coleman, Joe (1976)	31
Collins, Bob "Rip" (1940)	39
Collins, Ripper (1937–38, 1961–63)	3,55
Collum, Jackie (1957)	15
Comellas, Jorge (1945)	36
Compton, Clint (1972)	34
Connally, Fritzie (1983)	26
Connors, Billy (1966, 1982–86,1991–93)	45,3,38,4
Connors, Chuck (1951)	40
Coomer, Ron (2001)	6
Cooper, Mort (1949)	34
Cooper, Walker (1954–55)	25
Corriden, Red (1932–40)	41,51,56,19
Cosman, Jim (1970)	32
Cottier, Chuck (1988–94)	5,15
Cotto, Henry (1984)	28
Cotts, Neal (2007–08)	48
Covington, Wes (1966)	43
Cowan, Billy (1963–64)	20
Cox, Larry (1978,1982, 1988–89)	6,9,35
Craft, Harry (1960–61)	3,53
Creek, Doug (1999)	37
Crim, Chuck (1994)	32
Crosby, Ken (1975–76)	39
Cross, Jeff (1948)	6,18
Cruz, Hector (1978,1981–82)	24,27,30
Cruz, Juan (2001–03)	51
Culler, Dick (1948)	7
Culp, Ray (1967)	37

Cunnane, Will (2002)	49
Curtis, Jack (1961–62)	42
Cusick, Jack (1951)	37
Cuyler, Kiki (1932–35, 1941–43)	3,38,42
D	
Dahlgren, Babe (1941–42)	16
Dallessandro, Dom (1940–44,1946–47)	31,7,46
Daniels, Kal (1992)	28
Dark, Alvin (1958–59,1965,1977)	17,55,5
Darwin, Bobby (1977)	12
Dascenzo, Doug (1988–92)	29
Davis, Brock (1970–71)	29
Davis, Curt (1936–37)	24,22
Davis, Jim (1954–56)	22
Davis, Jody (1981–88)	7
Davis, Ron (1986–87)	39
Davis, Spud (1950–53)	47,52
Davis, Steve (1979)	29
Davis, Tommy (1970,1972)	29,24
Dawson, Andre (1987–92)	8
Day, Boots (1970)	20
Dayett, Brian (1985–87)	24
Dean, Dizzy (1938–41)	22
Decker, Joe (1969–72)	36,37
DeJesus, Ivan (1977–81,2007–08)	11,59
DelGreco, Bobby (1957)	5
Demaree, Frank (1932–33, 1935–38)	51,6,9
DeMerritt, Marty (1999)	38,48
Dempster, Ryan (2004–08)	46
Dernier, Bob (1984–87)	20
DeRosa, Mark (2007–08)	7
Derringer, Paul (1943–45)	30
DeShields, Delino (2001–02)	16
Dettore, Tom (1974–76)	32,31

Diaz, Mike (1983)	15	Eckersley, Dennis (1984–86)	40,43
Dickson, Lance (1990)	33	Edens, Tom (1995)	33
DiFelice, Mike (2004)	19	Edmonds, Jim (2008)	15
Dillard, Steve (1979–81)	15	Edwards, Bruce (1951–52,1954)	8,5
Dilone, Miguel (1979)	32	Edwards, Hank (1949–50)	16
DiPino, Frank (1986–88)	33	Elia, Lee (1968,1982–83)	19,4
Distaso, Alec (1969)	45	Elko, Pete (1943–44)	8,52
Dixon, Walt (1964–65)	62	Ellis, Jim (1967)	34
Dobernic, Jess (1948–49)	17	Ellis, Sammy (1992)	46
Donnelly, Ed (1959)	22	Ellsworth, Dick (1958,1960–66)	31,37
Dorsett, Brian (1996)	4		
Douthit, Taylor (1933)	31	Elston, Don (1953,1957–64)	36
Dowling, Dave (1966)	46	Encarnacion, Mario (2002)	15
Downs, Scott (2000)	35,37	Engel, Steve (1985)	49
Drabowsky, Moe (1956–60,1994)	26,39,42	English, Woody (1932–36)	1
Drake, Sammy (1960–61)	19	Epperly, Al (1938)	56
Drake, Solly (1956)	47	Erickson, Paul (1941–48)	32,37
Drott, Dick (1957–61)	18,30	Ernaga, Frank (1957–58)	5,17
Dubiel, Monk (1949–52)	26	Errickson, Dick (1942)	21
Dubois, Jason (2004–05)	4	Essian, Jim (1991)	41
Duncan, Courtney (2001–02)	55	Estes, Shawn (2003)	55
Dunegan, Jim (1970)	32,34	Estrada, Chuck (1966)	47
Dunlap, Harry (1976)	4	Eyre, Scott (2006–08)	47

E

Eaddy, Don (1959)	18
Earley, Arnold (1966)	47
Easterwood, Roy (1944)	12
Eastwick, Rawly (1981)	49
Eaves, Vallie (1941–42)	41,14
Echevarria, Angel (2002)	12

Dunn, Ron (1974–75)	28,22
Dunston, Shawn (1985–95,1997)	12
Dunwoody, Todd (2001)	11
Durham, Leon (1981–88)	10
Durocher, Leo (1966–72)	2
Dyer, Duffy (1983)	8

F

Fanning, Jim (1954–57)	48,1
Fanzone, Carmen (1971–74)	23
Farnsworth, Kyle (1999–04)	44
Fassero, Jeff (2001–02)	13
Fast, Darcy (1968)	38
Faul, Bill (1965–66)	13
Fear, Vern (1952)	30,37
Felderman, Marv (1942)	2,43
Felske, John (1968)	24
Fermin, Felix (1996)	2
Fernandez, Frank (1971–72)	47
Figueroa, Jesus (1980)	17
Filer, Tom (1982)	50

Fitzsimmons, Freddie (1957–59,1966)	33,3
Flavin, John (1964)	38
Fleming, Bill (1942–44, 1946)	30,46,36,32
Fletcher, Scott (1981–82)	20
Flores, Jesse (1942)	30
Floyd, Cliff (2007)	15,42[a]
Fodge, Gene (1958)	24
Foley, Marv (1994)	43
Fondy, Dee (1951–57)	40
Fontenot, Mike (2005, 2007–08)	29,17
Fontenot, Ray (1985–86)	31
Foote, Barry (1979–81)	8
Fossas, Tony (1998)	44
Foster, Kevin (1994–98)	31,32
Fox, Chad (2005,2008)	47,44
Fox, Charlie (1983)	4
Fox, Jake (2007)	9
Foxx, Jimmie (1942,1944)	16,26
Frailing, Ken (1974–76)	47
Franco, Matt (1995)	15
Francona, Terry (1986)	16
Franks, Herman (1970, 1977–79)	37,3
Frazier, George (1984–86)	39
Freeman, Hersh (1958)	32
Freeman, Mark (1960)	31
Freese, George (1961, 1964–65)	8,63
French, Larry (1935–41)	14
Frey, Jim (1984–86)	8
Frey, Lonny (1937,1947)	15,22
Friend, Owen (1955–56)	3
Frisch, Frankie (1949–51)	3
Fryman, Woodie (1978)	35
Fukudome, Kosuke (2008)	1
Fuld, Sam (2007)	57

Fyrhie, Mike (2001)	31
G	
Gabler, Bill (1958)	24
Gabrielson, Len (1964–65)	12
Gaetti, Gary (1998–99)	15,8
Gagliano, Phil (1970)	19
Galan, Augie (1934–41)	31,51,7
Gallagher, Sean (2007–08)	36
Gamble, Oscar (1969)	20
Gamboa, Tom (1998–99)	39
Garagiola, Joe (1953–54)	11
Garbark, Bob (1937–39)	39
Garces, Rich (1995)	57
Garciaparra, Nomar (2004–05)	8,5
Gardner, Rob (1967)	41
Garibay, Daniel (2000)	76
Garman, Mike (1976)	44
Garret, Adrian (1970,1973–75)	23,25,5,28
Garriott, Cecil (Rabbit) (1946)	22
Gassaway, Charlie (1944)	—[c]
Gaudin, Chad (2008)	57
Geisel, Dave (1978–79,1981)	46,40
George, Greek (1941)	24
Gerard, Dave (Jug) (1962)	31,45
Gerberman, George (1962)	30,33
Gernert, Dick (1960)	12
Gerut, Jody (2005)	9
Gigon, Norm (1967)	15
Gilbert, Charlie (1941–43, 1946)	4,22
Gill, Johnny (1935–36)	18,8
Gillespie, Paul (1942,1944–45)	2,24,10
Girardi, Joe (1989–92, 2000–02)	7,8,27
Giusti, Dave (1977)	44
Glanville, Doug (1996–97, 2003)	1,8,4
Gleeson, Jim (1939–40)	24

Gload, Ross (2000)	6	Guthrie, Mark (1999–00,2003)	30,31
Glossop, Al (1946)	27	Gutierrez, Ricky (2000–01)	12
Glynn, Gene (2000–02)	3	Guzman, Angel (2006–08)	37
Goetz, John (1960)	31	Guzman, Jose (1993–94)	29
Gomez, Leo (1996)	12	**H**	
Gomez, Preston (1980)	18	Haas, Eddie (1957)	37
Gonzalez, Alex (2002–04)	8	Hack, Stan (1932–47,	31,49,34,39,
Gonzalez, Jeremi (1997–98)	54,30	1954–56,1965)	6,20,25,54
Gonzalez, Luis (1995–96)	25	Hacker, Warren (1948–56)	17,18
Gonzalez, Raul (2000)	30	Hairston Jr., Jerry (2005–06)	15
Goodman, Ival (1943–44)	51	Hairston, Johnny (1969)	43
Goodwin, Curtis (1999)	19	Hall, Drew (1986–88)	44
Goodwin, Tom (2003–04)	5,24	Hall, Jimmie (1969–70)	23
Gordon, Mike (1977–78)	23	Hall, Mel (1981–84)	32,27
Gordon, Tom (2001–02)	45	Hamilton, Steve (1972)	37
Gornicki, Hank (1941)	20	Hamner, Ralph (1947–49)	22,35
Goryl, Johnny (1957–59)	4	Hands, Bill (1966–72)	49
Gossage, Rich (1988)	54	Haney, Chris (1998)	44
Grabarkewitz, Billy (1974)	10	Haney, Todd (1994–96)	20,24
Grace, Mark (1988–00)	28,17	Hansen, Dave (1997)	25
Grammas, Alex (1962–64)	11,55	Hanyzewski, Ed (1942–46)	45,34,49
Grant, Tom (1983)	38	Harden, Rich (2008)	40
Greenberg, Adam (2005)	17	Harder, Mel (1965)	59
Greene, Willie (2000)	39	Hardin, Bud (1952)	41
Gregory, Lee (1964)	28	Hardtke, Jason (1998)	19
Grieve, Ben (2004–05)	29,4,45	Hargesheimer, Alan (1983)	50
Griffin, Mike (1981)	50	Harkey, Mike (1988,1990–93)	48,22
Grimes, Burleigh (1932–33)	16,21	Harmon, Tom (1982)	8
Grimm, Charlie (1932–38,	6,7,8,1,38,	Harrell, Ray (1939)	16
1941,1944–49,1960–63)	40,50	Harris, Brendan (2004)	19
Grissom, Merv (1975–76)	46	Harris, Lenny (2003)	29
Gross, Greg (1977–78)	21	Harris, Vic (1974–75)	4
Grudzielanek, Mark (2003–04)	11	Hart, Kevin (2007–08)	55,22
Gudat, Marv (1932)	22	Hartenstein, Chuck (1965–68)	42
Gumpert, Dave (1985–86)	45	Hartnett, Gabby (1932–40)	7,9,2
Gura, Larry (1970–73,1985)	40,32	Hartsock, Jeff (1992)	44
Gustine, Frankie (1949)	6	Hassey, Ron (1984)	15
		Hatcher, Billy (1984–85)	22

Hatten, Joe (1951–52)	53,19
Hatton, Grady (1960)	20
Hawkins, LaTroy (2004–05)	32
Hayes, Bill (1980–81)	16
Hayworth, Ray (1955)	46
Heath, Bill (1969)	19
Hebner, Richie (1984–85)	18
Hegan, Jim (1960)	9
Heist, Al (1960–61)	18,22
Hemsley, Rollie (1932)	8
Henderson, Ken (1979–80)	24
Henderson, Steve (1981–82)	28
Hendley, Bob (1965–67)	33
Hendrick, Harvey (1933)	8
Hendricks, Ellie (1972)	39
Hennessey, George (1945)	27
Henry, Bill (1958–59)	19,37
Henshaw, Roy (1933–36)	34,22
Heredia, Felix (1998–01)	35,49,94
Herman, Babe (1933–34)	4
Herman, Billy (1932–41)	2,4
Hermansen, Chad (2002)	3
Hermanski, Gene (1951–53)	48,22
Hernandez, Chico (1942–43)	9,12
Hernandez, Jose (1994–99,2003)	18,15
Hernandez, Ramon (1968,1976–77)	33,36
Hernandez, Willie (1977–83)	38
Herrmann, Leroy (1932–33)	23,21
Herrnstein, John (1966)	7
Hiatt, Jack (1970,1981)	21,4
Hibbard, Greg (1993)	37
Hickerson, Bryan (1995)	41
Hickman, Jim (1968–73)	28
Higbe, Kirby (1937–39)	49,29,25
Hill, Bobby (2002–03)	17

Hill, Glenallen (1993–94,1998–00)	34,4,6
Hill, Koyie (2007–08)	36,55
Hill, Rich (2005–08)	53
Hiller, Frank (1950–51)	45,30
Hillman, Dave (1955–59)	53,21,31
Himsl, Vedie (1960–64)	4,54
Hiser, Gene (1971–75)	16,21
Hoak, Don (1956)	7
Hobbie, Glenn (1957–64)	28,40
Hoeft, Billy (1965–66)	40
Hoffman, Guy (1986)	50
Hoffpauir, Micah (2008)	6
Hollandsworth, Todd (2004–05)	28
Hollins, Jessie (1992)	32
Holm, Billy (1943–44)	12,10
Holt, Goldie (1961–65)	57
Holtzman, Ken (1965–71, 1978–79)	30
Hooton, Burt (1971–75)	44
Hornsby, Rogers (1932, 1958–59)	9,35
Hosley, Tim (1975–76)	6
Houston, Tyler (1996–99)	7
Howe, Cal (1952)	43,53
Howell, Jay (1981)	45
Howry, Bob (2006–08)	62
Hubbard, Mike (1995–97)	6
Hubbard, Trenidad (2003)	45
Hubbs, Ken (1961–63)	33,16
Hudson, Johnny (1941)	12
Hughes, Jim (1956)	25
Hughes, Roy (1944–45)	23
Hughes, Terry (1970)	17
Humphreys, Bob (1965)	36

Hundley, Randy (1966–73, 1976–77)	9,5,4
Hundley, Todd (2001–02)	99,9
Hurst, Don (1934)	41
Huson, Jeff (2000)	29
Hutson, Herb (1974)	40

I	
Ilsley, Blaise (1994)	51
Irvin, Monte (1956)	39
Izturis, Cesar (2006–07)	3

J	
Jackson, Damian (2004)	19
Jackson, Danny (1991–92)	32
Jackson, Darrin (1985,1987–89)	30
Jackson, Larry (1963–66)	46
Jackson, Lou (1958–59)	22,42
Jackson, Randy (1950–55,1959)	2,16
Jackson, Sonny (2003–06)	16,15,6
Jacobs, Tony (1948)	2
Jaeckel, Jake (1964)	39
James, Cleo (1970–71,1973)	24
James, Rick (1967)	38
Jansen, Larry (1972–73)	3
Jeffcoat, Hal (1948–55)	19,4,3
Jelincich, Frank (1941)	21
Jenkins, Fergie (1966–73, 1982–83,1995–96)	31
Jennings, Doug (1993)	53
Jennings, Robin (1996–97,1999)	39,29
Jestadt, Garry (1971)	16
Jimenez, Manny (1969)	23
Johnson, Ben (1959–60)	45
Johnson, Bill (1983–84)	37
Johnson, Cliff (1980)	7

Johnson, Davey (1978)	31
Johnson, Don (1943–48)	20
Johnson, Footer (Dick) (1958)	12
Johnson, Howard (1995)	20
Johnson, Ken (1969)	46
Johnson, Lance (1997–99)	1
Johnson, Lou (1960,1968)	24,33,41
Johnson, Reed (2008)	9
Johnson, Roy (1935–39, 1944–53)	61,20,42
Johnstone, Jay (1982–84)	21
Joiner, Roy (1934–35)	21,23
Jones, Clarence (1967–68)	27,29
Jones, Doug (1996)	27
Jones, Jacque (2006–07)	11,42[a]
Jones, Sam (1955–56)	27
Jones, Sheldon (1953)	26
Jurges, Billy (1932–38, 1946–48)	11,8,5,45

K	
Kaiser, Don (1955–57)	45
Karchner, Matt (1998–00)	52
Karros, Eric (2003)	32
Kelleher, Mick (1976–80)	20
Kellert, Frank (1956)	5
Kelly, Bob (1951–53)	18,33
Kelly, Mike (1934)	56
Kelton, David (2003–04)	24,28,27
Kendall, Jason (2007)	18
Kennedy, Bob (1963–65)	61
Kennedy, Junior (1982–83)	15
Keough, Marty (1966)	28
Keough, Matt (1986)	33
Kessinger, Don (1964–75)	11
Kieschnick, Brooks (1996–97)	19
Kilgus, Paul (1989)	39

Kim, Wendell (2003–04)	3
Kimball, Newt (1937–38)	43,26,32
Kimm, Bruce (1979,2002)	7,10
Kindall, Jerry (1956–58, 1960–61)	23,16
Kiner, Ralph (1953–54)	4
King, Chick (1958–59)	20
King, Jim (1955–56)	48
King, Ray (1999)	56
Kingman, Dave (1978–80)	10
Kirby, Jim (1949)	36
Kitsos, Steve (1954)	12
Klein, Chuck (1934–36)	6,4
Klein, Lou (1960–65)	3,60
Klippstein, Johnny (1950–54)	36
Kmak, Joe (1995)	7
Knowles, Darold (1975–76)	32
Koenig, Fred (1983)	51,9
Koenig, Mark (1932–33)	9,12
Koonce, Cal (1962–67)	34
Koronka, John (2005)	49
Kowalik, Fabian (1935–36)	24
Kraemer, Joe (1989–90)	43
Kramer, Randy (1990)	38
Kranitz, Rick (2002)	36
Kravec, Ken (1981–82)	37
Kreitner, Mickey (1943–44)	11
Kremmel, Jim (1974)	49
Krug, Chris (1965–66)	25
Krug, Gene (Gary) (1981)	47
Krukow, Mike (1976–81)	40,39
Kuenn, Harvey (1965–66)	7
Kunkel, Jeff (1992)	11
Kush, Emil (1941–42, 1946–49)	20,22,29
L	
Lachemann, Rene (2000–02)	5
LaCock, Pete (1972–76)	24,25,22,23

Lade, Doyle (1946–50)	19,22,23
Lake, Steve (1983–86, 1993)	16,29,10
Lamabe, Jack (1968)	40
Lamp, Dennis (1977–80)	47
Lancaster, Les (1987–91)	50
Landrith, Hobie (1956)	15
Landrum, Bill (1988)	47
Landrum, Ced (1991)	28
Landrum, Don (1962–65)	27,20
Lanfranconi, Walt (1941)	3
LaRoche, Dave (1973–74)	17
Larose, Vic (1968)	22
Larsen, Don (1967)	40
Larson, Dan (1982)	32
LaRussa, Tony (1973)	42
Lary, Al (1954,1962)	31,46
Law, Vance (1988–89)	2
Lawton, Matt (2005)	50
Lazzeri, Tony (1938)	15
Lee, Bill (1934–43, 1947)	19,15,11, 31,24
Lee, Derrek (2004–08)	25,42[a]
Lee, Don (1966)	43
Lefebvre, Jim (1992–93)	5
Lefferts, Craig (1983)	32
Leiber, Hank (1939–41)	9
Leicester, Jon (2003–05)	63[b],51
LeMay, Dick (1963)	30
Lemonds, Dave (1969)	48
Lennon, Bob (1957)	9
Leonard, Dutch (1949–56)	32,20
Leonette, Mark (1987)	32[b]
Lewis, Darrin (2002)	6
Lezcano, Carlos (1980–81)	30
Lieber, Jon (1999–02,2008)	32
Lillard, Gene (1936,1939)	3,27
Lilly, Ted (2007–08)	30

Lindstrom, Freddie (1935)	7
Liniak, Cole (1999–00)	18
Littlefield, Dick (1957)	34
Littrell, Jack (1957)	6,39
Livingston, Mickey (1943,1945–47)	38,11
Locker, Bob (1973,1975)	36
Lockman, Whitey (1965–66, 1972–74)	50,5,16
Lofton, Kenny (2003)	1,7
Logan, Bob (1937–38)	39,41
Long, Bill (1990)	37
Long, Dale (1957–59)	27,8
Lopes, Davey (1984–86)	12,15
Lopez, Juan (2003–06)	59
Lorraine, Andrew (1999–00)	55
Loviglio, Jay (1983)	17
Lowe, Q. V. (1972)	5
Lowery, Terrell (1997–98)	10
Lown, Turk (1951–54, 1956–58)	35,31
Lowrey, Peanuts (1942–43, 1945–49,1970–71, 1977–79,1981)	43,47, 7,2
Lucchesi, Frank (1987)	53
Lum, Mike (1981)	33
Lundstedt, Tom (1973–74)	8
Lynch, Danny (Dummy) (1948)	20
Lynch, Ed (1986–87)	37
Lynn, Red (1994)	39
M	
Mabry, John (2006)	17
Machado, Robert (2001–02)	29,72
Macias, Jose (2004–05)	1
Mack, Ray (1947)	49
MacKenzie, Gordy (1982)	5
Macko, Joe (1964)	64
Macko, Steve (1979–80)	12

Maddern, Clarence (1946,1948–49)	54,22
Maddux, Greg (1986–92, 2004–06)	31
Madlock, Bill (1974–76)	18
Madrid, Sal (1947)	21
Magadan, Dave (1996)	16
Mahay, Ron (2001–02)	54
Mahomes, Pat (2002)	52
Mahoney, Mike (2000,2002)	58
Mairena, Oswaldo (2000)	40
Maksudian, Mike (1994)	7
Maldonado, Candy (1993)	25
Malone, Pat (1932–34)	15,18
Mancuso, Gus (1939)	12
Manders, Hal (1946)	13
Mann, Garth (1944)	38,45
Manville, Dick (1952)	19
Marmol, Carlos (2006–08)	49
Marquez, Gonzalo (1973–74)	19
Marquez, Luis (1954)	48
Marquis, Jason (2007–08)	21
Marshall, Jim (1958–59, 1974–76)	27,12,2,25
Marshall, Sean (2006–08)	45
Martin, Fred (1961–65)	58
Martin, J.C. (1970–72,1974)	12,6
Martin, Jerry (1979,1980)	28
Martin, Mike (1986)	41
Martin, Morrie (1959)	45
Martin, Pepper (1956)	19
Martin, Stu (1943)	22
Martinez, Carmelo (1983)	12
Martinez, Dave (1986–88, 2000)	1
Martinez, Jose (1988–94)	3
Martinez, Ramon (2003–04)	7,6
Martinez, Sandy (1998–99)	8,15

Marty, Joe (1937–39)	8	Meoli, Rudy (1978)	12
Martz, Randy (1980–82)	34	Merced, Orlando (1998)	25
Mason, Mike (1987)	41	Mercker, Kent (2004)	50
Massa, Gordon (1957–58)	9,22	Meridith, Ron (1984–85)	38
Mateo, Juan (2006)	51	Merriman, Lloyd (1955)	28
Mathews, Nelson (1960–63)	12,23	Merullo, Lennie (1941–47)	27,35,21
Matthews, Gary (1984–87, 2003–06)	36	Mesner, Steve (1938–39)	21,15
		Metkovich, Catfish (1953)	22
Matthews Jr., Gary (2000–01)	51,19	Metro, Charlie (1962)	63
Mattick, Bobby (1938–40)	29,15	Metzger, Roger (1970)	16
Mauch, Gene (1948–49)	33	Meyer, Dutch (1937)	43
Mauro, Carmen (1948, 1950–51)	41	Meyer, Russ (1946–48, 1956)	38,28, 34
Maxwell, Jason (1998)	50	Meyers, Chad (1999–01)	20,40
May, Derrick (1990–94)	27	Michael, Gene (1986–87)	4
May, Jakie (1932)	19	Mickelson, Ed (1957)	39,46
May, Scott (1991)	39	Mieske, Matt (1998)	20
Mayer, Ed (1957–58)	40,20	Mikkelsen, Pete (1967–68)	40
McAnany, Jim (1961–62)	20,22	Miklos, Hank (1944)	39
McCall, Dutch (1948)	27	Miksis, Eddie (1951–56)	21
McClain, Scott (2005)	9	Miller, Bob (1970–71)	45
McClendon, Lloyd (1989–90)	10	Miller, Damian (2003)	27
McCullough, Clyde (1940–43, 1945–48,1953–56)	21,5,10,9,8	Miller, Kurt (1998–99)	53
		Miller, Ox (1947)	24
McDaniel, Lindy (1963–65)	43	Miller, Wade (2006–07)	52
McElroy, Chuck (1991–93)	35	Minner, Paul (1950–56)	24
McGehee, Casey (2008)	27	Mitre, Sergio (2003–05)	52
McGinn, Dan (1972)	30	Mitterwald, George (1974–77)	15
McGlothen, Lynn (1978–81)	40	Moisan, Bill (1953)	26
McGriff, Fred (2001–02)	29	Molina, Jose (1999)	19
McKnight, Jim (1960,1962)	6,15	Molinaro, Bob (1982)	29
McLish, Cal (1949,1951)	12,27	Monday, Rick (1972–76)	7
McMath, Jimmy (1968)	24	Monroe, Craig (2007)	27
McNichol, Brian (1999)	33	Montreuil, Al (1972)	29
McRae, Brian (1995–97)	56	Moore, Donnie (1975, 1977–79)	49
Meers, Russ (1941,1946–47)	27,17		
Meier, Dave (1988)	20	Moore, Johnny (1932,1945)	5,38
Mejias, Sam (1979)	32	Moore, Scott (2006–07)	15,4

Mooty, Jake (1940–43)	25,33
Morales, Jerry (1974–77, 1981–83)	24
Morandini, Mickey (1998–99)	12
Morehead, Seth (1959–60)	41,38
Morel, Ramon (1997)	33
Moreland, Keith (1982–87)	6
Morgan, Bobby (1957–58)	12
Morgan, Mike (1992–95, 1998)	36,38
Morgan, Vern (1954–55)	30,5
Morhardt, Moe (1961–62)	25,11
Moryn, Walt (1956–60)	43,7
Moskau, Paul (1983)	37
Mosolf, Jim (1933)	31
Moss, Les (1981)	6
Moyer, Jamie (1986–88)	49
Mudrock, Phil (1963)	33
Mueller, Bill (2001–02)	33
Mueller, Ray (1957)	22
Mulholland, Terry (1997–99)	45
Mumphrey, Jerry (1986–88)	22
Muncrief, Bob (1949)	11
Murcer, Bobby (1977–79)	7
Murphy, Danny (1960, 1962)	20,42,27
Murray, Calvin (2004)	17
Murton, Matt (2005–08)	19
Muser, Tony (1993–97)	40
Myatt, George (1957–59)	52,34
Myers, Billy (1941)	5,10
Myers, Randy (1993–95)	28
Myers, Richie (1956)	10
Myers, Rodney (1996–99)	59

N

Nabholz, Chris (1995)	53
Nation, Joey (2000)	52
Navarro, Jaime (1995–96)	38

Neeman, Cal (1957–60)	30,11
Nelson, Lynn (1933–34)	23
Nen, Dick (1968)	15
Nevin, Phil (2006)	40
Newman, Ray (1971)	45
Newsom, Bobo (1932)	27
Nichols, Dolan (1958)	27
Nicholson, Bill (1939–48)	8,43
Niekro, Joe (1967–69)	48
Nieves, Jose (1998–00)	11
Nipper, Al (1988)	45
Noce, Paul (1987)	16
Noles, Dickie (1982–84,1987)	48,47
Nordhagen, Wayne (1983)	20
Noren, Irv (1959–60,1975)	20,5
Norman, Fred (1964,1966–67)	45,41
North, Billy (1971–72)	25
Northey, Ron (1950–51)	10
Norton, Phil (2000,2003)	50
Nottebart, Don (1969)	38
Novikoff, Lou (1941–44)	19,26,14,45
Novoa, Roberto (2005–06)	44
Novotney, Rube (1949)	9
Nunez, Jose (1990)	39
Nye, Rich (1966–69)	32

O

O'Berry, Mike (1980)	6
O'Dea, Ken (1935–38)	41,12
O'Farrell, Bob (1934)	12
O'Leary, Charley (1932–33)	42
O'Leary, Troy (2003)	25
O'Malley, Ryan (2006)	48
O'Neil, Buck (1962–65)	53
O'Neill, Emmett (1946)	19
Oates, Johnny (1984–87)	9
Ohman, Will (2000–01, 2005–07)	35,50, 45,13
Ojeda, Augie (2000–03)	55,57,1

Oliver, Gene (1968–69)	12
Oliver, Nate (1969)	15
Oliveras, Mako (1995–97)	3,2
Olsen, Barney (1941)	19,29
Olsen, Vern (1939–42,1946)	23
Ontiveros, Steve (1977–80)	16
Ordonez, Rey (2004)	13,29
Orie, Kevin (1997–98,2002)	15
Ortiz, Jose (1971)	20
Osborne, Donovan (2002)	31
Ostrowski, Johnny (1943–46)	47,50,27
Otero, Reggie (1945)	51
Ott, Billy (1962,1964)	19,28
Otto, Dave (1994)	53
Owen, Dave (1983–85)	19
Owen, Mickey (1949–51)	9,10,12

P	
Pafko, Andy (1943–51)	33,48
Pagan, Angel (2006–07)	29
Page, Vance (1938–41)	41
Pagel, Karl (1978–79)	45
Pall, Donn (1994)	47
Palmeiro, Rafael (1986–88)	25
Pappas, Erik (1991)	37
Pappas, Milt (1970–73)	32
Parent, Mark (1994–95)	8
Parmalee, Roy (1937)	24
Passeau, Claude (1939–47)	13
Patterson, Bob (1996–98)	35
Patterson, Corey (2000–05)	27,20
Patterson, Eric (2007–08)	3,4
Patterson, Ken (1992)	34
Patterson, Reggie (1983–85)	52
Paul, Josh (2003)	29
Paul, Mike (1973–74)	35
Pavlas, Dave (1990–91)	46
Pawelek, Ted (1946)	32
Peden, Les (1965)	64

Pedre, Jorge (1992)	53
Pena, Roberto (1965–66)	7,41,28
Pentland, Jeff (1997–02)	55,2,4
Pepitone, Joe (1970–73)	8
Perez, Mike (1995–96)	47
Perez, Neifi (2004–06)	13
Perez, Yorkis (1991)	33
Perkowski, Harry (1955)	43
Perlman, Jon (1985)	35
Perry, Gerald (2007–08)	28,42[a]
Perry, Pat (1988–89)	37
Petrick, Billy (2007)	56
Phelps, Babe (1933–34)	61
Phillips, Adolfo (1966–69)	41,20
Phillips, Taylor (1958–59)	29,41
Phoebus, Tom (1972)	36
Pico, Jeff (1988–90)	51,41
Pie, Felix (2007–08)	17,20
Pierre, Juan (2006)	9
Pignatiello, Carmen (2007–08)	63
Piktuzis, George (1956)	50
Pina, Horacio (1974)	36
Piniella, Lou (2007–08)	41
Pisciotta, Marc (1997–98)	41
Pizarro, Juan (1970–73)	46
Platt, Whitey (1942–43)	48
Plesac, Dan (1993–94)	32,37
Plummer, Bill (1968)	8
Poholsky, Tom (1957)	29
Pole, Dick (1988–91, 2003–06)	34,46,39
Pollet, Howie (1953–55)	16
Popovich, Paul (1964, 1966–67,1969–73)	11,22
Porter, Bo (1999)	35
Porterfield, Bob (1959)	43
Prall, Willie (1975)	37
Pramesa, Johnny (1952)	25

Pratt, Andy (2004)	29
Pratt, Todd (1995)	8
Pressnell, Tot (1941–42)	40
Prim, Ray (1943,1945–46)	39
Prince, Don (1962)	47
Prior, Mark (2002–06)	22
Proly, Mike (1982–83)	36
Putnam, Ed (1976,1978)	8,17
Pyecha, John (1954)	34
Q	
Quade, Mike (2006–08)	81,18,8
Qualls, Jim (1969)	42
Quevedo, Ruben (2000)	48
Quinn, Wimpy (1941)	4,16,18
Quinones, Luis (1987)	28
R	
Radatz, Dick (1967)	43
Rader, Dave (1978)	8
Radison, Dan (1995–99)	42,3
Raffensberger, Ken (1940–41)	14,16
Rain, Steve (1999–00)	41
Rainey, Chuck (1983–84)	30
Ramazzotti, Bob (1949–53)	5
Ramirez, Aramis (2003–08)	15,16
Ramos, Domingo (1989–90)	15
Ramsdell, Willie (1952)	30
Ramsey, Fernando (1992)	40
Randle, Len (1980)	21
Ranew, Merritt (1963–64)	7
Rapada, Clay (2007)	50
Rasmussen, Dennis (1992)	48
Raudman, Bob (1966–67)	27,24
Reberger, Frank (1968)	37
Reed, Jeff (1999–00)	16
Regan, Phil (1968–72, 1997–98)	27
Reich, Herman (1949)	22

Reiser, Pete (1966–69, 1972–74)	7,6,27,46
Reitz, Ken (1981)	44
Remlinger, Mike (2003–05)	37
Renfroe, Laddie (1991)	39
Renko, Steve (1976–77)	50
Restovich, Michael (2006)	28
Reuschel, Paul (1975–78)	43
Reuschel, Rick (1972–81, 1983–84)	48,47
Reyes, Jose (2006)	61
Reynolds, Archie (1968–70)	39,46
Reynolds, Carl (1937–39)	43
Rhodes, Karl (Tuffy) (1993–95)	25
Rice, Del (1960)	9
Rice, Hal (1954)	28
Rice, Len (1945)	8
Richards, Fred (1951)	6
Richbourg, Lance (1932)	56
Richmond, Beryl (1933)	42
Rickert, Marv (1942,1946–47)	46,35
Riggleman, Jim (1995–99)	5
Riley, George (1979–80)	33,37
Ripley, Allen (1982)	33
Rivera, Roberto (1995)	41
Roach, Mel (1961)	12
Roarke, Mike (1978–80)	4
Roberson, Kevin (1993–95)	19
Roberts, Dave (1977–78)	41
Roberts, Robin (1966)	36
Robertson, Daryl (1962)	19
Robertson, Don (1954)	52
Robinson, Jeff (1992)	38
Rodgers, Andre (1961–64)	18
Rodriguez, Freddy (1958)	22
Rodriguez, Henry (1998–00)	40
Rodriquez, Roberto (1970)	43

Rogell, Billy (1940)	5
Rohn, Dan (1983–84)	17
Rojas, Cookie (1978–81)	1
Rojas, Mel (1997)	51
Roof, Phil (1990–91)	48
Roomes, Rolando (1988)	27
Root, Charley (1932–41, 1951–53,1960)	12,19,14, 17,49,4
Rosello, Dave (1972–77)	17,29
Ross, Gary (1968–69)	33
Rothschild, Larry (2002–08)	47,41,40,50
Rowdon, Wade (1987)	18
Rozonovsky, Vic (1964–65)	8
Rudolph, Ken (1969–73)	8,15
Rusch, Glendon (2004–06)	33
Rush, Bob (1948–57)	30,17
Russell, Jack (1938–39)	28
Russell, Rip (1940–42)	32,12
Ruthven, Dick (1983–86)	44
Ryu, Jae–Kuk (2006)	20

S	
Salazar, Angel (1988)	18
Salazar, Luis (1989–92)	11,10
Samardzija, Jeff (2008)	29
Sanchez, Felix (2003)	62
Sanchez, Jesus (2002)	41
Sanchez, Rey (1991–97)	15,6,11
Sandberg, Ryne (1982–94, 1996)	23
Sanders, Scott (1999)	27
Sanderson, Scott (1984–89)	24,21
Santiago, Benito (1999)	9
Santo, Ron (1960–73)	15,10
Sauer, Ed (1943–45)	24,49,45
Sauer, Hank (1949–55)	43,47,9
Saul, Jim (1975–76)	2
Savage, Ted (1967–68)	25

Sawatski, Carl (1948,1950,1953)	18,11,15
Scanlan, Bob (1991–93)	30
Schaffer, Jimmie (1963–64)	5
Schaffernoth, Joe (1959–61)	46
Scheffing, Bob (1941–42, 1946–50,1954–55, 1957–59)	33,10, 46,25
Schenz, Hank (1946–49)	17,5
Schiraldi, Calvin (1988–89)	32
Schmidt, Freddy (1947)	34
Schmitz, Johnny (1941–42, 1946–51)	7,31,53
Schramka, Paul (1953)	14
Schroll, Al (1960)	43
Schult, Art (1959–60)	43,23
Schulte, Johnny (1933)	56
Schultz, Barney (1961–63, 1977)	41,6
Schultz, Bob (1951–53)	32,10,34
Schultz, Buddy (1975–76)	35
Schulze, Don (1983–84)	43
Schurr, Wayne (1964)	30
Schuster, Bill (1943–45)	21,22
Scott, Dick (1964)	38
Scott, Gary (1991–92)	25
Scott, Rodney (1978)	32
Secory, Frank (1944–46)	49
Segelke, Herman (1982)	43
Seibert, Kurt (1979)	17
Selma, Dick (1969)	39
Sember, Mike (1977–78)	10,29
Seoane, Manny (1978)	37
Serafini, Dan (1999)	33
Serena, Bill (1949–54)	27,6,1
Servais, Scott (1995–98)	9
Shamsky, Art (1972)	24

Shantz, Bobby (1964)	45	Sosa, Sammy (1992–04)	21
Shaw, Bob (1967)	33	Soto, Geovany (2005–08)	58,18
Shea, Merv (1948–49)	11,45	Spalding, Dick (1941–43)	37,41
Shields, Tommy (1993)	1	Spangler, Al (1967–71,1974)	21,20,3
Shoun, Clyde (1935–37)	23,21	Speake, Bob (1955,1957)	11
Shumpert, Terry (1996)	15	Speier, Chris (1985–86, 2005–06)	28,35
Signer, Walter (1943,1945)	50,27		
Silvera, Charlie (1957)	8	Speier, Justin (1998)	56
Simmons, Curt (1966–67)	39	Sperring, Rob (1974–76)	16
Simon, Randall (2003)	35	Spradlin, Jerry (2000)	37
Simpson, Duke (1953)	30	Spring, Jack (1964)	33
Sinatro, Matt (2007–08)	39	Stainback, Tuck (1934–37)	42,5
Singleton, Elmer (1957–59)	20,42	Stairs, Matt (2001)	24,30
Sizemore, Ted (1979)	6	Stanky, Eddie (1943–44)	25
Skidmore, Roe (1970)	38	Starr, Ray (1945)	32,38
Slaughter, Sterling (1964)	41	Starrette, Herm (1987)	3
Sloat, Lefty (1949)	20	Steenstra, Kennie (1998)	49
Slocumb, Heathcliff (1991–93)	51	Stein, Randy (1982)	43
Smalley, Roy (1948–53)	39	Stelmaszek, Rick (1974)	8
Smith, Bob (1932)	18	Stephenson, Earl (1971)	37
Smith, Bob (Riverboat) (1959)	43	Stephenson, Joe (1944)	50
Smith, Bobby Gene (1962)	23	Stephenson, John (1967–68)	6
Smith, Charley (1969)	19	Stephenson, Phil (1989)	11
Smith, Dave (1991–92)	42	Stephenson, Riggs (1932–34)	4,5
Smith, Dwight (1989–93)	18	Stephenson, Walter (1935–36)	42
Smith, Greg (1989–90)	16	Stevens, Dave (1997–98)	40,48
Smith, Jason (2001)	56	Steevens, Morrie (1962)	35
Smith, Lee (1980–87)	46	Stewart, Jimmy (1963–67)	19
Smith, Paul (1958)	19	Stewart, Mack (1944–45)	38
Smith, Red (1945–48)	52	Stock, Milt (1944–48)	41
Smith, Willie (1968–70)	25	Stoddard, Tim (1984)	49
Smyth, Steve (2002)	39	Stone, Steve (1974–76)	30
Snyder, Jim (1987)	5	Stoneman, Bill (1967–68)	36
Solis, Marcelino (1958)	20	Strain, Joe (1981)	17
Solomon, Eddie (1975)	40	Strange, Doug (1991–92)	1
Sorensen, Lary (1985)	42	Stringer, Lou (1941–42,1946)	15,12
Soriano, Alfonso (2007–08)	12	Strode, Lester (2007–08)	35,42[a]

Sturgeon, Bobby (1940–42, 1946–47)	28,38,7
Sturtze, Tanyon (1995–96)	34
Stynes, Chris (2002)	11
Summers, Champ (1975–76)	27
Sundberg, Jim (1987–88)	11
Sutcliffe, Rick (1984–91)	40
Sutter, Bruce (1976–80)	42
Swartzbaugh, Dave (1995–97)	36,38
Swisher, Steve (1974–77)	9

T

Tabb, Jerry (1976)	12
Tabler, Pat (1981–82)	19
Talbot, Bob (1953–54)	10
Tanner, Chuck (1957–58)	39,6
Tapani, Kevin (1997–01)	36
Tappe, El (1954–56,1958–65)	55,10,2,52
Tappe, Ted (1955)	4
Tate, Bennie (1934)	11
Tatis, Ramon (1997)	52
Tavarez, Julian (2001)	50
Taylor, Harry (1932)	19
Taylor, Sammy (1358–62)	15,7
Taylor, Tony (1958–60)	5
Taylor, Zack (1932–33)	34,14
Telemaco, Amaury (1996–98)	44
Terwilliger, Wayne (1949–51)	6,21
Tewksbury, Bob (1987–88)	42
Thacker, Moe (1958, 1960–62)	19,23, 22,8,25
Theriot, Ryan (2005–08)	55,3,7,2
Thomas, Frank (1960–61, 1966)	25,34
Thomas, Lee (1966–67)	8
Thompson, Scot (1978–83)	25,29,18
Thomson, Bobby (1958–59)	9
Thornton, Andre (1973–76)	12
Thorpe, Bob (1955)	26

Tidrow, Dick (1979–82)	41
Tiefenauer, Bobby (1968)	38,45
Timmons, Ozzie (1995–96)	30
Tinning, Bud (1932–34)	21,22
Todd, Al (1940–41,1943)	10,2,11
Todd, Jim (1974,1977)	39,31
Tompkins, Ron (1971)	38
Torres, Hector (1971)	21
Toth, Paul (1962–64)	39
Trachsel, Steve (1993–99, 2007)	46,52
Tracy, Jim (1980–81)	23
Trammell, Alan (2007–08)	6,3
Trebelhorn, Tom (1992–94)	41
Tremel, Bill (1954–56)	33
Trillo, Manny (1975–78, 1986–88)	19
Triplett, Coaker (1938)	32
Trout, Steve (1983–87)	34
Tucker, Michael (2001)	11,24
Tyrone, Jim (1972,1974–75)	27,29
Tyrone, Wayne (1976)	22
Tyson, Mike (1980–81)	2,18

U

Uhle, George (1940)	20
Upham, John (1967–68)	45,37
Usher, Bob (1952)	12

V

Vail, Mike (1978–80)	27
Valdes, Pedro (1996,1998)	28
Valdez, Ismael (2000)	59
Valentinetti, Vito (1956–57)	57
Van Buren, Jermaine (2005)	37
Van Poppel, Todd (2000–01)	47
Van Ryn, Ben (1998)	58
Vandenburg, Hy (1944–45)	35
Vander Meer, Johnny (1950)	34
Varga, Andy (1950–51)	33,23

Varsho, Gary (1988–90)	24
Verban, Emil (1948–50)	7
Veres, Dave (2003)	43
Veres, Randy (1994)	45
Veryzer, Tom (1983–84)	29
Villaneuva, Hector (1990–92)	32,19
Vizcaino, Jose (1991–93)	16
Voiselle, Bill (1950)	96
Vukovich, John (1982–87)	2

W

Wade, Ben (1948)	24
Wade, Gale (1955–56)	2,3
Waitkus, Eddie (1941, 1946–48)	27,36
Walbeck, Matt (1993)	9
Walker, Chico (1985–87, 1991–92)	30,29,24
Walker, Harry (1949)	43
Walker, Mike (1995)	39
Walker, Rube (1948–51)	8
Walker, Todd (2004–06)	7
Walker, Verlon (1961–70)	56,4
Waller, Ty (1981–82)	21,29
Wallis, Joe (1975–78)	28,27,9
Walls, Lee (1957–59)	2
Walrond, Les (2006)	55
Walton, Jerome (1989–92)	20
Ward, Chris (1972,1974)	20
Ward, Daryle (2007–08)	32,33,42[a]
Ward, Dick (1934)	15
Ward, Preston (1950,1953)	29
Warneke, Lon (1932–36, 1942–43,1945)	17,16,12, 19,32,36
Warner, Jack (1962–65)	38,33,34,40
Warstler, Rabbit (1940)	43
Warwick, Carl (1966)	23
Watt, Eddie (1975)	39
Weathers, David (2001)	41,49

Weaver, Jim (1934)	12,15
Webster, Mitch (1988–89)	28,33
Webster, Ray (1971)	23
Wellemeyer, Todd (2003–05)	40
Wells, Randy (2008)	36
Wendell, Turk (1993–97)	13
Wengert, Don (1998)	33
Whisenant, Pete (1956)	30
White, Derrick (1998)	25
White, Elder (1962)	19
White, Jerry (1978)	24
White, Rondell (2000–01)	22
Whitehill, Earl (1939)	31
Wiedemayer, Charlie (1934)	11
Wilcox, Milt (1975)	42
Wilhelm, Hoyt (1970)	39
Wilkerson, Curtis (1989–90)	19
Wilkins, Dean (1989–90)	38
Wilkins, Rick (1991–95)	2
Will, Bob (1957–58,1960–63)	16,38,28
Williams, Billy (1959–74, 1980–82,1986–87, 1992–01)	4,41,26
Williams, Brian (2000)	51
Williams, Dewey (1944–47)	12,6,20
Williams, Jerome (2005–06)	32,57
Williams, Mitch (1989–90)	28
Williamson, Scott (2005–06)	48
Willis, Jim (1953–54)	28
Wills, Bump (1982)	17
Wilson, Enrique (2005)	19
Wilson, Jimmy (1941–44)	1,40
Wilson, Steve (1989–91)	44
Wilson, Willie (1993–94)	6
Winceniak, Ed (1956–57)	12
Wise, Casey (1957)	7
Womack, Tony (2003,2006)	5,1
Wood, Kerry (1998,2000–08)	34

Woodall, Brad (1999)	31	Young, Anthony (1994–95)	16
Woods, Gary (1982–85)	25	Young, Danny (2000)	35
Woods, Jim (1957)	48	Young, Don (1965,1969)	23,29
Worrell, Tim (2000)	45	Young, Eric (2000–01)	7
Wright, Mel (1960–61, 1963–64,1971)	45,59,1	**Z**	
		Zahn, Geoff (1975–76)	38
Wrona, Rick (1988–90)	1	Zambrano, Carlos (2001–08)	38
Wuertz, Mike (2004–08)	43	Zambrano, Eddie (1993–94)	39,22
Wynne, Marvell (1989–90)	25	Zamora, Oscar (1974–76)	45
Wyse, Hank (1942–47)	45,33	Zeile, Todd (1995)	27
Y		Zick, Bob (1954)	38
Yelding, Eric (1993)	20	Zimmer, Don (1960–61, 1984–86,1988–91)	17,4
Yerkes, Carroll (1932–33)	49,41		
York, Tony (1944)	24	Zuleta, Julio (2000–01)	15

Notes:

[a] *These people wore #42 for one day in honor of Jackie Robinson.*

[b] *These people actually never appeared in a major league game wearing this number (they were on the active roster, but never got in a game with this number).*

[c] *Charlie Gassaway's uniform number is unknown.*

ACKNOWLEDGMENTS

Matt

As with all these books, there are many who have come before with key information. My Cubs library now overfloweth. These works include *The Cubs: The Complete Story of Chicago Cubs Baseball*, by Glenn Stout and Richard A. Johnson (New York: Houghton Mifflin, 2007); *Cubs Journal: Year by Year & Day by Day with the Chicago Cubs since 1876*, by John Snyder (Cincinnati: Emmis Books, 2005); *Miracle Collapse: The 1969 Chicago Cubs* by Doug Feldman (Lincoln: University of Nebraska Press, 2006); *Wrigley Field: The Unauthorized Biography*, by Stuart Shea (Dulles, Virginia: Potomac Books, 2006), and various versions of the Cubs media guide. Online, there are many stops along the way, but the most frequent and helpful are baseball-reference.com, retrosheet.org, baseballalmanac.com, chicago.Cubs.mlb.com, and, of course, my partners' portals to the Friendly Confines: bleedcubbieblue.com and Cubsbythenumbers.com.

Several people were helpful in making this book possible. Paul Lukas, of espn.com fame, did some key research about Cubs uniforms and also found some Cubs batting helmet information for me. James Walsh at Maple Street Press helped facilitate this collaboration. Also to Linc Wonham, who first told me I should start working on a numbers book about the Cubs. It took a while to get into print, but my material was waiting when the time was right. Mike Kaplan shared a passion for the Cubs and a house in North Carolina for the boys from Roanoke during a wonderful weekend that became forever marred by a visit from the Grim Reaper 3,000 miles west in San Diego. The weekend? October 5–7, 1984.

Debbie, Jan, and Tyler are always understanding and often patient as I chase baseball ghosts in my messy office. Oak Park's own Bob Marich takes in all our family matters with a Cubs eye. My brothers, Michael and Mark, who went to Northwestern in the seventies, first explained to me the greatness that is Wrigley.

This book would not be possible, however, if not for a similar project about a rival baseball club. Jon Springer's outstanding Mets website (metsbythenumbers.com) provided the framework, inspiration, and content to create the book *Mets by the Numbers* (Skyhorse Publishing, 2008), which I helped write. We proved that such a book could be done . . . and done well, if I say so. Thanks also to Mark Weinstein at Skyhorse, who gave the go ahead for both the Mets and Cubs books, had the patience to wait for the right team of authors for the Cubs, and had confidence that we could get such a book done over the course of a season.

While it's not traditional to thank one's coauthors, we three had never met before an e-mail in late April on the subject. Within hours we had an agreement, an arrangement, and a publisher. Thanks to Al and Kasey for showing faith even though we came from different time zones and baseball religions. Three is a lot of authors, but with time bearing down, we turned this like a 6-4-3 double play by three Cubs who didn't have a number between them, but who made quite a poem.

Al:

It's a strange feeling to give my first acknowledgment for this Cubs book to a Mets fan, Eric Simon. Eric is the proprietor of the SB Nation's Mets counterpart to my Bleed Cubbie Blue site, Amazin' Avenue (amazinavenue.com). He wrote a review of *Mets By The Numbers,* and, knowing that Kasey had been maintaining a similar list of Cubs numbers for many years, I thought, "We could do this for the Cubs!" Thanks to Kasey's contacts with Jon Springer, one of *MBTN*'s coauthors, and Matt, the three of us, as Matt noted, were able to get this project up and running in a matter of a few e-mails.

The books and websites that Matt mentioned above are among those I used; particularly baseball-reference.com, where I seemingly lived last summer when I wasn't at Wrigley Field. The online archives of the *Chicago Tribune,* accessible from my home just because I have a Chicago Public Library card, were invaluable in finding contemporary accounts of games and players and coaches and numbers.

You might think it's "dogs and cats, living together," for Cubs fans like Kasey and me, and a Mets fan like Matt (his Web site is even metsilverman.com), to get along, but all of it went very smoothly and for that, Matt and Kasey both get thanks from me. A special shout-out goes out to Matt, who I have still not met despite our best efforts to get together at the rained-out final Hall of Fame Game in Cooperstown in the summer of 2008. It was nice to know that a Cubs fan and a Mets fan could collaborate so effortlessly despite the teams' long rivalry on the field.

Personal thanks are due to many, beginning with Mark Weinstein at Skyhorse, who believed in this project and believed in us to get it done during a baseball season. Thanks to Peter Chase and Jason Carr of the Cubs' media relations department, who cheerfully answered my questions about things that happened decades ago; to Ed Hartig, who always had an answer to every question I had, no matter how trivial; to Gabriel Schechter at the Hall of Fame, who tried—unsuccessfully, as it turned out—to find Charlie Gassaway's number, the Holy Grail of Cubs numbers; to Matt Boltz of WGN Radio; to Pat Hughes for graciously agreeing to write the foreword to this book; to Jessica Rosner and Bruce Ladd for finding me the answer to a seemingly unanswerable question about Emil Verban (and extra thanks to Jessica for giving me more information than I ever needed to know about her favorite player of all time, Greg Maddux); to SABR members Rick Benner, Steve Boren, Steve Smith, Merritt Clifton, Cappy Gagnon, Maxwell Kates, Rich Klein, Rod Nelson, Pete Palmer, and Jeremy Simons, who answered various questions I posted to the SABR-L discussion list; to Mike Bojanowski, who knows everything (and if by some chance he doesn't, knows where to look it up), and to Miriam Romain, who has patiently helped with anything and everything I needed.

And finally, to my children Mark & Rachel, who didn't get to see much of me last summer while I was working on this book.

Kasey:

First off, I would like to thank Jack Looney, author of *Now Batting, Number...*, who had enough faith in my uniform number lists to ask for my help with his book, and also gave me the incentive to keep up with my lists. I would also like to thank Jon Springer, whom I have known for several years through his MBTN Web site (and helped him find proof of

Jesse Orosco's first number when he made his debut at Wrigley Field). Without Jon's help, this book would not have come together as quickly as it has. I would also like to thank Al, who when he thought of the idea for this book, came to me and suggested that we do this. And to Matt, who has provided guidance throughout this project. Lastly, but not the least, to Mark Weinstein at Skyhorse, who let us bring this book to life.

I would also like to acknowledge the books and Web sites that Matt and Al have previously mentioned. All of them were of immense help in compiling information for this book.

There are several people who have helped me out with my research. I would like to thank Don Stuart, who back in March of 1995 posted a message about old Cubs uniform numbers on alt.sports.baseball.chicago-Cubs that prompted me to start collecting my lists of uniform numbers. I would also like to thank Chuck Wasserstrom of the Chicago Cubs, who always answered my questions about who wore what uniform numbers over the years. Also, in addition to Al's thanks to Ed Hartig, I'd like to add mine: Ed put up with my questions, and to my amazement, answered them, no matter how dumb they sounded; to Mark Kanges, who with his extensive collection of Cubs videos helped me out; to AU Sports, who graciously allowed me to peruse their collection of scorecards; and to Bob Vanderberg, who insisted that he just *knew* that Ron Santo wore #15.

I would also like to thank my wife, Peggy, who, when we got married and found my stash of hundreds of old scorecards, listened to me and didn't toss them out (see, I told you that they would come in handy some day), and to my daughter, Angela, who put up with me postponing many things in order to "work on the book."